Nobody Else
is Perfect

Nobody Else is Perfect

Charles Hennessy

W. H. ALLEN · LONDON
A Howard & Wyndham Company
1980

*Printed and bound in Great Britain by W. & J. Mackay Ltd,
Chatham, Kent
for the Publishers, W. H. Allen & Co Ltd, 44 Hill Street,
London W1X 8LB*

ISBN 0 491 02771 0

Acknowledgements

I should like to acknowledge my debt to:
Anderson and Sheppard Ltd (my tailor)
Washington Tremlett Ltd (my shirtmaker)
Bill Murray (my landlord in France)
and others too numerous to list here. They know who
they are.
I should also like to thank Hubert Nicholson
and the Autolycus Publications for permission to quote
from the poems of A. S. J. Tessimond.

The wise have no authority, and those in authority are not wise.

Krishnamurti

If I were to say 'I love you', my teeth would crack.

Gauguin

Though leaves are many, the root is one;
Through all the lying days of my youth
I swayed my leaves and flowers in the sun;
Now I may wither into the truth.

W. B. Yeats

I've known what it is to be hungry; but I always went right to a restaurant.

Ring Lardner

Preamble

I was born an aristocrat. My parents, being peasants, were naturally a disappointment to me. The profound conflict nurtured then, between what is and what might be, set the pattern for my life. This book, besides creating a totally new literary genre — *fiction thinly disguised as autobiography* — is the story of my losing battle with reality. Now read on....

Amble I

Chapter 1

Most young people who opt for higher education arrive at their choice of establishment by considerations of various kinds: specialisation desired, reputation for learning, for social life, for sport, the availability of bursaries, family tradition and so on. In my own case the choice was based on a rather more eclectic criterion: the colour of my dressing-gown.

I had been conscripted, like millions of others in wartime, straight from school into military service. For reasons that are still not clear to me – though rebellion may have been a motive, since I had been brought up in Royal Air Force camps and, more significantly perhaps, my older brother had just won his wings, as they say – I elected to be a soldier, and not only a soldier but an infantryman. (Class, I now think, may have had something to do with my choice, as it has to do with almost everything in England: for an officer, which for reasons of comfort and snobbism I intended to be, the British Army – as Orwell pointed out in *England Your England* – socially outranks the other services.)

I had been head boy of my school, and captain of games, and secretary of the debating society, and co-founder of the school newspaper. (I had written to Bernard Shaw, as a fellow-Irishman, to ask for a contribution to the paper; he had replied, by handwritten postcard, 'Your paper will not be a success if you fill it with contributions from old gentlemen of eighty. Try an age limit of eighteen.' We ran this as the main story, or lead, under the headline, PLAYWRIGHT'S ADVICE TO EDITORS: TRY AGE LIMIT OF EIGHTEEN SAYS GBS.) This run of apparently effortlessly attained success continued in the army, after the grim cold shower of early training, and when I celebrated my twenty-first birthday (by, as it happened, and quite coincidentally, dining in his palace with the King of Jordan), I was commander of a company of the 1st Battalion of the Duke of Cornwall's Light Infantry, stationed in Palestine. And not only was I the youngest by far of the company commanders, I was also the only non-regular officer to command a company: indeed my second-in-command was a regular officer of the regiment and it may well have been the humiliation of this, as it were, subaltern role that led him, shortly after his appointment, to vanish, taking with him, for inscrutable reasons, the clean laundry of the entire battalion.

My achievements – amazing now to someone who would join no group nor fight for any cause or country, for I see my enemies as all within – did not stop at the purely military. I was elected Food and Wine Officer of the mess (chiefly as the result of some facetious remarks I contributed to the suggestion book to the effect that there were many ways of preparing eggs besides frying them: stung by this, the mess sergeant served boiled eggs the next morning, explaining to my enraged fellow-officers that he had merely followed Captain Hennessy's advice; their revenge was to put me in charge of the whole operation.) It was a role I enjoyed – far more anyway than trying to root out the Stern Gang, and Mr Begin and the rest of the Irgun Zvei Leumi. I found excellent wines in Rehovoth, including the workmanlike hock called Carmel, and in the kibbutzim there they were making convincing copies of most of the famous cheeses of Europe including, astonishingly, an admirable Jewish Stilton.

Our mess had two great assets, a couple of Italian prisoners, one of them a dessert man, the other an entrée man. With their combined talents at the furnaces, we ate well – but it was too good to last. Our Italians shared a tent behind the mess and one hot Mediterranean night the Meat man found himself obliged to defend his honour with one of his carving knives against the amorous advances of the Sweet man. One of them had to go. It was a hard decision. War can be tough.

I was also Sports Officer of the Battalion and during the period of my appointment we won, in indisputable fashion on the playing fields of the American University of Beirut, the football championship of the Middle East Forces. There were two reasons for this achievement, and neither of them, unfortunately, can be placed to my credit. When I joined the Battalion it was commanded by a pleasant, handsome and elegant man called Colonel Fletcher, known as 'Monkey', perhaps because, like monkeys I believe, he rarely wore a tie. 'Monkey' Fletcher had represented the British Army at soccer and now, while giving priority always to the military efficiency of his command, contrived to garner, from all over the army, men who had worn the 'strip' of famous professional clubs before being called to other colours. It was not, therefore, entirely by accident that our Corporal Hodges had been better known to the fans as Johnny Hodges, the demon striker of Arsenal, or that Private Rowley, whom I subsequently had the pleasure of promoting first to corporal, then to sergeant, was none other than big Arthur Rowley, solid and phlegmatic fullback of Manchester United.

The second, and more important, factor in our football success was the man who became my platoon sergeant when I joined the Battalion. The name of this man, who was my senior by three or four years, was Alf Ramsey. He now outranks me, having been knighted for his services to English football, and had the British Army not been resolutely based upon a feudal system he would undoubtedly have outranked me then. When he fell victim a few years ago to the same implacable caste system I wrote, for the first time in my life, a letter of angry protest to *The Times*. *The Times* kept my record virgin by declining to print it.

Ramsey was a man who possessed all the qualities required for leadership: he would not have been out of place as commander of the Battalion. His powers of diplomacy, even then, were such that when, each Wednesday, we sat down together to choose our team for the next match I invariably left the meeting with the feeling that my contribution had been not only vital but crucial.

10

Ramsey was one of nature's aristocrats, an intensely private man who must have thought that his special qualities, which, being a realist, he had not always displayed, had in recent years been truly recognised. If so, the fall from grace must have been cruel indeed. He has tried perhaps to become an English gentleman and been rebuffed by those who decide such things, but an English gentleman is what he has always been.

If I have seemed to lay emphasis upon my earlier successes it is not from any motive of self-aggrandisement (after all, as an earlier observer has noted, you can fool some of the people all of the time) but in order to try to understand why what followed was in such stark contrast. Not that my life has been without its worldly successes, but it may be that these have been wrongly based, on a groundwork of false values, for each of my projects has seemed to carry the seeds of its own failure, like a mechanism that contains its own self-destruct device. It is possible to see my life as a series of self-aborted flights.

When I was not choosing teams or cheese I was leading my Company in unconvincing midnight raids on sleeping settlements or walking the railway lines at dawn to clear them of mines before the citrus trains came through – a disagreeable way to start the day on an empty stomach. At the time of these sorties I shared a cell in a Greek Orthodox monastery with my fellow-officer and friend, then and later at Oxford, a parson's son called Tony Kelly. He enlivened mess nights by performing a violent crouching Cossack dance while holding in each hand two full pint glasses of beer. It is doubtful if his pupils at Windsor Choir School or Westminster Under School – institutions of which he became headmaster – were aware of this special talent, but in the Greek monastery it was greatly appreciated.

Another close friend, the Intelligence Officer, Norman Swallow, was an Oxford graduate who has been for many years a distinguished television producer. He was one of the few officers actually known to read books. Worse, he somehow contrived to edit, at that distance, a little literary magazine in England. When *Brideshead Revisited* appeared he flattered me, and frightened me,

11

by asking me to review it. I titled the work, inevitably, 'Waugh in Peace', but in spite of this it was well received and Louis MacNeice, or Stephen Spender, asked Norman who the writer was. (I have been asking the same question ever since.) Swallow paid me five pounds for this first literary effort and in gratitude I agreed to be his best man on my next leave in England.

Attached to Swallow's Intelligence Unit was a bright, pleasant, articulate Arab graduate of Beirut University. As an honorary member of the Battalion he wore our uniform, with the stripes of a sergeant on his sleeve. I have since followed his career with interest in the newspapers. His name was George Habash and he is now the leader of the Popular Front for the Liberation of Palestine.

I took my leaves alone, taking the sandy train to my favourite city – or rather, since I have known Paris – my spiritual home, Alexandria, which I had first seen as a boy. Perhaps it was in Alexandria that I first discovered France – in the restaurants, in the streets which were labelled *rues*, in the language when I sipped real, witty, black coffee and armagnac on a corniche balcony with new-found friends.

I am not good at picking people up, but in Alexandria I did it once. I stayed usually at the Cecil (or when it closed for the hot weather, along the coast in the Summer Palace at Ramleh, where fat Farouk and his sycophantic courtiers came of a warm night to make the calm terrace noisy and vulgar) and dined sometimes at the Officers' Club, a commandeered German bank. At a window seat there one night I looked up from my prawn mayonnaise to see a young and pretty girl standing on a balcony across the narrow alley. She was looking down, with what might have been yearning, from the velvet night into the golden light where couples, the men in uniform, were dancing in what had been the central well of the bank. She was swaying slightly to the music.

Just then the head of what might accurately be called a street Arab appeared at the open window beside me. He was selling red roses. Emboldened by my pre-dinner Tom Collins, I bought a bunch and asked him to take them up to the girl. He merged into the gloom of a doorway opposite, then reappeared, still with the flowers. He explained that the lady could not accept them because she did not know who I was. I found a piece of paper and wrote, 'With the compliments of Captain Hennessy' and then, cleverly, *'Avec les compliments du Capitaine Hennessy'.* The boy disappeared again. When I next looked up the girl was holding the roses against her face. She made a gesture as if telephoning and pointed to the club.

I went to the telephone and heard a young voice in clear English thank me for the beautiful roses. I asked her if she would care to dance. She would adore to. She would come in just a moment. I was no longer alone in Alexandria.

She was fresh and lovely and seventeen and she was the daughter of the manager of Barclays Bank. In the days that followed we ate, danced and swam together. She wanted to come back to Palestine with me and live near the camp. Or anyway she wanted my address, or at least to know what train I left on so that she could come and see me off. Craven, not for the last time, before the threat of responsibility, or the demand for commitment, or the fear of freedom lost, I ducked all of these demands and sneaked away from the hot city closing in on me. I can remember everything about her except her name.

The Battalion was ordered to Dekelia, near Larnaca, in Cyprus. Our role was to guard in barbed-wire-enclosed camps Jews who had been captured while fleeing the Europe of barbed-wire-enclosed camps for the promise of Palestine. Outside these camps, in my bunk beneath the watchtowers and the searchlights, for the first time in my life I knew insomnia and took to drinking too much beer before I went to bed. Inner conflict about a disagreeable task? Anxiety outside these muttering, rumbling camps, whose inmates greatly outnumbered us? Or the first fear of the looming, civilian future? Soon, if all went well, I would unbuckle my webbing belt and thump my revolver down for the last time. (Now when I hear the word revolver I reach for my culture.)

Down in Dekelia, below the seething compounds, our quarters

were fifty yards from the shore of a small round bay. When not on duty up the hill it was my habit each morning after my batman – Bill Davies, a London bus conductor – had woken me with a mug of strong, sweet tea, to walk naked from my bed into the blood-warm sea. Returning from this sensual treat I would put on my dressing-gown and sit on the veranda to read my mail. The mail was important these days. My continued education was at stake. I had no alternative plans.

A letter arrived one morning from the Master of Peterhouse, Cambridge. I had applied for entry to that institution because it was the oldest of the Cambridge colleges, it was modest in style and, perhaps most important of all, it was reputed, its kitchen having been richly endowed, to have the best table in the University.

No news is bad news that hasn't arrived yet. I had waited anxiously. Here now was the disappointing reply. First, the good news: the Master was happy to inform me that I had been accepted for entry into the college. Next, the bad news: owing to the post-war 'bulge', the college, presumably like colleges everywhere, was full and I would have to wait another year to enter.

This was undoubtedly a setback. I sat looking out at the Mediterranean, which in sympathy had turned Cambridge-blue. A voice said, 'What's the matter with you?' 'Nipper' Sharland, proprietor of the voice, was my good friend the Adjutant of the Battalion, a regular officer who was, untypically, an Oxford graduate. Dumbly I handed him the letter. As he read it he seemed to smile – a curious reaction, I thought. Wanting in feeling, even. He handed the letter back to me, still with this Giaconda smile, if an unshaven army officer may be imagined for a moment to be the Mona Lisa.

'Why don't you try Merton?' he asked. He went on to explain that Merton was the name of the oldest of the Oxford colleges, that it was an attractive place, with a good academic reputation. So far, and in spite of the early hour, I had followed his reasoning. One thing remained unclear, though. Oxford was stiff with colleges; Cambridge too. So – and here was the sixty-four dollar whammeroo – why this Merton?

'Well,' said 'Nipper' Sharland, 'for one thing, you're wearing the Merton colours.'

This surprised me. Perhaps I should explain that when I had joined the army my mother, ever thoughtful, had scoured the ritziest emporia of Aylesbury High Street and come up with a rather distinguished dressing-gown which she gave me as a going-away present. During my service as a private soldier I had prudently hidden this elegant garment in the bottom of my kitbag, for in the simple, democratic world of the barrackroom one was expected to be either in bed, wearing the regulation underpants, shirt and socks, or out of bed, fully clothed. Dressing-gowns, though undoubtedly *de rigueur* for the well-dressed officer, were distinctly *mal vues* among the lower ranks.

Now, however, this splendid vestment had been able, as it were, to come out of the closet and into its own. It was, and is for that matter, for I have had it these thirty years, a rather striking sight, in vertical broad magenta and thinner white stripes. And the devilish thing is, 'Nipper' was right: those are, as I have had ample opportunity to confirm, the official colours of *Collegium Mertoniensis in Universitas Oxoniensis*. This coincidence changed my life.

I wrote to the Warden of Merton to make formal application for entry into the college in October of that year. Shortly afterwards a letter bearing the Merton crest – in magenta – arrived. I was invited to present myself, upon demobilisation, at Merton College for an interview with Robert Levens, Senior Tutor.

'Demob' day came soon and I said my nonchalant goodbyes. The driver detailed to take me to the boat for Suez, seeking for something suitable to say, said 'I remember the day you joined us, sir.' It had been four years, a fifth of my life, each day twenty-four hours with the same men, in hard and easy times, the faults and foibles of each known to all. My eyes, unused to them and thus surprised, suddenly brimmed with tears and I stared ahead

15

through them, startled, embarrassed, as the ship loomed up like a mirage in front of us.

It was late August when Robert Levens, a tall, stooped, shambling crow of a man with that absent look that bookish people have, led me across the cobblestones of Merton Street to take tea under an apple tree in the gardens of the old Warden's Lodgings. The sun came dappling, Pissaro-like, through the leaves of the tree. The lawn was freshly barbered. We talked of this and that, about my army experiences ('It's so nice here when the warriors return') and about the theatre – his wife, Daphne, was active in university productions. The afternoon wore on most pleasantly but after a while I began to grow anxious and said nervously, 'I'm afraid I have a train to catch. You don't think perhaps that we should start the interview?'

Levens looked startled. Recovered, he gave a croaking laugh. 'My dear good chap,' he said, 'the only reason we ask people to come all the way to see us is so that we don't get any out-and-out bastards walking about the place and making it look untidy. See you at Michaelmas then.'

The hit songs that summer were 'Oh What a Beautiful Morning' from *Oklahoma* and Edith Piaf's 'La Vie En Rose' and I think I was singing one or the other of them almost all the time.

Chapter 2

The years 1947 to 1949, as they were in Burgundy and in Bordeaux, are generally admitted to have been vintage years at Oxford: the crop was abundant and the quality exceptional. This plethora, for me, could be regarded as a bonus, for my prime motive in going to Oxford, though only half-admitted, was to have been there.

The names of people that I first met then have leaped, increasingly, to my eyes in the English newspapers I have bought, in such abundance, on Times Square and in St Germain des Près. They form, to a great extent, the English Establishment of the sixties and seventies. Men of power like Tony Wedgewood Benn, Edward Boyle, and Peter Parker (and women like Shirley Williams – then Catlin); film and theatre people like Tony Richardson and John Schlesinger; writers like Kingsley Amis, John Wain, Francis King, Sandy Wilson, Alan Brien, Michael Davie, Ronald Payne, Kenneth Tynan; athletes like Chris Chataway and Roger Bannister; television 'personalities' like Robin Day and Ludovic Kennedy; aristocrats like Billy Wallace and Edward Montague; actors like Robert Hardy and Jack May; oddballs like Teddy Goldsmith and John Aspinall: most of these I knew, some I knew well, and a few became my closest friends. Other friends I found again: Tony Kelly, at Queen's had been in my battalion and so had Hugh Bax, whose jeep driver was up too, reading Divinity.

At my own college, Merton, I made new friends: Alan Cooke, then out of the Coldstream Guards and now a BBC television producer, with whom I first saw Paris; Hilary Rubinstein, who went to the top at Gollancz before becoming a literary agent; Anthony Curtis, authority on Somerset Maugham and Literary Editor of the *Financial Times*; James Cameron, who joined me at S. H. Bensons, the advertising agency; Digby Neave, brother of the politician, who helped me when I went to live in France, and after; and the first man I met at Oxford, who became my closest companion there, an Indian called K. S. Bajpai.

I arrived in Oxford a day or two before the beginning of Michaelmas term, thinking to become acclimatised – or maybe to get ahead of the others, those grand, brilliant and high-born unknowns. The porter had shown me to my rooms. At the foot of the staircase I saw first my name, then others, painted in white capitals on black boards. Michael Davie was above me, K. S. Bajpai beside me on the ground floor. It was dusk, but the building was dark and silent. Outside, beyond the college wall, a damp miasma hung over Christ Church Meadow. Young men had looked out at this dank view since 1264.

Inside, for this was England, and old England at that, the climate was about the same. Hooks for pictures were on the walls, but no pictures; there were bookless shelves, a bare table and a cushionless leather Chesterfield. I sat on this and looked gloomily around. Where was the life I had read so much about, had looked forward to – and feared – so much? Where were the young blades, the wits, the dashing handsome athletes? Where were the midnight feasts, the bookish talk, the fun? Where was the glamour that the very name of Oxford once evoked? Not here, not now.

There was a knock at the door. I opened it. Outside, alien here as curry in a cereal dish, a tall, slender, black-haired, brown-skinned, richly dressed young man was standing, feet together, hands joined in prayer, torso bent slightly forward, eyes lowered, like an earnest beginner on a diving board. From this exotic presence there emerged, like a benison, the sound of perfect English spoken with a lilt, as the Welsh speak our language.

'Forgive me please if I intrude. My name is Shankar Bajpai. We are neighbours, I think. I do not know if you have already

18

made plans for this evening. In the event that you have not I would be delighted if you would join me in my humble supper.'

I followed my strange visitor along the short passage to his rooms. The ambience was as different from mine as, well, as chalk from ghee. Incense hung heavily in the air. Through the tangible fumes floated the voice of Gallicurchi's Carmen singing 'Là-bas, là-bas dans la montagne'. Red and white spines of Penguins lined the walls, with other books, fatter and taller than any I had known, their jackets more strident, their imprints unfamiliar: Random House and Doubleday and Knopf.

Our humble supper began with Dubonnet and poppadum, waferlike spiced bread sweated and crisped before the fire, and ended with strange sweet mangoes. These exotic goodies, which merely bracketed our feast, had arrived, my host explained, by diplomatic pouch, a present from his mother. His father was Sir Girja Bajpai, Foreign Minister in Nehru's government and previously High Commissioner in Washington, where Shankar had attended school. He had come from there to Merton because this had been his father's college.

Shankar, he told me, was a brahmin, a member of the highest, priestly caste, the outer sign of which was, strangely, a piece of old string he wore round his neck. By such measurements I was a good deal closer to the untouchable caste and yet I sensed already that we shared what might be called an aristocratic view of life: an inner conviction that what was best was meant to be enjoyed by those most capable of appreciating it, whatever their origin.

Unlike most of us, subsisting on scholarships or the government grants allotted to returning servicemen, Shankar received a generous allowance which, however, like the less noble postal order of Billy Bunter, had the irksome habit of arriving late. Faced with the threat to the chosen lifestyle that such a hiatus posed, your ordinary remittance man would perhaps have tightened the belt and sat the crisis out. Such however is not the aristocratic way, and it was not Shankar Bajpai's.

Scattered throughout the ancient colleges of Oxford, it

19

transpired, were numerous compatriots of Shankar. It is probable that many of them were of a lower caste than he. Most of them, as I recall, were named Mukkerjee, although there may well have been an occasional Chatterjee among them. Whatever their names, without these men Shankar's life at Oxford, and with it mine, would have been even more fraught (to use a catchword of the day) with hazard than it was.

Shankar then was what would now be called a film buff, or freak. When he discovered that the University Film Society had access to many desirable films, he quickly joined, and, becoming Secretary, was able to influence its choice in favour of those we had not seen or wished to see again. Films shown in the town cinemas, however, had to be paid for, a problem when, as so often, the P & O liner carrying Shankar's remittance was delayed by storms in the Indian Ocean. This is where Shankar's compatriots were to prove so singularly useful.

One winter afternoon when funds, and therefore spirits, were low Shankar suggested that we go to a movie. When I pointed out that this would require money, however little, Shankar said, with that look of surprised disdain with which he invariably greeted such mundane or sordid objections, 'My dear boy, that is no problem.'

We walked down Merton Street, turned left at the finishing school (where Lady Caroline Blackwood was the current toast) and right at the Eastgate, our local pub, and headed down the High to Magdalen. The college once had housed the Duke of Windsor, then Prince of Wales. Earlier it had sheltered Oscar Wilde, and earlier still, Gibbon, who complained, 'I spent fourteen months at Magdalen College; they proved the most idle and unprofitable of my whole life.' One thing was certain: somewhere inside Magdalen today there lurked a Mukkerjee, unaware.

Shankar told me to wait at the porter's lodge and I examined idly, between the red double-deckers, the legs of the gowned and eager girls of St Hilda's, cycling back from some dull lecture to tea and Marks & Spencer's crumpets and the day's catch of invitations to dim sherry parties or Ethel Mannin at the English Club. Shankar, emerging from the cloisters, walked towards me with his usual imperious stride, his face as always solemn. (In our second year he broke his leg and walked for a while with an imperious limp.) Getting quickly down to the nub I asked, 'How much?' Shankar halted abruptly, as was his disconcerting habit, and said, 'Dear boy, fifty pounds. Will that be enough?'

Shankar devised other schemes for dealing with the recurring money crisis. In desperate circumstances there was the book caper. Blackwell's, one of the two distinguished bookshops on Broad Street, extended credit to undergraduates. This concession was useful for obtaining books when one had no money. In Shankar's hands it was useful for obtaining money when one had no money. He had discovered that the other bookshop, Parker's, which was just across the street, though more reticent in matters of credit, would buy new books at half price, for cash. Thus it was the work of a moment for Shankar to charge a few books at Blackwell's, stride across to Parker's and emerge with a handful of the ready. It was a costly procedure, but by the time Blackwell's bill had been submitted, say twice, the famous remittance would once more have safely made its passage from India.

The allusion, in the context of books, recalls the visit to Merton of E. M. Forster. Shankar had become, *noblesse oblige*, President of the University Indian Society, the Oxford Majlis. Since it was the year of Partition, and because he was an admirer of his work, Shankar, without too much hope of success, had invited Forster to come over from Cambridge to address the Society. Forster, surprisingly for one so notoriously self-effacing, accepted and I was recruited to help entertain him.

The Junior Common Room was jammed, a brown sea of expectant Mukkerjees and Bannerjees, when we escorted Forster in, a frail, grey, shoulderless figure, shaped like a Beerbohm caricature. Seated behind a large table, Forster began, not to talk but to chat, shyly, as one who expects to make a few remarks from politeness and then clear the platform for more important

21

people. And he chatted, not about India, or Partition, or even about his books, but, for inscrutable reasons, about the Wild West of America, and the Grand Canyon, and Niagara Falls, all of which appeared to have impressed him on a recent trip. He illustrated his little chat with coloured brochures, which he distributed, of the kind found in the offices of travel agents.

When this brief and baffling discourse had ended, or rather trailed away, we took the old man, who wore a look of secretive amusement, like one who has scored a point in some decisive but tangential way, to tea in Alan Cooke's rooms, which were adjacent. Then we put him on a sofa and wrapped him in a rug for a nap before taking him to the station to catch, perhaps to his relief, the train to Cambridge and the comforting safety of his rooms at King's.

Up Magpie Lane and across the roaring High in the sober splendour of Queen's I encountered again my army friend, Tony Kelly. As Wine and Food Officer I had found Tony to be one of my better customers and I was pleased to discover that his new-found academic duties had not diminished his appreciation of good beer – a commodity for which his college was renowned. Queen's was the last of the Oxford colleges to brew its own ale and on a chill winter night it was heartwarming stuff. One drank in the steamy buttery, standing, silver mug in fist, around the kind of potbellied stove supplied by Props for the general store scene in western movies. Among drying tea-towels and black-gowned undergraduates white-jacketed college servants moved to set the long tables in Hawksmoor's serene hall across the cloistered way.

Queensmen for centuries have been summoned to dinner by hunting horn and sometimes the thin archaic toot told me it was too late to sprint for Merton hall. In Hilary term, the first of the academic year, strange faces abounded and I would be smuggled into dinner disguised as a member of Queen's. The food was better than at Merton and the company of Tony Kelly's friends agreeable: one, a northerner called Russell Greenwood, became a diplomat and steered me into advertising.

During all this time lectures, I heard, were going on all over town. Ever an enemy of prejudice, and willing always to give the benefit of the doubt, I once attended one of these academic rites. The lecturer was Lord David Cecil, an English tutor at New College. He may well have had important things to say, or perhaps it is true that everyone loves a lord, for hundreds of women undergraduates crammed the hall and looked up at him the way dogs do when the roast is brought to the table. This girlish crush banished me to the back of the room and since His Lordship talked in a high, bird-like twitter (twitching his head to one side like a budgerigar confronted with a mirror), any gems he may have been scattering failed to reach me, and finding myself still near the door by which I had entered, I stole away.

My tutor, whom I saw once a week for an hour – this constituting almost the sum of my exposure to academic life at Oxford – only confirmed my low opinion of the lecture hall. 'If we have anything to say at all, Charles, we've either put it in a book or we're just about to. So why not stay in your rooms and read? Much cosier.'

When Hugo Dyson died not long ago *The Times* devoted almost a third of a page to his obituary, a lot for an obscure don – for Hugo had published almost nothing, nor was he one of the great eccentrics, like Spooner. There is reason to believe, however, that he was greatly loved, and by many. He was a small, pink, twinkling man who moved on dainty feet, like an academic Cagney. As he walked his hands were busy together, as if he were knotting string, or telling beads. His hair was white and he held his head slightly cocked, in courteous attentiveness, as if awaiting some sublime punch-line. He seemed always to have just stopped laughing or to be just about to start. In between he twinkled. He was a merry man as only the deep can be.

His rooms in Fellows' Quad looked out through a seventeenth-century dormer window past Dead Man's Walk to the unchanging Meadows, filled with seventeenth-century cows. I entered these noble chambers always with pleasurable anticipation. To be treated as an unquestioned equal by this man induced a god-like feeling.

'Charles – oh how nice! You do look well! Are you playing lots of games? Never thought of you as a *hearty*.'

He would twinkle away into a rear room and his voice would pipe through the doorway.

'What do you say. Madeira? What tempts you this lovely morning – isn't it beautiful – Worthington? Good!'

Returning with a drink for both of us, eyes Pickwickian and conspirational, he would chatter on.

'Now – what are you going to teach me today? You know, Charles, when you want to you can write like an *angel* – like poor Poll!'

At this point, too often, I would take a gulp from my glass and begin to explain that, grappling devotedly though I was with the longer narrative poems of Wordsworth, I was not absolutely ready to commit my views on them to paper and that the further intensive study needed before such commitment would demand a little more time – say, about a week. Hugo's reaction to this snivelling excuse was always the same. He would seem to brighten even more, his pale blue eyes would become large and round, like a child's before its first Christmas tree, and he would say, as if the thought had struck him for the first time, 'Then how about a little walk? A turn in the Meadows! What do you say?'

It was always the same walk, Hugo beside me, bright, eyes and feet twinkling, hands fiddling, talking or listening, his head cocked, with huge interest to my banalities, as we went out through Fellows' Gate, past the Gothic horror of Christ Church Meadow Buildings, where Auden had lived, blinds drawn, down Broad Walk, left at the river and the college barges, left again at the Cherwell, past the new buildings of Merton and the Botanic Gardens and out on to the High across from Magdalen. It was at the sight of this, the most glamorous of the Oxford colleges, that inspiration would strike Hugo. He would stop, turn towards me like one who has just been handed the Secret of Life on a plate, and as if realising for the first time that our path would take us past the Eastgate public house, he would say, 'Charles! Shall I

24

just pop into Magdalen and see if Jack Lewis is there? Bet he's in the Eastgate though. What do you say? Let's just look, shall we?'

Jack Lewis, better known perhaps as C. S. Lewis, was invariably there, and so was another don, called Tolkien, a name which, although he held the chair in Anglo-Saxon, meant nothing then to the world outside the university. Lewis, red-faced, portly, dressed always in the same double-breasted blue serge suit, looked like a farmer in town for market day. Tolkien, Slav-boned, white haired, ascetic, almost fugitive but with the slightest hint of secret arrogance: the high egocentricity perhaps of those who speak a private language. It is to me a melancholy fact that I always found the much-admired work of these two famous men completely unreadable.

These apparently haphazard encounters on Wednesday mornings, throughout term, during which I drank beer and exchanged views with Dyson, Lewis and Tolkien, comprised the major part of my tuition at Oxford. I use the word 'apparently' because it was not until recently, while leafing through a new biography of Tolkien, that I discovered that the distinguished trio had for years been meeting regularly, with the ostensible purpose of discussing Christianity, at a pub in St Giles on Sunday evenings, and in the Eastgate at noon on Wednesdays. The biographer, though in other ways commendably thorough, fails to mention the presence at these latter meetings of a shy, awe-struck, dark-haired undergraduate: a lapsus that will no doubt be rectified in future editions.

Lewis and Tolkien achieved world fame, Dyson almost none at all. He has, however, been seen by millions more than they. When John Schlesinger made the film that brought *him* fame, he invited his old tutor to join in the fun. Those who would like to see how our mentor was in the flesh should seek out the film *Darling*, in which Dyson plays the famous writer. Poetic, or at least filmic, justice had been done at last.

I had almost forgotten, the painful memory having been long suppressed, that I attended another weekly tutorial, this one of a much less agreeable kind. Perhaps because of the long-held

English belief that if you do anything pleasurable you must be punished for it, the school of English at Oxford included Anglo-Saxon as a compulsory subject. (Cambridge, more enlightened, had dropped it years since.) This ugly and rebarbative language drove me more often than was good for me and my academic progress to the snug buttery and forgetful beer of Queen's. Had my Anglo-Saxon tutor been more inspiring I might have applied myself more diligently to the deadly declensions or to the translation of the repellent *Beowulf*. Unfortunately, success in English Literature was inseparably tied to success in English Language. I knew, because he had told Alan Cooke and Anthony Curtis so, that Hugo confidently expected me to get a First – and C. S. Lewis had told me that he expected the same for his pupil, and my friend, Ken Tynan. In fact he got a second and I lay his (comparative) failure, and mine, squarely at the feet of Grendel and his disgusting mother.

I was close to Tynan in one other way at Oxford: I tended to inherit his cast-off girl-friends. I have never forgotten those splendid girls. How could one forget girls with names like Eileen Rabbinowitz, Liz Zaiman and Ellie Horowitz? Many was the game I played with these brainy beauties around the ping-pong table at Somerville (Tynan, among his many qualities, was a demon with the table-tennis bat) but it was never a love match. Love came though, in my second year.

There were graver matters. Something gave way when I went up to Oxford. An iron band began to compress my skull. My arms became stiff and heavy. Anxiety floated round me like an invisible cocoon. I took these puzzling symptoms to the doctors. They diagnosed a 'mild anxiety state' and prescribed phenobarbitol, forerunner of the tranquillisers. Nobody mentioned conflict, or the unconscious, or psychiatry. I would have scorned them if they had. I was a healthy, normal chap. Always had been. Why should I change now, in this paradise of youth, this beautiful free state, this goal of my dreams attained?

Faced for the first time with a world where there were no, or few, rules to break or to obey, I failed to impose my own.

Confronted for the first time with real competition – in brains, in charm, in wealth, in looks, in talent – I elected to play possum or the waiting game. Threatened with the revelation of my own inferiority in these fields, I defended myself with wit and protected myself with self-deception. I had begun my slow withdrawal from life. From then on, I said to my friends, with that famous, desperate wit, it was neuroses, neuroses all the way.

Her name (what else could it have been?) was Mary and she was an English rose of the smaller, pink and bud-like kind. She was neat, petite and slender (absolutely the right size). Her hair was *chatain* (though she, the darling, called it mouse) and wavy-curly and cut close to the head, the way that women wore it the year that I was born (aha! Dr Freud). Under the high-arched brows, perfect parentheses, the eyes were two blue ponds to drown in: myopia gave devoted intensity to her gaze. The lips were the little-girl lips of the heroines of silent movies. No make-up insulted that blameless skin – dairy cream, strawberry-tinged. Botticelli, Greuze and Boucher had made rough sketches for this face: here was the finished work. She was seventeen, she had never been kissed and she was mine.

Our gaze had met, as Hammerstein had foretold, some enchanted evening, across a crowded room. The room, large, low-ceilinged, on the High, was crowded with the guests of Robin Beatson, a Merton friend, who shared it with his old chum from Charterhouse, an Exeter man called Colin Hunter. Tony Kelly was there, and Shankar Bajpai, and the blond, outrageous James Cameron. But I had smoke-filled eyes only for her, and I could see, for one senses those things, that she was interested in me, or anyway, was interested in the interest I showed in her, which gave me a base to work from.

I did not make much progress, for by discreet inquiry I discovered that she was Colin Hunter's sister and chaps tend to be protective about their little sisters. It so happened that Colin regarded me, in his phrase, as 'anti-social'. (That he also regarded her as anti-social I only discovered the other day, when, thirty years later, he told me so.) I asked him to introduce us – such was the custom then. He contrived not to. The frustration was ended when the bold young thing, frustrated too, I liked to think, strode across the room to where I stood and asked me if I had a light. I did not have a light: I do not smoke. It did not matter: nor did she. It gives you the measure of the girl.

She invited me to the annual dance of her art school, at High Wycombe. She – the fair, the chaste, the inexpressive she – invited me! I went, and I held her in my arms, as one did for dancing then, and at midnight she took me, reckless girl, anti-socially into the modelling room, and I kissed her and she kissed me back, in a spirit of reciprocity, while all around this passionate scene, the Greek and Roman statues stood unmoved.

Whenever she could she came to Oxford, to tea in my rooms, for walks in Merton gardens, for parties, to dance all night, at Digby Neave's twenty-first at his aunt's house on Box Hill, at college Commems where we drank champagne for breakfast. When we could not meet we wrote, impossibly long letters every day. Hers were not giddy *billets doux*. At times she could be gravely Austenish: 'We see each other as often as is tactful: I should not be allowed to see you more and I would not want to see you less'; at other times precociously perceptive: 'I think I like the way your friends like you more than the way you like your friends.'

There wasn't anyone who knew her who didn't love her. Where I had the advantage was that she loved me. Shankar said, 'My dear boy, I love you dearly, but if you ever harm that girl ...', and 'My dear fellow, do not think that you are the only one who has feelings about a certain young lady....' He gave her a silk scarf, blue like her eyes, which was a credit, in every sense, to his London shirtmaker, Washington Tremlett.

When Shankar's father came to London with Nehru and his daughter Indira the party would be lodged in regal apartments at Claridges. This lavish accommodation was always reserved for several days in advance, to give the High Commissioner, Krishna Menon, and his minions, time to fill the place with flowers and pianos. In the hiatus it was Shankar's custom to move into the empty suite to await his father. A warm, affectionate man, Shankar disliked being alone and, generous, he liked to share his good fortune. It was thus that Mary and I found ourselves installed, as guests of an unwitting Government of India, in the Prime Ministerial suite at Claridges.

When one is young, and in love, though penniless, the mere presence of the loved one is sustenance enough. A loaf of bread, a glass of wine, and so on. However, to prolong the metaphor, there is nothing wrong either with what the French call *un peu de beurre sur les épinards*, if that happens to be the dish you've ordered. And while between the three of us we did not have the price of a plate of fish and chips down the road we could, and we did, lift the white telephone and order up, in sufficient quantities, those staples of the high political diet, smoked salmon, foie gras and champagne, with the trimmings. There was a Steinway grand, for sentimental Chopin. There were flowers everywhere. I remember it all now. So does His Excellency Shankar Bajpai, for we talked about it only the other day. But does Mary? There was another line in Hammerstein's song: 'When you have found her, never let her go.' Strange how potent cheap music can be.

Chapter 3

When young Americans leave home to make their way in the world they share apartments: 'room-mate', like almost all innovations in our language, is an American idiom. The French never leave home at all: the terrible obstacle of the *bac* surmounted, they move into the *chambre de bonne*, and then, a suitable marriage having been arranged, transfer to the *appartement* of an aunt or grandparent who, with French practicality, has come to a timely end.

In England, as in most other matters, such things are differently arranged. In the early 1950s, when the belief that an Englishman's home was his castle still had, so to speak, tenancy, the young man or woman leaving the parental home moved into a single room, ill-equipped for even the most basic hygiene and warmed by a gas fire which glowed only when shilling pieces were fed into a meter's insatiable maw. Such miniature machines for living were called bed-sitting-rooms by the politely educated, bed-sitters by their unfortunate inhabitants and bed-sits by their money-grabbing owners seeking to save space in the advertising columns of the evening papers. Whole houses, whole streets of houses, all over London were rabbit-warrened with these cheerless cells. From grim Oakley Street on the fringe of acceptable Chelsea to smoky Pimlico on the wrong side of the Victoria railway line, they spread like cancer in the city bone. In all bed-sitterdom, no street took precedence over Ebury Street, which hugged the grand purlieus of Belgravia. Mozart had lived there; George Moore had lived there; so had Noel Coward. And so did I.

My room was on the top floor front of a house distinguishable from the others in the street only by its number, 64. Mary, who had been accepted as a student at St Martin's School of Art in Charing Cross Road, had taken a similar room a few doors away. This chaste arrangement reflected the social pattern of the time.

Depressing and familiar then to the young job-seeker as the two words 'Ebury Street' were the two names 'Gabbitas' and 'Thring' ('Church and Gargoyle' in *Decline and Fall*). This ancient establishment was a place of last resort for young men and women who either did not know what career they wanted to pursue or, having given thought to the matter and made their choice, found that thousands were there before them, for the choice was always the same: journalism, publishing or the BBC.

Gabbitas, Thring were specialists in the plugging of holes in the educational fabric with suitably shaped pegs. At a shaming interview one's few credentials would be noted and a few days later buff envelopes containing roneo'd typewritten slips of coarse white paper would begin to arrive in the post for one's consideration. The kind of slip I would have regarded with favour would have announced something along these lines:

> Widowed Italian lady seeks cultivated, personable young Englishman as tutor to her two daughters (15 and 17). Knowledge of English essential; some Italian an advantage. Should be prepared to give private tennis and swimming instruction. Application, with photo, to: Contessa Crespi, Villa Borghese, Piccolo Marina, Capri.

What I got was rather closer to the kind of slip that the unfortunate Paul Pennyfeather received:

> ... first-class games essential
> Status of school: school
> Salary offered: £120 resident post
> Reply promptly but carefully to Dr Fagan ('Esq., Ph.D.' on envelope) enclosing copies of testimonials and photograph, if considered advisable....

My school was in one of those large Victorian terrace houses

31

that huddle together near West Hampstead Underground station in the desperate but forlorn hope of being mistaken for Hampstead proper. Apart from the ageing and ague-ridden headmaster and his long-defeated wife, I was the only staff. There were about fifty boys, up to the age of twelve, and my duties were to teach all subjects, to supervise and referee games in a sad little field across the road from the house and, in the lunch hour, to invigilate chess tournaments among the brainier of the little beasts. For these activities my salary was to be £4 10s. a week, paid in cash each Friday. My rent in Ebury Street, also payable in cash on Fridays, was £2 10s. It seemed a long way from the officers' mess, from Oxford and, though geographically closer, from Claridges.

The boys were rich, spoiled, fat and filled with low cunning. They were the sons of the better-heeled sort of *New Statesman* reader and those European immigrants who had managed to bring their jewels with them. They despised me effortlessly when they discovered that I did not own a television set. Sensing the lack of a vocation, they were always trying to catch me out. In the case of Latin this was easy enough, for although it had been required for matriculation at Oxford, that was long ago and by now Latin was Greek to me. I was saved from exposure and the boot by Mary, whose studies in the field had been more recent than mine. I took the set textbook home and she wrote the answers to the questions in an exercise book and I kept this crib on my knees when the boys handed in their work for correction. The boys, missing nothing that might be turned to evil use, knew what was going on, but I needn't have worried. Appreciation, respect even, gleamed in their piggy eyes.

Art, also proposed in the curriculum, remained untaught in the absence of a qualified instructor, leaving the boys dangerously free to kick each other on Friday afternoons − their preferred mode of self-expression. Inspired, I proposed Mary for the post and, there being no other applicants, the offer was accepted. Since Friday was now a double pay-day we were able to splurge on a meal (baked beans on toast in the ABC) and even a movie on

Friday nights on our way home. That winter term, the big hit was Carol Reed's *Third Man* with Joseph Cotten and Orson Welles, and London jangled to the sound of the zither.

Weekends and nights of Ebury Street's genteel squalor, the early morning rush to meet the rigid hours of a job I violently disliked, the mean diet – all this, after the warm wombs of army and university, came as a disagreeable shock. Humankind, as Eliot noted, cannot bear too much reality, and I was only human. Mary had found a vacation job filing income tax returns in Vincent Square for five pounds a week. I quit the dreaded school and joined her there (even more time together!). We were fired, after a while, for smooching on the job, but by that time I had been pointed in another, and unexpected, direction.

Flush with funds from our jobs as temporary civil servants, we went out one night to offer ourselves a beer. We chose a pub called the Antelope, because it was near, and chic. In the saloon bar that night was a man I had last seen in quite another watering hole: the Buttery of Queen's College, Oxford. Russell Greenwood, friend of Tony Kelly, was a tall, stooped man with the face and posture of a failed eagle. He spoke with a swallowed, glottal accent that could have got him an audition with a Liverpool rock group. Curiously, for a man with a dry wit, he always looked as if he was about to drool, like a sated baby. He was a nice man withal and had a keen brain, which was as well, for he was about to take up a post as Second Secretary in one of our embassies.

He wondered amiably what I was doing. When I told him, struggling manfully as always to keep the self-pity to a minimum, he said, 'I'd have thought you'd do well in advertising.' Elaborating on this theme, he explained that advertising, which I had assumed was produced by manufacturers, was in fact 'created', in organisations called advertising agencies, by quick-witted jokers with a gift of the gab – people, in short, like me. What was more, he knew one or two of these people, and they were damned well paid.

Feeling already rich, and with that reckless improvidence that

33

comes so easily to me even when poor, I ordered another round of that warm English beer that tastes of pennies. The good Greenwood beatled on. You could try, he said, Rumble, Crowther and Nicholas. Or Young and Rubicam. Or Colman, Prentice and Varley. Or J. Walter Thompson.... I stopped him. A joke was a joke. Not bad, for a list of fictitious companies, improvised on the spot. But this was serious. I needed a job. Greenwood, injured by my tone, protested. These agencies were real. Ask around. Look in the book. Convinced, I wrote the names down.

When, next day, I checked at the Post Office (for bed-sitters have no telephones and hence no telephone books), I found that he had indeed been telling the truth. These surreal establishments existed and although I did not know what were the qualifications for employment in them, I decided to present my candidature. What, I would have said had the saying existed then, have I got to lose? (My freedom, I might now reply.)

Chapter 4

It is an immutable rule of advertising agencies that they will employ only those who are already employed by advertising agencies. Absolute beginners, innocently persuaded of their intrinsic and obvious worth, quickly stumble on this Catch 22. There was no difficulty in obtaining interviews: agencies, having nothing to offer their clients except talent, can no more afford to miss a budding Shakespeare than a publisher can risk losing a potential *Gone With The Wind*. But talent needs to be demonstrated and a witty film review in a university magazine – even supposing I had one to show – is no proof that its author is capable of discovering the fifteen words that will incite a working girl in search of true love to select some particularly repellent shade of lipstick from a Woolworths' counter in Grimsby.

As I made the nervous round of agencies the pavements seemed harder and the streets chillier after each warming glimpse of debutante receptionists, smooth executives, languid copywriters and carefully raffish art directors. Get some experience, I was courteously advised, and come back and see us in a year or two. I doubted if I could wait that long. Baffled, discouraged but increasingly desperate, I decided to change my tactics. The polite exchange of letters was ineffective, wasteful of time and money. I would choose an unvisited agency and, one more unfortunate, rashly importunate, put my shirt on the one last gamble and simply turn up on the doorstep.

With the courage of despair, or whatever the cliché is, I strode one afternoon down the sedate slope of Hertford Street, a snooty thoroughfare that connects Park Lane, with its heavy traffic, to

Shepherd Market with its lighter traffic of top tarts. Turning and mounting a few steps in front of a serene Georgian facade I pressed a bell beside a well-mannered plaque that bore the legend EVERETTS ADVERTISING. Returning my hand to the pocket of my Burberry, for warmth and also for poise, I waited.

The girl who opened the door was the kind of girl who opens the door in places like that. Not the first rank in the secretarial pecking order but it would do until something better came along. She invited me in and asked me whom I would like to see. I said I would like to see the Chairman. Like someone who already knew the answer she asked me if I had an appointment. It was now my turn in our little rondel and I answered no. That cleared that up and, showing me to a seat behind a glass-topped table with the magazines I'd read a dozen times that month, she disappeared to wherever receptionists disappear to.

Another girl came down the stairs and from a higher plane. She carried a shorthand notebook like a badge of office in a hand manicured for the boss's eye.

'Mr Everett Jones is in a board meeting, I'm afraid,' she said poshly. 'Can I help you? What was it about?' she added helpfully.

This was going better than I had hoped. 'I'm looking for a job,' I said. 'As a copywriter,' I added, helpful in my turn.

Her reaction surprised me. Her nicely-sketched eyebrows shot up, her non-notebook-laden hand rose to conceal her mouth and she began, unmistakably, to giggle. Recovering her composure – one is not a chairman's P A for nothing – she said, 'Do forgive me. They thought you were God, you see. It was your name. Now I have to go back and tell them you're not a big brandy account. Do you mind waiting a little longer?' Grinning to herself, she climbed back up the stairs.

Some moments later the girl came swinging, smiling back. 'They think its a scream,' she said. 'They're dying to meet you. Could you possibly come back tomorrow, this time?'

I said I thought I could manage that. 'Who should I ask for?' I added, efficiently, if ungrammatically.

36

'Mr Harling. Robert Harling,' she said, and smiled encouragingly. I went out into the street, where strangely it wasn't cold, and headed home to tell Mary the wonder of it all.

Next day, an old hand now, I rang the bell beside the porticoed door in Hertford Street. The neat receptionist, buddy-buddies today, led me down a corridor to the open doorway of a calm, light, high-ceilinged room. There, sideways on to me, a man stood, legs braced and apart like a captain on the bridge watching a squall come up. He wore no jacket and his trousers, of unusual cut, were supported by braces of a spirited design. They were braces meant to be seen; show braces. The trousers were of point-to-point tweed, cut so narrowly that they clung like ballet tights at the thighs, wrinkled slightly behind the braced knees and followed the form of the calves down to the spread feet, which were sheathed in brown country shoes whose narrow length bespoke bespoke.

Seen in profile, this figure, not tall, not short, resembled one of those caricatures of nineteenth-century notables drawn by 'Spy' and used to decorate the gaming rooms of gentlemen's clubs. Indeed, partly because of the importance given to the strong head and powerful torso by the tapering away of the rest of the body, partly because of the prominent but fine nose and assertive chin, Robert Harling (as I took him to be) closely resembled Mr Punch – but a Punch disciplined, ascetic, handsome, lean: a Punch with punch.

Oblivious, apparently, of my presence, Harling continued to gaze at the drawing board, his hands gripping it on either side like an athlete about to vault. He was studying the design of a large black capital 'A' with what looked like hatred. Ignored, I occupied myself by removing my Burberry, a good tactical move, for under it I was in better shape to meet the vestimentary challenge posed by my interviewer's idiosyncratic garb. My response was to play the classical card, believing as I do, like Beau Brummel, that if people notice a man's clothes he is badly dressed. This calls for great art and I was a little shocked to find that Harling, whom I knew to be one of the nation's leading typographers, should subscribe to an opposing school; for the role of type is to exalt the word, so that good typography is self-effacing and attains at its highest to invisibility.

The most elegant man I had met was my Oxford friend, Shankar Bajpai. Only when I inquired further into the reasons for this elegance did I discover that artists had been at pains to achieve it, so that his suits were not like others' suits, nor his shirts like others' shirts. It was Shankar who, at my request, introduced me to his tailor and his shirtmaker. I have been faithful to them ever since. Accompanying me, then, on this fateful morning were Anderson and Sheppard of Savile Row, represented by a tasteful grey flannel three-piece, and Washington Tremlett, of Conduit Street and (then) the Rue de Rivoli, represented not only by a made-to-measure cream poplin shirt but by a made-to-measure tie too, for in those days you chose your square of silk at Tremlett's and they made it up, layer on rich layer of the stuff, with no recourse to your modern hessian filler.

This then was how Robert Harling and I squared off sartorially for our confrontation. It was to be a short but drama-packed bout. Harling straightened from his drawing board, turned his piercing, slightly mocking gaze on me – the look of one who has cruelly learned not to believe in human goodness or decency but who is obliged by some relic of deeply buried hope to go on looking for them all the same – and said, 'What is the minimum you can live on?'

With insane recklessness I added ten shillings to the only salary I had ever earned.

'Five pounds,' I said.

'Can you start tomorrow?'

'Yes.'

He nodded dismissively and returned to the big black A. And I shrugged on my Burberry and walked out of the room and into the street and home to tell Mary that I had passed whatever test it was you had to pass to become a copywriter in a London advertising agency.

Chapter 5

Advertising, like everything else, begins with the word. A Savignac poster is a visual pun. Behind even a silent commercial there is a script. It follows that the star of the advertising world, the most sought-after, the highest-paid and the most indulged of employees, is the copywriter. What the pilot is to the mechanic, what the prima ballerina is to the corps de ballet, what Mick Jagger is to the Rolling Stones, the writer, *primus inter pares*, is to the rest of the agency. Had I been aware of this heady fact during my interview, or rather anti-interview, with Robert Harling I might have asked for, say, six pounds a week instead of five. On the other hand, had I done so I might never have met the two representatives of that élite who together formed the Copy Department of Everetts Advertising.

Of this odd pair, one was male, one female; one a poet who wrote of cats and unrequited love, the other a worshipper of dogs and horses; one spoke with an accent best described as cultivated Liverpool, the other with the clear gong-like tones of the Oxford blue-stocking; one is dead and one has been gravely ill and both became my friends.

When I entered the first-floor room that housed the Everetts Copy Department, A. S. J. Tessimond and Margaret Evans (*née* Flannery) were sitting face-to-face at desks that jutted out in parallel from a large bay window that overlooked the quiet backyards of Hertford Street. Margaret Evans's legs, of stunning symmetry and reckless length, rested, crossed and nylon-sheened, on the surface of her desk. The legs of John Tessimond, no less long, stretched out from under his desk and the feet that completed them were shoeless.

Ironically, advertising, that enemy of promise, has always attracted poets, for the poet's gifts are useful in the copywriter's trade, and slim volumes do not pay the rent. The three men who became my closest friends in advertising were all poets. The first of these was before me now, the first poet I had ever met, and I raised my eyes from my leg-inspection to look at him.

Tessimond's hair, straight, fine and abundant, was flaxen going grey. It fell, like Auden's or that of the young Yeats in the Augustus John portrait, over his right eye from where occasionally a long-fingered bony hand would sweep it back. His eyes, deep-set under albino brows and lashes, were like Slav-sloping cat's eyes. When he blinked the upper and lower lids seemed to meet in the middle over grey-green pupils like Colchester oysters. His face was long, lean, almost gaunt, like the face of Pasternak. Standing, as he was to meet me now, he was not quite tall but seemed so because he was so slim. There was something Scandinavian in his look: with a guitar in his hands he could have passed for Carl Sandburg. He was simply, elegantly dressed, in a charcoal-grey pinhead suit. (This suit, I discovered, was made by Huntsman, which meant that two-thirds of the Copy Department of Everetts were dressed by Savile Row, almost certainly a world record in the advertising business.)

I came to know him as well as most. His father had been a branch manager of Martins Bank. Tessimond had run away from Birkenhead School, but had gone on to take a degree at Liverpool University. Lowry-like, he had worked in offices – in advertising agencies – ever since, writing what he always called his verse in his spare time. He was utterly modest, free of all false notes and frugal in his habits. Although as a copywriter he was well paid, and though he had a small private income from the rent of a row of houses in a Liverpool suburb, he chose to live in a dark, one-room basement flat that looked out on a coal-heap in Jubilee Place, off the King's Road in Chelsea. His dinner, which I often shared, was always the same: sausages and Brussels sprouts (an honorable but unpoetic dish).

He drank sparingly, claiming that the principal effect of alcohol was to send him to sleep. He liked both classical and popular music which he played on a radiogram that occupied about an eighth of his apartment; a table with two upright chairs, two easy chairs, a single bed and book-shelves filled most of the remaining space. Modigliani prints hung on the walls. His favourite author was the novelist R. C. Hutchinson to whom untypically he wrote a fan-letter, starting a correspondence between the two. He spoke of Gerhardi and Djuna Barnes as admired contemporaries. His poetic master was Yeats.

His recreations were on a modest scale. Every Sunday at 4 o'clock he walked around the corner to the Classic cinema, an art house that specialised in French films. Sometimes on Sunday nights he would be persuaded to take a bus to Epsom, where the novelist Hubert Nicholson held poetry readings in his home: Tessimond hated being, as he inevitably was, the star but he felt a duty to poetry. Clifford Dyment, fellow-poet, the typographer Bea Ward and the painter Ceri Richards were the only other friends of his I met – apart, that is, from his rather unusual girl-friends.

Tessimond had been impotent, or more exactly, incapable of sexual intercourse, all his adult life. (I am giving away no confidences: he discussed his problem freely, as if it was back-ache.) He explained to me that at the moment of penetration his partner turned into his mother, whom he hated. In his constant effort to find the solution to his sexual problem, chasing girls was an activity to which he devoted a considerable amount of time and ingenuity. He specialised in good-hearted sluts and he found them by spending hours in the kind of sleazy night club that employs 'hostesses' who cajole customers to buy them fake drinks at prices that are all too real. Three factors commended Tessimond to such girls: he was kind, he fell romantically in love, and he was a source of money, a commodity for which they had an urgent, profound and insatiable need.

It seemed that he sought to be romantically ensnared and then disillusioned. The pattern was depressingly the same with each new conquest. Tessimond – 'Tessie' to his girl-friends – would

41

question the latest discovery about her life and problems, which were the same each time, then offer to help, even pressing money on her in the shape of loans which for the form were sometimes covered by a series of post-dated cheques. There would follow a rosy period in which the girl would demonstrate her gratitude in the way for which her professional training had best equipped her. She would allow him to buy her records, to be played first on the monstrous radiogram while she teetered about to the music, drinking too much of his gin; she would be taken to smart restaurants before her evening stint, during which Tessimond would sit obscurely, a Craven 'A' between long fingers, in the smoky corner of some revuebar; she would be taken to Paris or even to Juan les Pins, where the bikini had just made its daring début.

Then would come the weeks or months of doubt, and later dismay, as Tessimond discovered that his loans were not repaid, would never be repaid. Anger would follow, though anger in him was never convincing, harsh telephone calls, fierce letters. The girl would disappear and he would haunt the night-clubs looking for her. He rarely, if ever, recovered either his girl or his money, yet, after a while, he was ready for the next disaster. The pattern, formal as a sonnet, of kindness, generosity and love, followed by disillusion, recrimination and bitterness, would start again.

Any money that escaped the hot and scented grasp of these young floozies went into the pin-striped pockets of Mayfair psychoanalysts; for depression hung on Tessimond like the cloak of Death. He had often contemplated suicide but rejected it on the reasonable, if dispiriting, grounds that there was no way of being sure that what followed would not be worse than that which one had fled. He was constantly revising his will and I would witness it, noting with mixed feelings that in some versions I was left his radiogram.

In his verse he showed a wisdom that failed to help him in his life. (It has helped me though, and probably others.) Of the psychoanalytical experience he wrote:

His fees are large, his cares are light,
His analytic eyes are bright,
He glows with pride as well he might.
The analyst is always right.

He knew about money, and lost his own:

Money talks with a voice that's thinned
To a rustle of chequebooks in the wind.

Money talks with a voice as dry
As an auditor's enquiring eye.

He knew about the English, and failed in his relationships with them: 'We are a people/Easily made uneasy....', he wrote; we are fearful of one day saying

... all, all, all we did not mean to,
All, all, all we did not know we meant.

He understood cats, and like a cat, walked alone:

Cats, no less liquid than their shadows,
Offer no angles to the wind.
They slip, diminished, neat,
Through loopholes less than themselves ... are seldom
Truly owned till shot and skinned....

He knew about other animals, including the human:

Fish do not smile, nor birds: Their faces are not
equipped for it. A smiling dog's the illusion
And wish-fulfilment of its owner. Cats where
Permanent smiles inspired by mere politeness....

But the human kind had that unsought, unbidden '... gracenote of a smile.'

Regular, desperate and unspeakable electroconvulsion therapy at St Thomas's Hospital seemed to lift the intolerable weight of the cloak for a while, but it always settled again, more heavily each time, it seemed. Vacations did not help. He announced that he was going to Jamaica, a long and arduous journey then, and

43

hideously inappropriate as a resort for the Tessimond we knew. Three days later he was back in the office, appalled and shaken. There was a 'verse' in that, though, too, and one good enough, I note now, to be included in Philip Larkin's *Oxford Book of Twentieth-Century English Verse*.

This, my first poet, was also my first professional mentor. He claimed that writing copy was a painful process for him and shook his head in rueful admiration of my apparent facility. But I am a good mimic, and I had Tessimond to imitate. (At Everetts there appeared to be no other way of learning this strange new trade.)

He worked on the Ferranti account and claimed gloomily (the word recurs when one thinks of Tessimond) that the only slogan he had ever invented in advertising was 'Clearly Ferranti for sight and sound'. He also invented the word 'Waspie' for a waist-pinching corset. He proposed 'Slyboots' for a range of womens' footwear and for the same brand advised readers that the latest models were already the rage among Italian women but 'in England they are fore-runners. Firstfruits. Finds.' He was called upon, and I after him (terrified), to produce light verse to announce the services rendered by a firm of office cleaners. Beneath an illustration of a tycoon pacing about while dictating he wrote

> Even the slow, majestic beat
> Of Managing Directors' feet
> Can make a rose-red rug from Turkey
> Grim and grey, besmirched and murky:
> But we've a scientific knack
> For putting those brave colours back.

To show how class tells, even at this level of literary production, here for comparison is my own first effort in the series, under a picture of a dirty hand-bowl:

> Pray tell us, Sir, is that a basin
> You'd care to wash you hands and face in?
> For shame, it seems the care of bowls

Is not among your cleaner's roles:
But we will clean, in half a wink,
Everything *and* the kitchen sink.

It should be remembered in my favour that I was being paid
five pounds a week for this stuff by a hard task-master of whom
Tessimond wrote, in a series of clerihews published under the title
'ad-verse' in the office magazine:

Robert Harling
Is fond of snarling,
But won't, if you treat him right,
Bite.

But if I regarded myself as underpaid, Tessimond was
convinced that he was overpaid; and being a man of painful
integrity, insisted on raising the matter, complete with figures and
suggestions for cuts, before the board of directors, not only on
one occasion but frequently, to the board's embarrassment and
everyone else's disbelief. Tessimond's attitude in this matter, as in
much else, is unique in my professional experience.

When Tessimond gave a copy of one of his books (either *Walls
of Glass* or *Voices in a Giant City*) to his colleague, the dedication
read, 'To Margaret, without whom my life at Everetts would
have been even more gloomy, lack-lustre and glum.' The
sentiment was typically Tessimondian, in its style and in its
appropriateness. Margaret Evans, sitting opposite Tessimond, was
in most ways his opposite. You would have said, on meeting her,
that she was one of those healthy, practical, no-nonsense girls
produced by the English upper-middle-class to take in hand its
Finknottles and its Woosters. You would have been wrong. For
one thing she was Irish, and convent-reared. For another, your
healthy, practical, no-nonsense girl does not become an
advertising copywriter, even in a Mayfair agency.

She had that near-beauty which has the advantage over classic
beauty of being human and therefore easier to live with. Her
straight dark auburn hair was worn pulled back, emphasising the
high cheekbones and the eager, almost rapt look of a rider taking

a fence at speed. The eyebrows were not the usual female arch but the horizontal tick of the male, like the eyebrows of Lauren Bacall. The determined mouth grinned rather than smiled. Her slim, slightly angular figure looked as if it had just stepped out of jodhpurs and into a dress and was itching to get back into jodhpurs again. She had the hip-swinging stride of Garbo in *Queen Christina*; one of those girls who is also one of the boys.

She claimed to like horses and dogs and to find one or two people tolerable. She took some pains to conceal her considerable intellectual powers and her more womanly qualities. It was as if, having registered with Central Casting as a hard-riding, hard-drinking, thigh-slapping type from the Shires, she had accepted, *faute de mieux*, a temporary role as a sophisticated West End female executive.

Inevitably, of the various accounts Margaret worked on, her favourite was Bob Martin's Dog Powders, which she referred to, though not in the presence of the client, as Dog Martin's Bob Powders. It was not the most important account in the agency – Boots the Chemists spent far more money – but it had its prestige value and it had been with the agency for many years. This year, though, things were not going well at all. The bone, so to speak, of contention was the price of the Dog Powders. The agency held the view that this was too high for consumer acceptance, there being, in the jargon of the trade, a 'psychological ceiling' for the price of any product. The client, understandably loth to see his profit-margin reduced, resisted the agency's arguments.

While the battle raged, amid the acrid smell of powders, a full-page newspaper advertisement had been prepared: that is, a layout had been made by the studio, based on copy written by Margaret Evans; these two elements having received the client's approval, a proof had been prepared and was being circulated in the agency, by the Traffic Department, for the signatures of the heads of departments before transmission to the newspaper for publication. Pending the outcome of the heated discussion, a white space had been left in the 'base-line' of the advertisement, where the price of the product is usually mentioned. The text, or

46

copy, now read: 'Bob Martin's Dog Powders will cost you [blank] a packet at your local chemist or pet-shop,' or that is how it should have read. Unfortunately a conscientious compositor at the printers', ignorant of the bloody war engaged between agency and client, and seeing a blank space where no blank space should be, had closed up the line. Since it now made, grammatically at least, perfect sense, every head of department, and Margaret Evans as the copywriter responsible, had initialled the proof. Only the uncontrolled giggles of the messenger-boy sent to take the okayed proof from Harling's office to the newspaper, attracting its occupant's cold anger but also his attention, saved the account for the agency by preventing the following message from appearing at the astonished breakfast-tables of the nation the following morning: 'Bob Martin's Dog Powders will cost you a packet at your local chemist or pet-shop.'

Relationships with another client were also temporarily soured when Margaret, asked for a name evocative of ballet for a particularly armour-like corset, proposed 'Casse-noisette'. She had the good sense not to show another *jeu d'ésprit* of hers to the client concerned, but she showed it to me and in spite of twenty-five years of intensive effort I have been unable to erase it from my memory:

> O Lilly has stolen my luncheon;
> O Lilly has stolen my dinner;
> She's left me with nothing to munch on;
> I'd like to catch Lilly and Skinner.

Margaret lived alone, except for a handsome Irish setter, in a basement in Pimlico. (If you were an Everetts copywriter you lived in a basement.) Pimlico being not far from Ebury Street, we would often walk home together after work. Sometimes we would call in at my local pub – the Prince of Wales. Occasionally, after a drink, she would invite me back for dinner. The meal, if I was lucky, would be cooked, supremely well, by what might have been called her steady boy-friend, did not that adjective convey the reverse of the truth.

47

Patrick Kirwan was a slim, black-but-greying-haired Irishman with a fine but faintly ravaged face that, had its ruin been more advanced, would have resembled one of those faces seen on the benches of the Embankment, under the bridges of Paris or on the hard stoops of the Bowery. He was a courteous, quiet and scholarly man with a sly wit which was, alas, too often lost in the depths of an impenetrable brogue. He had, one was told, published a slim and well-received volume of hagiography, and had become film critic of the London *Evening Standard*. Now he was a scriptwriter and his current project was an episodic comedy set in the Western Desert during the war and starring, among others, Yvonne de Carlo and Peter Ustinov. Script conferences were held in the back bar of the Café Royal and the concensus at the last of these was that if the script was ever to be completed it would be necessary to lock Kirwan in a room for at least two weeks – a plan which, though *in extremis*, proved successful.

Kirwan lodged on what was called a 'play-street' but had been obliged to seek shelter elsewhere after being unnerved, and almost unmanned, by what he graphically called 'T'ose bullet-headed little bastards coming at you ball-high.' He was the almost inseparable (except, that is, when locked in a room) drinking and racing companion of Liam O'Flaherty, author of *The Informer* and other notable works. He introduced me to O'Flaherty one night in the French Club, a watering-hole favoured by the bohemian literati largely because it was open when the bar of the Café Royal was closed. O'Flaherty's hair was whiter than white, his skin baby-pink, and his eyes were the transparent blue of the fanatic. He held himself rigidly, unnaturally upright, like von Stroheim in *La Grande Illusion*. When we met his eyes glared palely at me and he barked, 'Where would you be from, Hinnissy?' I said that my parents came from Carlow, in the county of Carlow. He pierced me with another dose of the blazing blue. 'Thin you're a gintleman, Hinnissy!' he shouted and turned on his heel.

Kirwan had his own assessment of me. The psychological symptoms that had begun to manifest themselves at Oxford flared from time to time. I felt I ought to talk to somebody about them, but to whom? For someone like Margaret, I felt, the recommended treatment would be a good gallop and a rub down afterwards. Kirwan may have been closer to the mark. When she recounted my problems to him, he gave the matter some thought, while adding a dash more *estragon* to the sauce and said, with quiet finality, 'Sure, there's nothing wrong with Hennessy that a five pound note won't cure.'

Chapter 6

Living with a neurosis is like swimming in an overcoat: one is disadvantaged, but it can be done. Do not expect the swimmer, though, to strike out for distant shores. All his resources will be engaged in simply staying afloat. So it has been with me. Self-circumscribed by fears, of failure, of rejection, weighed down by guilt, I strived to do nothing that might provoke authority, that might expose my inadequacy, that might attract attention. I was farther out than they thought, but I wasn't waving, and I wasn't drowning.

Tessimond had written, in 'Song of the Psychiatrist':

> Learn to know the mind-behind-
> Mind that sees when you are blind;
> Learn to know the mind-below-
> Mind that's wiser than you know....

and I recognised wisdom there, but couldn't see its application to my case. I just wanted to be a healthy, normal fellow, like everybody else.

I went, as I had at Oxford, to see a doctor, recommended to me by a colleague at Everetts. He was a handsome, dashing, pin-striped pederast, with pink cheeks and a red carnation and a way with the flirty mink-muffled Mayfair matrons. For the insomnia, he said, 'Too many pillows! It's *always* that.' But he knew about fear, this boy, and about concealment, and about not being like other chaps, and he wrote me a note to take to the Psychiatric Unit of St George's Hospital. ('They have some awfully good people there. You'll love it.')

50

So I went to see Dr Maurice Partridge, a chain-smoking prefrontal lobotomy freak with a face like a tired toad who sat across a desk from me in a bare room that looked as if it had been commandeered by the army, and took non-stop notes, using grunts for punctuation. He asked me if I had many friends and when I said yes, he said, *'Friends?'* Then he asked me, 'Have you ever tried to do anything you couldn't do?' which was a good one and called for no answer. When he showed me to the door, he shook his head and said with a sad, hang-frog expression, 'It's a vale of tears, old boy, a vale of tears.'

And so it was just then, in the Ebury Street sector. Somebody said somewhere that if writers idealise women it is not because they see less than other men but because they see more. Well, I wasn't a writer, only a copywriter, but I knew that nothing was as good as I saw that it could be. What's more, you'd hardly expect a practically certified neurotic, who set unattainably high standards for himself, not to set unattainably high standards for what is often called, revealingly, his better half. Neither as elemental as Byron, who couldn't bear to see his women eat, nor as fundamental as Swift, who had his hang-ups, I found plenty to chip away at in my near-perfect mate. Near-perfect is just not good enough, ideal-wise. Such demands put more strain on the liaison than the liaison had it in it to take. When you put a love-object on a pedestal and take your chisel to improve the shape of things, something is going to crack.

Mary fled, leaving, as such scenarios demand, a note forbidding me to try to find her, the kind of note that always means the opposite of what it says. I traced her, with some dismay, for I would have preferred a script with more romantic locations, to Blackpool, where her married sister lived. In the movie version our hero would have leapt in hot pursuit on to the earliest train. So indeed would I, had I not been obliged to scout around a bit for the fare. Encouraged in my project by my friend Ron Terry, an art director at Everetts, and with eight pounds of his salary in my pocket, I headed north.

In Blackpool, euphoric, for once in command, I telephoned her and instructed her to meet me at the Tower, the workers' Tour Eiffel. She protested, sticking to the dialogue, but I knew she was impressed by my romantic dash (or rather I guessed she was: I knew I was). She arrived, the one unstrange sight in Blackpool, bursting with beauty, with just contained excitement, like a debutante at her coming-out ball. With the juice still up I swept her off (only the cliché will do) to the ballroom high in the Tower. In the 1950s, people still danced with, rather than at, each other, and couples swirled around the vast space, negotiating the corners with cunning, show-off reverse steps. I did some more sweeping and we swirled too, she with her eyes lowered, silent, for there was nothing she needed to say; she was savouring an inner feast.

I looked around at the hundreds in our heat of the marathon and up at the hundreds more on the balcony that surrounded the floor. Then I noticed a strange thing. All those people, with twice as many eyes, were watching us, were following our every step. Granted, we made a handsome couple; admittedly my lessons at the Arthur Murray Dance Academy, bought at frightening cost, were now paying off: *mais, il ne faut pas exagérer*. Was there perhaps a visible aura, special to people in love, that made us a sudden cynosure? Was it our state of grace that focused this human spotlight on us? It wasn't. It was Mary's hat.

Alone among these holidaying mill- and factory-girls Mary was wearing a hat − a small white woollen bonnet or beanie that sat like a saucer on her chestnut curls. And all those eyes were fixed on this moving disc, as helplessly as they would have been on a magician's glove or the ball at a tennis tournament.

Sobered, we talked and made up and decided we should see less of each other for a while and that she would accept a long-standing invitation to go and stay with Tony Kelly's mother in Devon while we took a cooler look at our feelings. We kissed and parted as day broke. As the poet put it in another context, bliss was it in that dawn to be alive, and to be young was very heaven.

Back at Everetts, with both salary and confidence increasing, I went on writing copy, for Chubb Locks, for General Cleaners, for Ferranti. I wrote a two-part playlet for Bob Martins (now friends again) to teach their salesmen how to, and how not to, sell their products to the retailers. I knew nothing of such matters, but my guesses were good: the client wrote a letter of congratulations to the Managing Director, Everett Jones (a small, feisty Welshman, like a jollier, blue-chinned Harry Truman, himself a failed Liberal politician and man of culture *manqué* who claimed to have a friend with a garden landscaped by Calamity Brown), adding that it was clear that the author was someone well versed in the lives and problems of dog-powder salesmen. Ha! I thought, he doesn't know what old Willie Maugham had to say about that: that for a writer to describe a sheep, it is not necessary for him to have eaten a sheep, but it will help if he has tasted a lamb chop.

With Hamish Nimmo, an art director who had a gift for caricature, I invented the Tycoon, as representing the typical reader of the *Economist*, to sell advertising space in that magazine. The notion had a certain *succès, d'éstime* at least: I was telephoned by the head of Time–Life, a competitor of the publication, and Hamish was hired to be its art director.

Robert Harling, among other things, designed the *Sunday Times*, which won prizes for its typography, not surprising when one considered that Harling also edited a rich and glossy magazine called *Alphabet and Image*, later called *Image*. (Advertisements for this first featured a large 'A', and it was this that Harling was designing when I interrupted him with an interview.) He startled me, and flattered me, by asking me to write a piece for the magazine on the graphic work of Edward Ardizzone, best known for his children's books. Apart from my five pound commission from Norman Swallow for the definitive work on *Brideshead*, literary work was, as it were, a closed book to me; but I needed the money and I accepted the job. I was saved in my ignorance by two things. Ardizzone, who cooked me a spaghetti dinner in his home, was a charming, literate and helpful man (although, like many an illustrator, and like Sullivan with his symphonies, he was convinced that he was truly a serious painter obliged to do illustrations for a living).

My other saviour was V. S. Pritchett. I discovered that he had written a monograph on Ardizzone as an introduction to a Pelican edition that Penguin for economic reasons had decided not to publish. With Pritchett's kind, spontaneous and generous permission, I got hold of the page-proofs of this article and, without his permission, I lifted most of it. Since it is mostly Pritchett's work, it remains the best thing I have published.

Pleased with my plagiaristic piece, Harling asked me to write a short book on Eric Gill, the artist and typographer whose Gill Sans face sets, on bus stops, tube stations and posters, the undating house-style of London Transport. Gill's widow turned down the idea. It has taken twenty-five years for the book to appear – written, I note, by Robert Harling himself.

For all Harling's extra-mural help, and although my salary increased greatly in the next two years, there was a limit to what this small, pleasant, civilised company could pay me, and a limit to what I could learn there. Besides, I now had the one essential qualification for employment in an advertising agency: employment in another advertising agency. I was ready for the big time.

The two top, blue chip, glamour-stock advertising agencies in London, it was generally agreed, were J. Walter Thompson, the English branch of an American multinational, and S. H. Benson, a homespun, native outfit of some antiquity. The locations of these two companies almost defined what would now be called – thanks, if that is the word, to David Ogilvy – their brand-image.

JWT, as it was known to insiders, was situated in Berkeley Square, at the throbbing heart of ritzy Mayfair. Its secretaries were debutantes, its account executives were Old Etonians and its directors members either of the House of Commons or, like my Oxford friend Edward Montague, of the House of Lords. Bensons was in Kingsway, a dull and ugly artery that segregated the West End from the City, forming a kind of buffer zone where bowler hat and trilby met. It was staffed by ex-naval officers, Oxford graduates in the arts and poets, whose eccentricities were suffered by a secretariat dredged, by way of the Holborn tube, from the dimmer suburbs.

This then, for I was aiming high, was the choice before me. I wrote to both and was received by both. In the airy early nineteenth-century premises of Thompsons an elegant and casually efficient lady with the title of Head of Personnel sat me at a desk and gave me ink-blot and intelligence tests. I enjoyed myself at these pleasant games and at the bell I had scored, she told me, as high a mark as had ever been recorded. Next came the bad news: I must now be interviewed by their psychiatrist. A couple of days later, old hand that I now was at the unburdening caper, I bared my soul to this bird, throwing light cheerfully over the murkiest recesses of my rich and dark unconscious. This, in retrospect, may have been a mistake. Shortly afterwards a letter informed me that J. Walter Thompson could find no use for my talents. (I took my revenge later by joining their Paris office.) A little disappointed, I addressed myself to the other contender for my services.

Halfway up Kingsway from Aldwych an awning announced the entrance to a high, long and totally anonymous passage. This was the entrance to Kingsway Hall, seat of the Methodist Church in England. It was also the entrance to S. H. Benson Ltd, Advertising Agents. A door on the left led to a caged lift under the command of an attendant whose choker-collared dark-blue uniform was bedizened with red-and-gold sergeants' stripes and the vulgar postcard-sunset tones of medal ribbons. At the lift's terminus a regimental comrade of the lift-man stood behind a reception counter. On the wall to his right, alarmingly, hung a clock and a machine to be punched by the arriving workers. Welcome to Bensons.

I was led up a flight of stairs, along a pale grey corridor, past the head of a spiral staircase whose sinister history I then ignored, and shown into a room which looked less like an office than the wheelhouse of a Channel ferry. The officer of the watch was standing, his back towards me, at a long sloping shelf against the wall and studying, for all I knew, his charts and weather forecasts. He turned and walked towards me and said, with a shy

55

smile, 'Stobo.' It sounded like a password and I didn't have the answer. I tried 'Hennessy,' and he said, 'Come on in.' He was a man of average height and middle age with a sallow, pointed face; from a low forehead the straight white Onassis hair was brushed back without a parting. He looked like a kindly weasel who had sustained a bad shock. He wore a good grey flannel suit each element of which appeared about to fall off his slim frame. It was as if, like a schoolboy, he had been neatly dressed when he left the house but that it hadn't lasted, and never would. He was Philip Stobo and he was Creative Director of S. H. Benson Ltd.

He was handsome, distinguished, a sort of inarticulate Alistair Cooke: when he tried to speak he made little mouthing movements, like a baby watching the spoon approach. It was a tic that wouldn't have had to work too hard to become a full-grown stammer. When he managed to produce speech it had a Scottish burr on it.

Shy and inarticulate myself – in situations like this anyway – I quickly showed him my 'book', containing my 'specimens' (English usage) or 'samples' (American): proofs of advertisements and brochures mounted on black, cellophane-covered pages. Stobo examined my work with close attention, with relish even. This surprised me. At Everetts nobody had pretended that our work was anything but an amusing chore which might on occasion entertain and which, while unlikely to do any good, was unlikely to do much harm either.

Such sophistry would not appeal to Stobo. As he staccatoed on (like Pinter, he was also a master of silences) it became clear that advertising for him was a high calling, a force for good in the world, a way of improving the lot of the housewife (as the expression went) and her family by introducing her to products of whose existence she might otherwise have been quite unaware. More, since advertising prepared the way for the mass distribution of such life-enhancing products, it also helped reduce their price – another benefit to the community!

Here was a man with missionary zeal. For him, advertising was a kind of universal education, lifting clouds of unknowing

56

from over the heads of the huddled masses, bringing the light of knowledge where before there had been ignorance, darkness, doubt, even disease. Not rows of books, but shelves of detergents, would bring enlightenment; not music but the hum of the washing-machine would lift the hearts of the consumers; not art but advertising would bring truth to the people.

As I was musing on this startling new conception of my role in society, Stobo began to jerk his head about, then thrust it forward on its long, Spiro Agnew neck, like a tortoise mapping out the next day's hike. He picked up my book and in what seemed like a tone of suppressed excitement said (twitch, jerk), 'C-c-come along with me.' I followed him from the bridge along the grey passageway and into the captain's cabin. The ceiling was low. The window was round, like a port-hole. Sea-scapes and paintings of scudding yachts hung on panelled walls. At any moment a tuniced steward would step past the bulkhead, or whatever, and bring me a pink gin.

'Bobbie Bevan,' Philip Stobo managed. Captain of the ship. Embodiment of Bensons: when he left, the great ship went off course, was boarded by pirates and finally sank without trace.

On top of a powerful body, and attached to it by a narrow neck, was a head about one size too large. This massive feature was topped by steel-grey hair whose waves and curls had fought a winning battle with the brush and comb. Beneath the bushy grey brows, grey-blue sea-bleached eyes peered out from under half-moon eyelids and from over half-frame glasses. Those eyes could be dull and leaden and also merry. The pink skin of the face glowed as if it were trying to sweat and could only manage a glow. The mouth looked as if it would like to crack a joke but was wondering if this was the moment: it decided to smoke a pipe and think about it.

Bevan wore a well-cut, navy-blue suit (what else? I thought) easily and well and stood squarely, or almost, for one shoulder was slightly raised, on powerful legs. He seemed both shy and sure of himself, a mixture often found in the only child, and yet he had the easy authority that comes with the unquestioned exercise of power.

He asked me about my war service, hinting playfully that not everybody could expect to be accepted by the navy, and about Oxford, remarking agreeably that if one couldn't be at Christ Church, Merton was a perfectly acceptable second choice. Like Stobo, he was good at protracted silences too. I would like to have seen the pair of them in *The Caretaker*. Neither had the social smoothness I would have found at Thompsons. Both seemed highly intelligent and, for businessmen, reasonably honest. There might be worse places to spend a year or two than Bensons. Would they want me? And how would Everetts react? I went back to Ebury Street and the grim atonement of a London weekend.

On Monday morning, a time when those who work in offices hope that nothing very important will come up, I was summoned to Harling's. Apprehensively I descended the stairs: such a call was rare. As usual, he was standing, legs braced, in front of his drawing-board. He turned his head as I walked in and gave me a sardonic smile – the only kind he ever had in stock.

'So you want to leave us for Bensons,' he said, enjoying it, and returned to his sketching.

Calling on reserves of aplomb not usually available until later in the week, I asked him how he knew. He and Bevan, ex-naval officers both, were also friends and neighbours in Essex. Over the weekend they had discussed my case. Bevan wanted to take me on. Harling explained that though he would like to keep me I had reached a salary ceiling at Everetts.

So it was that, powerless as a professional footballer, I was transferred from one club to another: from the steady second-division team of Everetts to the dashing leaders of the first, S. H. Benson. There would be more money, bigger crowds, tougher opposition, and farther to fall. But it was the big time and maybe I'd become a star.

The continued existence of the ideal Mary, a creature of my unconscious yearning, was increasingly threatened, in our daily

58

cheek-to-jowl lives, by disturbing manifestations of the living, breathing girl, possessed of desires and feelings of her own. Rigid attitudes which might have been just the thing for a successful relationship with a Dresden doll shattered against the spirited defence of a girl who knew very well her own worth, a girl whose very imperfections, as I achingly knew, were as close to perfection as I was ever likely to find. By a process that curiously resembles Groucho Marx's resigning from his clubs because he didn't want to belong to any club that would take him as one of its members, I reviled, in effect, the baffled Mary for giving herself unquestioningly to someone as detestable as me. Self-loathing led to self-destructiveness (providing *au passage* one more reason for self-loathing) and the exhausting push-pull of dependence-rejection soured our existence.

Returning from her stay in Devon, in a sweet, tender time of reconciliation and renewed self-discovery, she said one evening in Ebury Street, 'Charles – why don't you ask me to marry you?' I contrived not to respond to this simple, sensible question until it was too late.

That summer her brother Colin invited her to go, with his girlfriend and his Oxford room-mate Robin Beatson, on a motoring trip to the Italian lakes. She wanted me to approve, to share her pleasure in the excursion. Darkly jealous, pettily fearful that once having tasted freedom she might not want to return to the possessive yoke, I violently opposed her going. I was both wrong and right. When she came back she was free. We met once, she left, and I never saw her again.

I saw her picture though. On my way from Bensons to catch the No. 11 bus in the Strand I bought as usual the *Evening Standard*. Thumbing through it, I came across a series, just beginning, called 'The Ten Most Beautiful Women In England', by the society photographer Baron. There she was. Miss Mary Hunter. Somebody else had noticed. I saw her picture often after that: as a top model; her marriage, which my friends – Shankar, James Cameron, Jeffrey Simmons – attended, morning-coated, at St Peter's, Eaton Square; her divorce; her re-marriage. It was all in the papers. I kept every relic of her: her letters, which I bound, her drawings, photos of us together, the usual things. It's been twenty-five years; one of these days I must open the trunk and look at them; silly not to, really.

Chapter 7

In this day of hot-shops, brain-storming, trouble-shooters and think-tanks it amazes me to recall that when I joined the Copy Department of S. H. Benson there were still ancient retainers of that company who referred to it by its earlier title of Literary Department. There were other singularities. Large agencies elsewhere had found it expedient to organise their Copy Departments into manageable groups. At Bensons the Copy Department was not only not organised into groups: it was not organised at all. True, small fiefs existed, of which the most prestigious was the Guinness enclave. But otherwise, to the newcomer, the Department seemed to consist of a loose gathering of quiet and disparate eccentrics who had made the office a second home, or at least a second study. Since neither time nor money seemed important — for we were generously paid, and insulated against client pressure — the climate was one of ancient privilege, and an aristocratic code prevailed. I found it all most congenial.

It couldn't last, and it didn't. The arrival of Omo, the first detergent account, signalled the beginning of the end of the old Bensons. But the old rule, and the old rules, lingered on. Received wisdom held, for example, that if you could not think of what to say in an advertisement you should draw a little man: if that failed to do the trick, you should draw a little man *with a hat on*. Older connoisseurs will recall that Bensons advertising of the epoch was thronged with little men, with or without hats. (Urged on by Stobo, I added to this gallery myself: a little *woman* called Daisy Jute.)

Benson's advertising, like much English advertising then and now, leaned heavily on the pun. In a major Bensons breakthrough, *two* little men, with *caps* on, were shown playing golf on a hot afternoon. One says, 'I feel like a Guinness.' His partner replies, 'I wish you were.' A little bullock, drawn as an animal on a carousel, proclaimed, 'Roundabout mid-morning – Bovril.' The nation was asked, 'Did you Maclean your teeth today?' Under an exotic bird with a couple of bottles in his capacious beak you read,

> If he can say as you can
> Guinness is good for you
> How nice to be a toucan –
> Just think what toucan do.

One annual task, which fell to me, was to fill the top and bottom of each page of the Royal Tattoo programme with puns for Bovril, each with, so to speak, a military bearing. You would think that time, the old wound-healer, would have erased them from my memory. No such luck:

> The general is rotten to the corps until he's had his Bovril.
> What cadet my Bovril sandwiches?
> Has the sergeant-major Bovril yet?
> Bovril is full of good in tents.
> Never let a Weekend Pass without Bovril.
> Corporal punishment: take away his Bovril.

Visitors to the Tattoo may be unable not to recall many others; I had to produce twenty of them every year.

There were famous Benson campaigns then, for Bovril, for Colmans Mustard, for Macleans. But the most famous by far was for Guinness. It was the account whose personality most influenced the style of Bensons. It was the account by which all other accounts were measured, and it was under the direct control of Bobbie Bevan, who had, as it were, been weaned on Guinness.

To anyone brought up in England, Guinness advertising seems to have been there for ever. It may be a measure of Bensons' achievement that the first Guinness advertising in England was placed by Bensons in 1937. If Guinness can be said to have had an image before that, it was that of a drink consumed by black-garbed Dublin shawlies in bars with sawdust on the floor. And while the objective of these ladies in pouring the stuff down in such generous libations was to give themselves a quick and inexpensive lift, they had also convinced themselves that it was doing them a spot of good.

Having acquired the account, Bensons was faced with two problems: how to 'trade up' the unfortunate image of the product (the shawlie market holding no great promise in England); and how to capitalise on the product's existing image of 'goodness'. The first goal was achieved by associating Guinness with upper-class food. Lavish display material in the posher restaurants, and colour advertisements in glossy magazines like *Illustrated London News*, *Tatler*, *Sketch* and *Country Life*, showed glasses of rich, dark stout (though never called stout, like commoner dark beers) alongside oysters, lobsters and salmon, in what amounted to a visual assertion that for the gourmet there was now a civilised alternative to the glass of Chablis.

The second theme, that of the potion's alleged 'goodness', was handled in a more subtle way: an intensive campaign was directed not at the consumer, but at the consumer's doctor. Lavish, amusing and flatteringly literate booklets, illustrated by well-known artists, became, unlike the pharmaceutical and other junk mail with which they were showered, collector's items among the nation's doctors. What the doctors were asked to swallow in this pleasantly coated pill was the claim that clinical evidence proved that Guinness was good and nourishing and could not only be recommended to patients, but could and should be prescribed. The medicine was further sweetened by accompanying six-packs of the product with the artful message, 'and five for your patients ...'.

Both campaigns were highly successful. In London, in restaurants like Scotts, Wheelers and Pruniers, and in the clubs of St James, trencher-men were seen sluicing down their dozen Whitstables or Colchester Royals with draughts of the dark and creamy-headed stout. And all over England, under the impact of slogans like 'Guinness is good for you' and 'My Goodness, my Guinness', people, and especially the elderly, and especially elderly women, with the approval, tacit or otherwise, of their doctors, were getting a gentle buzz on, happy with their rationalisation that they were taking care of their health. By the time I arrived at Bensons the Guinness advertising was indisputably the best known in Britain with the result that those responsible for the creation of Guinness advertising became an élite within the élite which was the Copy Department of Bensons; and the first of these was Stanley Penn.

Penn was a tall, slim, slightly stooping, almost foppish figure, with drooping hands and long, flat, out-turned feet. He walked, or rather sauntered, like Hulot in slow-motion, with a slightly forward tilt from the hips. Seen in the corridor from behind it was as if, with a cloth under each foot, he were abstractedly polishing the floor. It was the walk of the old soft-shoe man. His hair was gingery-brown, thin and straight and his eyes protruded slightly, like those of Leslie Henson or of Eddie Cantor, from under sleepy Max Beerbohm lids. He was as beardless as a teenager but his face had acquired in middle-age Audenesque lines, like a parched river-bed. He kept this face straight until he told a joke, when it would fold, using its whole network of lines, into the triumphant and faintly self-approving beam of the born funnyman.

He arrived each morning, as a mark of status, even later than the rest of us, and strolled off earlier. We would watch his serene, unhurried progress down the corridor, rolled umbrella over one arm, *The Times* under the other. His office attained, he would hang up his hat and umbrella, kick off his shoes and put on his carpet slippers, which he never removed, client or no client, while he was at the office. Seated in his green leather armchair, unmoved by sounds or signs of crises, he would complete the crossword before turning to the less pressing matters on the day's agenda.

If the Benson Copy Department of those days was a gentleman's club, Stanley Penn was its oldest member, and its wiliest. Through all this apparent inactivity, the brain teemed and ideas surged, not just on Guinness but on any other problem that seemed to present a challenge. He had nothing but fun, the whole working day. About market research, the cost of space, the measurement of impact, aided and unaided recall, consumer panels, test marketing, hidden offers and all the other cumulus of modern advertising, he knew little and cared less. Before the phrase had joined those other jargon words, he was an ideas man, of the rarest vintage.

With Sidney Irwin, a shy and self-effacing art director whose favourite activity was fishing, Penn worked on the posters that became part of the landscape in England at that time: the workman carrying the huge girder, the other workman lifting a man-hole cover to reach his lunchtime Guinness, unaware that he is also lifting a steamroller parked on top of it – the slogan being 'Guinness for Strength'. Then there were the hundreds of verses, many of them brilliant parodies of Lear or Carroll; or to accompany mock-naturalist illustrations of exotic animals, like the hungry lion,

> Insatiable carnivore:
> Oh how voraciously you roar!
> Is it because, like us, you feel
> You need a Guinness with your meal?

or the thoughtful kangaroo,

> Ma supials have a pouch or bin
> To stow their little treasures in:
> Not strange if Momma Kangaroo
> Should Poppa Guinness in it too.

(Those who feel that it is easy to turn out stuff of that calibre to order, and to meet deadlines, and to re-write because the client, or the client's wife, doesn't like this word or that, are welcome to apply for employment in an advertising agency, having first, of course, taken the necessary step of securing employment in another advertising agency.)

In the Guinness fief or kingdom there was a dauphin. John Chenevix Trench shared with Stanley Penn the distinction of being among those few Benson copywriters who were not graduates of the older universities. He had, through some aberration, held his majesty's commission in the army, but his aspect was more scholarly, with a tinge of the clerical, than military.

Trench was a little remote from the rest of the Copy Department, though less remote from the women than from the men. He had a kindly face, with a high-brow's high brow and hair that had never really taken. His eyes were flat-based half-moons, like Mr Chad's, with Malteser pupils and laughlines at the outer corners. It was withal a face more apt for smiling than for frowning. He lived in the country, near Beaconsfield, and baked his own bread in an ancient oven. On the commuter train he wrote thrillers: his first success was *What Rough Beast*. From yeast to Yeats, as it were.

This mild and pleasant man was one of the modern masters of English light verse. An example of his work at Bensons is included in the Penguin collection, *More Comic and Curious Verse*: possibly the only piece of advertising copy to be found in a literary anthology.

> *The Sensible Sea-Lion*
> The sea-lion, naturalists disclose,
> Can balance balls upon his nose,
> And some, so neatly does he judge it,
> Ask, 'If a ball, why not a budget?'
> No head for figures is his knob –
> His eye's not on the Chancellor's job.
> He doesn't balance gains with losses,
> But pleasure on his own proboscis.
> And rightly, he prefers to win his
> Spurs by demonstrating Guinness.
> Perhaps this very session he'll
> Be chosen as Lord Privy Seal.

On the other side of Penn from Trench sat a wholesome and

quiet lady called Helen Bonington. She was rarely seen, or heard, outside her office. I suppose she worked for Bensons. I don't think we ever discussed the matter. She had a pleasant, strong face and wore her greying hair in plaited buns like ear-muffs against the cold, a fashion which may well have had an influence on her son, Chris, who, fearless among the elements, charged up Everest one day in a fit of peak, and having got a big fat best-seller out of it, charged up again, incessantly.

Farther along the corridor, chain-smoking and chain-thinking, in profile behind a glass wall, sat Julian Yeatman, a man who shared with two slightly earlier Benson copywriters – Dorothy L. Sayers and the poet Norman Cameron – the distinction of being a Real Writer. The title of his best-known book, *1066 And All That*, has become part of English English. But he was a modest and retiring man; he stayed behind his glass, quizzically smoking, his hair the same faded auburn as his tobacco-stained fingers.

I never heard him say a funny thing, and I never say any copy he had written. He saw mine though, for I showed it to him, and always regretted that I had, for Julian was a pedant. His office had dictionaries the way others had telephone books. My copy, for him, was simply a point of departure for an excursion into the meaning of words and their origins that would take foot-hopping hours. It may just possibly be that this gamesmanship was his way of cutting a pretentious and over-ambitious beginner down to size.

If I needed building up again, there was Bill Spencer, the only scientist in the Literary Department. He had joined Bensons from Cambridge, where he had turned down a fellowship in nuclear physics in order, as he put it, to try his hand at commerce. This decision was the more mysterious in that Bill Spenser, apart from being a scientist, was also a mystic, and greatly given to trance-like meditation, an activity for which the purlieus of the Benson Copy Department came very close to being the ideal setting.

It was good casting. He had long straight kohl-black hair that fell from a centre parting over each eye, like the Dead End Kid Alfalfa. The face was lean and ghostly pale, with long-lashed, grey-pupilled eyes behind steel-rimmed National Health glasses: long before it became fashionable he looked like John Lennon in his guru phase. He was a man who had achieved outer peace – not everything, perhaps, but a start.

Bill persuaded me to write down my dreams, of which he provided long written interpretations that had the effect, like popular horoscopes, of being deeply penetrating, utterly personal and completely reassuring. He also introduced me to the Tao, to the works of Gurdjieff and his pupil Ouspensky, and more importantly, to the writings of Krishnamurti, possibly the only Messiah to have had his shoes made by Lobb and his shirts by Hawes and Curtis.

Like most other members of the department, I wrote my copy in longhand, using a pencil (it was rumoured that the copywriters on Guinness used quills). When the copy typist was surcharged, my copy was sometimes typed by a girl called Joan Kennedy, who was Philip Stobo's secretary. She was a marmalade-haired, blue-eyed Scottish tomboy and nobody's fool. She didn't think much of some of my copy, and said so. I suggested that she show me how it should be done, and she did; no sweat. When Stobo had approved a fair amount of her copy, on the assumption that it was mine, I apprised him of its authorship. Thus Stobo lost a secretary and Bensons gained a copywriter – and Miss Kennedy an increase in her emoluments.

She had a boy-friend who had also been, though with such brevity that his sojourn might better be described as a flying visit, a Benson copywriter. He was a shortish Irishman called Derek Driscoll. He had the fair, wavy, brushed-back hair and the slightly pop-eyed, eager, even hungry look of a *Daily Mirror* whizzkid, which is what he was.

Driscoll was a well-read man and not without cultivation but he was chiefly remarkable for the success with which he concealed these admirable qualities. He affected a foreign-correspondent trenchcoat with the collar turned up, smoked cigarettes in an urgent way, as if it were forbidden by law, and like an old lag talked furtively out of the corner of his mouth while looking ceaselessly around for the approach of the prison guard. In the bar of the Ritz, it is the kind of thing that can draw attention.

John Mellors was a lean man with mild blue eyes, sandy hair and a sandy Yorkshire accent, a graduate of Queen's College, Oxford. He was a decent man, dourly cheerful, quietly sociable, with a quizzical but kind regard. He was not competitive and I believe remained a stranger to office intrigue when it spread like dry-rot through the corridors of Bensons.

Though we came to share the supervision of the Copy Department, including its unthinkable partition into manageable groups, our styles were different, though perhaps complementary. I was the quick study, the artful dodger, the facile pen; he was the steady worker, the conscientious craftsman, the careful scholar; I was the romantic, he the classicist. I was Denis Compton to his Len Hutton.

Our hiring styles reflected the difference. We both saw every candidate. We did not always agree: Mellors was more tolerant than I. A case in point was a most engaging young man just down from Cambridge. His name was Jonathan Gathorne-Hardy. I thought that Jonnie Gathorne-Hardy, although a man of charm and of romantic, even poetic aspect – the Rupert Brooke *de nos jours* – was not ideally equipped to handle the bricks and mortar of advertising copy. Mellors thought otherwise and took him under his wing. Perhaps because his later judgement about his role in the advertising industry came to concur with mine, Gathorne-Hardy left Bensons and became quite famous for two books: a study of the English nanny, and a survey of that other British contribution to the feudal system, the ironically named public school. Before that, however, he had published a novel, and in it there is mention of both Mellors and me.

The young, romantic and poetic hero is being interviewed for a job by the head of a large advertising agency:

'First,' said Claw, 'great advertising men, the real greats, men like Oglethorpe of Oglethorpe, Press and Coulden, or Chas.

69

Hennessy of Hennessy and Mellors Ltd, are born, not made. They come one or two a century, like Beethoven, like Puccini.'

Well, yes – but *Puccini*?

I don't know who hired Gavin Ewart. One pleasant day he just seemed to be there, his peaceable profile on public view behind the glass wall of the office next to the verbophile Yeatman. His work was supervised by Mellors and I was thus spared the awkwardness of having to pass judgement on the output of an established poet who was also my senior by ten years.

Gavin belonged to the generation of the red rebels of the public schools, of Philip Toynbee and Giles Romilly (who sped off with one of the Mitford girls). He had come to Bensons from the world of the little magazines and the big drinkers of Fitzrovia, the Carsons, the Maclaren-Rosses and the Tambimuttus. It was also, more seriously, the world of *New Writing* and *Horizon*, of John Lehmann and Cyril Connolly, and of the war-poets, Alun Lewis, Bernard Spencer and Bernard Gutteridge.

Gavin's contribution to English literature had got off to a good start with the publication of his first poem while he was still a schoolboy at, of all places, bellicose Wellington. It was happily entitled 'Phallus in Wonderland' and firmly established him as a comer, though his reputation had shrunk a little in later years.

He was a sturdily built man of above-average height. His eyes were deep set and had the Slavic upward slant of Tessimond's, but where his were pale and cat-like, Gavin's were dark and flickered like the eyes of a horse which has just smelled smoke and is wondering if the stable door is locked. Above these fear-flecked eyes, abrupt and bushy eyebrows glowered. Above the brows the dark brown, unwavy hair fell to the forehead, like the hair of Auden and Day Lewis: Yeats had set not only a poetic but a hair style for a whole generation of English bards. Below the eyes the high cheekbones jutted and the jawline was heroic, like Dick Tracy's. The lips were firm and wore the secret semi-smile that poets and the Giaconda have, the smile of those who have a hot-line to the truth. Surprised at his desk, Gavin would look up with dreamy recognition, like someone who had been profoundly elsewhere and would need a little time to surface.

He fitted admirably into the world of Bensons. He was reserved but sociable, infinitely courteous but watchful, quietly deliberate in speech and gesture (this is something of an understatement: Gavin is the slowest eater I have ever met). He was an athlete and won the Bensons squash championship from Hadley, a dapper director. It is possible that the presentation to a poet, in the precincts of an advertising agency, of a cup for sporting prowess, constitutes an event unique in literary history.

Chandler's poetically-named hero neatly sums up my feelings about the Bensons of that era. Returning to his bleak pad after a typical day of being beaten up by thugs, insulted by cops and betrayed by clients, Marlowe sets himself a ferocious chess problem. 'A greater waste of talent,' he muses, 'you wouldn't find anywhere outside an advertising agency.'

Chapter 8

The house on the corner of Elizabeth Street and Ebury Street was a frontier-post on the right side of the Pimlico–Belgravia border. I had rented a large room on the third floor. There was a kitchen that I shared with my neighbour, a pleasant man who stays in my mind chiefly because, incensed one day at some real or imagined slight or sneer, he mouthed, 'My God, Hennessy, why can't you be decent?'

My watering-hole was the pub around the corner in Elizabeth Street where I had sometimes shared a drink with Margaret Evans on our way home from Everetts. It was known formally as the Prince of Wales and familiarly as 'Charlie's', after its tall, ruddy and handsome landlord – an eternally youthful-looking man with the aspect of one who had left the farm to become a PT instructor in the Brigade of Guards.

Although the English pub is to the French bistro what Brown Windsor soup is to *consommé madrilène*, Charlie's was for the moment all I had. Wodehouse said that he wrote for the pleasure and to keep himself out of pubs: I went to pubs not for the pleasure but to keep myself out of my room. A psychoanalyst might have said I was seeking to avoid myself and, as my friend Tessimond observed, the analyst is always right.

It would not have been difficult to obtain the opinion of an analyst on the matter, for one of that calling had conveniently opened a restaurant across the road. Dr Hilary James was a nice, shy, private man who had the distinction, if that is the word, of having, single-handed, invented the *faux*-bistro, a mode that swept through London with the speed, and not a little of the effect, of the Great Plague.

His first creation, the Matelot, purported, as its name suggests, to be French: that is, its menu featured garlic bread, a comestible totally unknown in France, and chicken-in-a-basket, a dish whose provenance, whatever it may be, is not French, and whose *raison d'être* has always escaped me. Portugese plonk *en carafe* was plonked on Portugese-wine-stained red-check table cloths, to the accompaniment of cracked records of Edith Piaf, by out-of-work chorus boys in red football shirts and desperately-clinging black satin trousers. This improbable formula proved so successful with the pseudo *bon vivants* of rich Belgravia that its Freudian creator was encouraged to open another, almost identical place almost next door to handle the overflow, and nightly could be seen scampering between the two, gaily ringing up the tills.

If I ate at the Matelot it was for the same reason that some fool gave for climbing Everest: because it was there. (The image is not all that far fetched: the prices were steep.) On nights when I felt the call of something more traditional and less chi-chi I would walk down to Eaton Terrace where a quiet, comfortable Edwardian (in spite of its name) restaurant called the Queens offered sound English food with vaguely Greek overtones. Old waiters in greening black tails served stuffed vineleaves and Welsh rarebit savouries to retired colonels and their ladies living within nostalgic earshot of the Chelsea Barracks' bugles, to tweedy and twin-setted middle-aged couples up from the country to see their bed-sitting-roomed progeny, and to Augustus John, tottering, white-maned, listening with exquisite courtesy and looking with undisguised lechery as his very young, very beautiful and very eager groupies chattered on.

As in most pubs, there was an assortment of regulars at Charlie's and the centre, the moving force, the unifying element among them was a short, dark, green-eyed woman with high colouring and a determined mouth, like Elizabeth Taylor with cheekbones, who entered the saloon bar with the mien of one of nature's hostesses and with a slight limp. Her name was Antoinette Watney, she was known to her friends as Toinette, and she lived, with her son Marcus and her husband John, in a house in Chester Row, catty-corners from the Prince of Wales.

Toinette was a painter and had been the designer of Ken Tynan's production of Thornton Wilder's *Winterset* at Oxford, among the cast of which were Robert Hardy, Tony Richardson, Peter Parker and Sandy Wilson.

Apart from her son, what Toinette liked best in life was parties and the parties she liked most were the parties she gave herself. Parties fulfilled her, parties made her glow and dance, parties made her sing her favourite song, 'Time after Time', time after time. Her guests, not always the case with dedicated hostesses, were her friends and they were friends worth having: Arthur Koestler, Stevie Smith, Lynn Chadwick, Sandy Wilson, the Tynans – creators, contributors, originals. With all of these people Toinette was attentive, concerned, available. Kindness is easy enough to fake: the vocabulary and gestures are rapidly acquired. Toinette was not a phoney. She could not help being good, even when she was being kind.

A friend of Toinette's who became a friend of mine was Robin Jacques, an illustrator who then lived and worked in a studio in Ebury Street, across from my room. His work, unmistakable in style and built up of thousands of painstaking little lines or dashes, had been appearing in the *Radio Times* (always an enlightened patron) for many years and he had illustrated, among other books, Joyce's *Portrait of the Artist as a Young Man*. His sister was the plump and plump-hearted comedienne Hattie Jacques, then married to the actor John Le Mesurier, a man that I always saw as physically a more melancholic version of myself.

Robin was a handsome man with dark, straight hair brushed back unparted from a fine high forehead above kind but penetrating eyes which were, as Baudelaire said of his own, as bright as coffee-beans. The strong but shy-seeming head, with its nobly Roman nose, clean jaw and sensitive mouth, was set on a powerful torso supported by shortish but quick and muscular legs.

He was a man both private and gregarious, timid but

74

affectionate, given to long bouts of hard work ('doing my dots') punctuated by parties at which the guests were always people one was glad to meet, many for the good reason that they were young and beautiful girls. At one of these parties, in the sky-lighted upstairs studio, I was introduced to a very pretty blond girl, the Lady Jane Vane-Tempest-Stewart. This name enchanted me and when we were separated I murmured it to myself from time to time for the pleasure of the euphony. Finding myself face-to-face with her again I said, with that idiocy that alcohol so often induces, 'Ha! Jane Vane-Tempest-Stewart, I believe.' There was a long pause, during which she gave me the kind of thoughtful but clinically detached look that a dentist might bestow on a hopelessly decayed tooth. Then, raising almost imperceptibly one perfect eyebrow, she spoke. 'That is correct,' she generously conceded. 'But who are you?'

Perhaps because of his sister's calling, Robin's acquaintance was to some extent theatrical and he had acquired some of the verbal mannerisms of stage people. Friends were addressed, in his mellifluous, almost unctuous, voice, as 'sweetie'. (On the telephone: '*Hello* sweetie? *Robin*. How *are* ya love?'). Occasionally and reluctantly he worked half-time as an art director in the advertising agencies: like me, for Everetts (Harling, he had decided, was 'on the side of the angels'), for Bensons and for J. Walter Thompson in Paris.

From Thompson's London office came another advertising man, the poet Bernard Gutteridge, who lived with his pretty, exotic and volatile Franco-Egyptian wife Farah in a plush apartment just up the road in Eaton Square. Elegant and observant as most poets are, Bernard had asked me for the name of my tailor, thereafter adding to his own natural elegance and to Anderson and Sheppard's natural worries. 'Copy Chief', in our trade paper, *Advertiser's Weekly*, had said that a piece of my (anonymous) copy was 'the best prose being written in advertising today'. Copy Chief, I discovered in Charlie's, was Bernard Gutteridge.

Though many of the regulars at Charlie's were no doubt trying,

75

in another line from a Tessimond poem, to 'make the cunning clock-hands pause', one of them, Dr McManus, never seemed to have time to linger. Niall McManus was a shortish man whose costume, invariably, was black jacket, striped trousers and a hard white collar that seemed too tight. Dark tufts of whisker bloomed like sage-brush on his cheeks and his large round almost popping eyes (the collar perhaps?) looked anxiously but distantly around, like a man who, having left his house that morning with an umbrella, is trying to recall when he had it last.

His style, like his short, barking laugh, was staccato: he did not linger long. A pink gin or two – an old Royal Naval custom – and he was off across the tracks, black bag in hand, to his family in Pimlico. This kind, respected and restless man had a habit, when talking, of punctuating his phrases with clicking noises emanating variously from nose or throat: a tribal technique since successfully exploited on the stage by the African singer Miriam Makeba but not, at that time, frequently encountered in the saloon bars of Belgravia.

People who wear cloaks appear to sweep rather than walk into places. Our sweeper at Charlie's was Lewis Way, who sported a Middle-European loden job that Costumes or Wardrobe would have hung unhesitatingly in the rack marked 'Viennese psychoanalysts'. They would have been right, for Lewis had been a pupil of Adler, who not only invented the inferiority feelings, as he was the first to call them, and the theory of compensation, whereby he showed that Napoleon became so big because he was so miffed at being so small and that musicians chose wind instruments because they had weak lungs and not, as one might have supposed, the other way round, but also adumbrated the 'middle-child complex', which interests me more.

According to the wily Adler, the infant who has never received the cosy rewards of being the first-born, and who, while just about to adjust to this vexatious situation, is deprived by the unexpected arrival of a usurper of the pleasures that accrue to the baby of the family, attempts to ensure his share of love by attention-getting efforts, often taking the form of creative endeavours. Speaking as a middle child, I think Adler may have something there.

Where Niall McManus tended to click, Lewis Way, a man with long and thinning fairish hair and an eager, windswept face, like a figure on a ship's prow, specialised in the giggle, of a particularly unselfconscious kind. He was a highly strung man and a demonstrative one: years on the couch, I supposed, had released him from those bonds that, like so many umbilical cords, confine the expression of our inner feelings within socially dictated limits. When Lewis was around, joy, together with most of the other emotions, was unconfined.

These two men, Cambridge graduates both, were soon joined in Charlie's pub by an Oxford man beside whose hyperactivity they looked about as jumpy as a pair of tombstones. Had there been a three-sided competition for the greatest consumption of nervous energy in the Prince of Wales, Michael Morris would have left the others standing – and they were men of international class. He seemed ready for such a race, for he had a habit, while talking, of hitching up his trousers with his wrists, like a runner waiting for the starter to fire his pistol.

Michael was a tall, powerfully built, red-headed man with the red-head's high complexion. High tightly waved hair, beginning low in a point on his brow, swept straight back. His eyes below the upward slanting orange brows were closely set and cunning. The mouth went humorously up at the corners, matching the angle of the brows and hair-line. Had his hair been black and his complexion sallow and you were looking for someone to play Mephistopheles you would have needed to look no further.

There was nothing criminal about Michael Morris, who was in fact a partner in a distinguished firm of solicitors. His mind was, as I have indicated, hyperactive, and finding, as it seemed, ordinary English inadequate to convey to a listener the complexity of his thought, he had invented a variant of it, the better to express himself. While this chosen form of speech – impossible to reproduce in print, but combining back-slang, baby talk, jabberwocky and scat-singing – may well have provided him

77

with welcome release from the pressures of a racing intellect, it had one serious disadvantage: it was totally incomprehensible to his listeners. To all, that is, save one, and to her it was, literally, love-talk.

Margaret Evans's relationship with Patrick Kirwan had been a notably free and easy one, the ease being rather on her side and the freedom on his. He would disappear for days and weeks at a time – to Longchamps with the unnerving O'Flaherty, around the bars with film or literary cronies – leaving Margaret alone in her basement flat: alone, that is, except for the company of her Irish setter, Sean. This entailed no suffering for her, for she had long regarded animals – or anyway, horses and dogs – as in every particular superior to human beings who, though undoubtedly worse Abroad than at home, were pretty unspeakable anywhere.

It was only when I introduced her to Michael Morris, in Charlie's pub, that I was able to admire in her that quality that Scott Fitzgerald proclaimed to be the mark of a first-class mind: the ability to hold in view two opposing ideas at the same time. That Michael was a human being was manifest; that he was also a desirable partner was seen as in no way in contradiction with that fact. Anyone not knowing that such a thing was impossible would have confidently attributed her intellectual confusion to the fact that Margaret Evans was in love.

When she became Margaret Morris the couple moved into a house conveniently located halfway between the pub and my lodgings. Their first child was always referred to as the Horse.

Michael had for many years been the proprietor of another house, this one in the dreaded Abroad. It was situated in Ramatuelle, a citadel village in the foothills above the bay of St Tropez, and a nodal point in Palinurus' Magic Triangle – that area (in France of course) within which ideally one should live. When Michael proposed to drive to France with furniture for the house, there was naturally no question of Margaret, loyal though she was, accompanying him on any expedition intending to penetrate the Continent beyond the port of Calais, which for her, as for any sensible Englishwoman, represented the furthest reaches of civilisation. My friend and colleague Gavin Ewart and I however, having wrapped up a good deal of Europe on previous trips, were looking now towards fresh woods and pastures new and agreed to go along, as the phrase has it, for the ride.

The English on holiday often seem to be on safari, even to the extent of travelling in two vehicles, to keep all angles covered while traversing hostile territory. We also had two vehicles but they had been combined into one, a hybrid called a Dormobile which contrived to unite, on one chassis, the less desirable features of a truck and a car. Surrounded by wardrobes, commodes and fuel for the driver in the shape of crates of Gordon's gin, we were sealed in this slow, noisy and sweltering pantechnicon for two days, arriving on the evening of the second at the sea's edge on the Plage de Pamplonne. My two companions, trained to the inch at the finest public schools and seeing water before them, stripped and sprinted for the Mediterranean's warm embrace, while I, ever the observer and made of feebler stuff, gazed as four white English buttocks, looking as if they had been kept under a paving stone for the last year, waddled off into the sunset.

Ramatuelle is to me now, like Alexandria, a touchstone, a place by which other places are measured. I have been in love there, I have lain with a broken neck there, I have failed to be married there, I could live the rest of my life there. It has changed less than most places since the summer I first saw it, with Michael Morris and Gavin Ewart.

The village is built in concentric circles, one street within the other, the streets interconnected by archways. Michael's house was on the second street in from the *place*, through an arch that joined a church that dated from the fifteenth-century to a post-office-store which had not yet reached the twentieth. A second arch, between the bead-hung doorways of a butcher and a baker, led to the front door of the tall, narrow house. At the top of all the stairs a small terrace overlooked the orange-russet roofs of the outer houses, whose small terraces looked down past the vineyards and the olive groves to St Tropez. In the corner of the terrace a screen concealed a chemical toilet: there were no sewers

79

or electric lights in Ramatuelle then, and the two telephones were in the post office and the Café de l'Ormeau.

The village, as villages are, was noisy with the voices of black-clad, white-haired, sallow-faced old women talking in the narrow high streets. Odours of hot olive oil and ratatouille hung in the air and shutters slammed shut for the siesta hour. Later, around the 800-year-old *ormeau* on the *place* the pale villagers stared politely at the tanned tourists and greeted the local boy made good, Gerard Phillipe, Keats of actors, too truthful and too beautiful to live, as he circled the tree in his 1930s open Renault tourer.

When I returned to the grey chill of London, along with the usual angst of the returning voyager there was a feeling that something remained abroad, a part of myself that had been left in Ramatuelle like a deposit to ensure my return.

Chapter 9

'Down this staircase was flung to his death', read the plaque, a gentleman whose name now escapes me but who was the villain of a book called *Murder Must Advertise*. The staircase in question was the wrought-iron spiral job that connected the 'creative' floor of S. H. Benson Ltd to the 'executive' floor, and which I had glimpsed on my first visit to the agency. The plaque, as it announced, had been unveiled by the author of the book, Miss Dorothy L. Sayers. When she created her rather yucky hero, the aristocratic detective Lord Peter Wimsey, she had been a copywriter at Bensons, where she shared an office with a young man called Bobbie Bevan, now Managing Director of the firm. She often, at his invitation, appeared at functions – such as the sixtieth anniversary of the firm which we were then celebrating – dressed invariably in a mannish though skirted suit and a flat black wide-brimmed hat of the romantic-artist style favoured by such as Hilaire Belloc for walking, reading and boozing tours in the Pyrenees.

On either side of the corridor in which the spiral staircase stood were housed, or officed, the account executives, known, in distinctively Benson style, as 'account managers'. Their function was to visit, write to or telephone the clients, to report their needs to the creative people and to explain and justify, in formal ceremonies known as 'client presentations', the graphic responses of the creative people to those needs. The reactions of the clients were then conveyed, both verbally and in written reports, to the creative people, with demands for appropriate action where necessary. Copywriters occasionally slummed along this corridor,

81

descending, in every sense, to take to task some manager for an ill-timed request in a report of a client meeting, or to explain, with forbearance, why a piece of copy that had been refused by some pointy-headed ignoramus in the murky and barbaric Midlands should be presented again, unchanged – so perfect had it been in its conception, its style and its technique.

Walking along the corridor on such a painful but necessary mission, a copywriter such as myself could not fail to see a display of advertisements framed in a glass-covered panel on one of the walls. These advertisements, for products as disparate as Helena Rubinstein, Schweppes, Viyella and the British Tourist Association, were the work not of Bensons but of its affiliate in New York, then known as Hewitt, Ogilvy, Benson and Mather. It would be no exaggeration to say that from the moment I began to see these advertisements, constantly renewed as the latest proofs arrived from New York, I began to become dissatisfied with my work, and hence my life at Bensons. I thrive on excellence, and I know it when I see it, even in advertising.

Apart from the heady flights of Guinness and the occasional pleasing *trouvaille* for Bovril, the work we did was honest, journeyman stuff which had too often the grey look that comes from repetition and from compromise. The writing, layout and typography were unimpeachable, as they had been at Everetts, but the results, though handsome enough, lacked distinction.

By contrast, these new advertisements shone with originality. Although they had been prepared for different and widely-varying products they shared a common distinction, as a suit from a great tailor will bear his stamp whether worn by a tall or a short, a fat or a thin man. What gave these advertisements their distinctiveness, apart from the originality of the content, was the high quality of their presentation, their elegant and hand-sewn look. Whereas the Benson advertisements seemed to reach out to tap the reader on the shoulder, if not punch him on the nose, these HOBM advertisements, by their modesty and good manners, seemed to charm the reader into lending his attention. Rich and compelling, they enhanced the grey walls of Bensons,

82

like a row of old masters in the passageway of a battleship.

Nothing better than these campaigns was being done in the business I was in, and nothing but the best is all I have ever demanded. As I walked along the executive corridor I brooded about how I might become associated more closely with work like this which, though mere advertising, had for me some of the appeal of fine clothes, fine food, fine wine. And I wondered how, as a mere tyro, I might sit at the feet of the master of this dubious trade, *il miglior fabbro*, the already legendary David Ogilvy.

Chapter 10

I was sitting, as usual, with my feet on my desk – an affectation that might be analysed as a rejection of the work-ethic, or of authority, or of both – when authority and the work-ethic, in the shape of the sleek, white otter head of Philip Stobo, appeared in my doorway. After a mandatory thrust or two of his head, like, to change the metaphor, that of a tortoise wearing a shell one size too small, speech painfully emerged.

'E-e-h, Charles, There's a girl downstairs.'

'How nice.'

'I thought you might like to look after her for a bit. Show her around. Let her sit in on a meeting.'

'What kind of a girl?'

'American.'

'Oh God.'

'From our New York office.'

I removed the feet, thoughtfully, from the desk.

'Aha!' I said, and to underline the point, 'Aha!' I said again. 'What's her name?'

'Reva Fine.'

'Once more, please.'

'R-E-V-A. Fine like just fine.'

'Oh God.'

This girl with the improbable name – improbable, that is, to someone who had not yet seen a New York agency's list of employees – was, it seemed, a copywriter with HOBM, in Europe on holiday, who had decided to look in on the founding fathers. Mather and Crowther had borne the brunt. Bensons was next in the firing line.

Well, maybe she wouldn't be awful, the way all American women were. (I had never met an American woman: nothing nourishes a good healthy prejudice like a large dose of ignorance.) Anyway, if she was one of the authors of the advertisements I so much admired in the corridor below she couldn't be all bad.

'Wheel her on then,' I said graciously and rose, languidly I hoped, to my feet.

The girl who appeared in my doorway would have been called cute in America and *mignonne* in France: in England she was sweet. She was young, small, neat, with straight failed-blonde hair cut in the short, fringed, *gamine* style the girls on the cover of *Elle* were wearing. The face was heart-shaped and had the pale, almost steamed complexion of the native New Yorker. The eyes were blue-grey and bright as buttons. The mouth was small and thin-lipped and opened in a smile that showed teeth no bigger than a child's milk-teeth. It wasn't a face you fell in love with at first sight but you wouldn't slam a door on it either.

'Hi,' it said. Nobody had ever said that to me before. My horizons were broadening. It was heady stuff.

'Hallo,' I said, not to be outdone.

Reva Fine (for such, however improbably, it was) seemed both cool and warming, still but sparkling, like a *blanc de blancs*. She had that nothing-to-hide openness which stamps the American life-style: the unhedged garden, the never-closed office door, the voice unlowered in public places, the count-them smile. What you saw, as they say there, was what you got, and what I saw before me now was one quick, bright, foxy lady.

She had the unforced wit that, with the musical comedy and the bagel, seems to have been the Jewish gift to New York. Her father had emigrated from Europe, she told me, and when he heard she was sailing for that continent on the cheapest ticket she could find he shook his head tragically and sighed, 'From steerage to steerage in one generation....' She had started in Macy's, writing the kind of store advertising that seems to occupy 90 per cent of the column space in the New York newspapers. David

Ogilvy had rescued her from this bargain basement of advertising and with the perceptiveness, or the perversity, of genius decided that she would possess just the touch needed for the writing of his very suave, very English, Schweppes and British Travel Association campaigns. (She had never, of course, seen England and when, later, I took her to Oxford, she looked around in wonder and said, 'Gee, it's terribly BTA.')

I became close to this twinkling Jewish New Yorker (we had established, shall we say, a rappaport), alien among the homespun broadcloth of Bensons. It was sad that she was soon leaving. America seemed a long way off – chiefly because, in those days, it was a long way off. Reva would be returning by way of Majorca. Having in previous excursions pretty well wrapped up Ischia, Capri and St Tropez, Gavin and I had decided that summer to take on Monte Carlo.

That is, Bernard Gutteridge had suggested that we take the villa of his father-in-law. Well, not the villa, exactly, but a sort of gardener's cottage in the grounds. A bit run down, but perfectly serviceable. No beds or anything but a lovely view from the outdoor privy over the Jardins Exotiques to the sea. We could pick up the keys and mail at the Hotel Metropole down in the town.

I tried to persuade Reva to join us there. She said gee that would be great but she didn't see how.... She would write and let me know, but I shouldn't count on it. Better to say goodbye now. And she left.

I don't know how it is with your unconscious, but mine is both cleverer and harder working than its more visible and noisy twin. Send down the trickiest problem and it disappears like a fish thrown into a porpoise's smiling maw. Wait a day or two and up pops the solution. Never fails. So it was this time. What Tessimond called 'the mind-behind-mind', drawing on a lifetime's diet of Hammett, Chandler and Hollywood B-features, produced a draft cable for my approval. 'BE THERE COMMA IS ALL', it read and it seemed about right to me. Changing not a word of this masterpiece I sent it off to Reva in

Majorca.

When, a few day's later, Gavin and I ambled in to the Metropole to pick up the keys to the gardener's cottage, the *concierge* handed me two communications. The first was a letter from Reva, four fraught and deeply moving pages saying how spiffing everything had been in England and how much she would love to come and join us but, alas, it was out of the question and so this time it was really goodbye. The second communication was a telegram, dated a few days later. It said, 'ARRIVING NICE AIR FRANCE FLIGHT 127 MONDAY 1400 LOVE REVA.' For a moment there I thought I heard my unconscious purr.

The gardener's cottage was bare of furniture and in the night the air-filled mattresses we had lugged from England deflated sneeringly, leaving our hips and shoulders to grate on the tiled and sandy floor. But the view from the doorless toilet through the olive trees and past the spiky palms and plump cactuses of the Jardins Exotiques down to the siesta-still, blue and yacht-flecked bay was food for the soul; and body-food in the shape of fuzzy peaches dropped ripely from our trees, soft drum-beats in the ceaseless cha-cha-cha of the cicadas.

I rented a Renault Quatre and we beetled hotly past the rose-red walls and green shutters of Italianate old Nice and up to a St Paul-de-Vence not yet tourist infested and down to naval Villefranche and Cocteau's camp chapel and the terrace of the Hotel Welcome where we ate *crevettes grises* with fingers that smeared the glasses and dulled the cool gleam of the *rosé de Pierrefeu*. We went, defiantly for we were poor, into the Monte Carlo Beach Club and swam in the pool with the international fat-cats and their slim-pussy accessories. We bought oily black olives and *saucisson sec* and still-warm *baguettes* and melty butter and the kind of wine that comes in litres with tear-off tops; and for dessert reached out a sated hand for our own squishy peaches.

And at Nice airport my devilling unconscious surfaced again and fed me the line I needed. 'See you in New York for New Year's,' I said recklessly, but knowing that the phrase had come from somewhere deep, where perhaps truth hides, for mostly, up here, we are false.

Back in autumnal Kingsway I resigned from Bensons, explaining with head-spinning simplicity that I wished to go and live in America. I had no plan. But, I thought, some people live their lives and keep their fantasies for the Sunday afternoon doze or the dull commuter train. I would live my fantasies now and keep my life for living later, in the Sunday afternoon of my days. What was it anyway, my life, but a piece of fiction? The facts were quite other, and elsewhere.

For the first, and the last, time Bobbie Bevan invited me to lunch at the Garrick, that swinger among the London clubs. Peering bluely over his half-moon glasses and under eyebrows that looked as if they had escaped from the prison of a mattress he explained, between sips of the club claret, that although Bensons, with Mathers, had put up the money to start the New York agency, this gave them no authority over David Ogilvy: however, if I was really set on going to America, he could write to Ogilvy and ask him to accept me, with the condition that I return after my stay to Bensons, there to spread the gospel that I had learned at the Master's feet. Bensons would pay half my salary, and my fare.

It has long been my contention, flying as I do in the face of everything the Englishman is taught, that the world owes me a living. This seemed to me the only dignified stance to take once the first startled screams had registered my disapproval of the abrupt and unheralded translation from my blood-warm first abode to the cold and cruel outer brightness. Torn as I was from paradise and finding no way back, sinned against but guilty of no crime (and yet so charged by the Catholic church), I now demand redress: it is, as it were, my birthright.

Here, now, was a little on account. I had taken the risk, and I had won. It was no more than my just deserts. Anyone else at Bensons, desirous of an expenses-paid trip to America, could have tried the same ploy. How very true, I murmured to myself in an ecstasy of self-approbation: none but the brave deserves the fare.

I was to see Roger Lloyd, the Research Director, who also sat on the board of the New York company, to discuss my travel arrangements. Lloyd was a lean, taciturn, word-biting man with a cold, accusatory eye. He looked like a male Anthony Perkins. He said that since presumably I would be going First Class (I always travel First Class for the simple reason that if I travel Second I feel so sick at not travelling First it simply isn't worth the money saved) I could get a berth on a Pan Am Constellation, which would take twelve hours, with a stopover in exotic Gander, Newfoundland; on the other hand, if I wasn't in a hurry, why not go by sea? The Bensons travel agents would arrange all that.

Some shrewd observer has pointed out that when you fly you go to places and when you sail the places come to you. I chose to steer the latter course. The travel agents sent me a deck plan of the *Queen Mary*, which was leaving conveniently soon, and I picked a stateroom (heady word!) on 'A' Deck, adjoining the ritzy suites. They also sent me some quietly loud red, black and sky-blue Cunard labels with sticky backs, and plain black-and-white ones that said, with simple arrogance, 'FIRST CLASS'. The better to display these notices, I bought a second-hand black metal steamer trunk, the kind that stands upright and opens to reveal drawers on one side for shirts and socks and a wardrobe for your cheviots, flannels and midnight-blue on the other. Among these labels, I emblazoned this antique object with an imperious 'Wanted on voyage'.

Was I running away? Well, yes. But Robert Frost said somewhere, 'Running away isn't necessarily bad. It all depends what you're running away from, and what you're running away to.' I had five days, stolen out of time, to think about that, before the cloud-capp'd, terrible towers of that advertising Mecca, Manhattan, came to fill the vacant portholes of my stateroom.

Amble II

Chapter 11

A glance at the passenger list confirmed that, though a neophyte in such matters, I had chosen well: my outside stateroom on 'A' Deck of the *Queen Mary* was next to that of the Duke and Duchess of Windsor. To be more precise, it was next to the stateroom of the Windsors' servants. To be deadly accurate, it was next to the stateroom of the Windsors' dogs and therefore two removed from the ducal pad. But for an absolute beginner, and a peasant at that, it wasn't bad going at all.

Heeding the advice of Philip Stobo, I had already reserved my deckchair for mid-morning bouillon on the Promenade Deck. And, though failing to make the Captain's table, I had obtained a place at that of the·Chief Engineer, which Stobo had assured me was the next most desirable slot. Stobo had made one other helpful suggestion for my well-being, of a rather more fleshly nature, and I looked forward to acting on it that very night.

A veteran of First Class trans-Atlantic travel, Stobo had explained that on the first night out from Southampton one did not dress – a fact that was crucial to the success of his scheme. The advantage of being in mufti was that one could descend into the saloons and bars of Second Class and rub shoulders with the hoi-polloi without drawing attention to the fact that one was a First Class passenger. The purpose of this incognito reconnaissance was beguilingly simple: unattached girls, having usually neither private fortune nor access to expense accounts, tended to travel Second Class. (Those travelling in First were accompanied by at least one parent, which for my purposes was one parent too many.) The beauty part of the scheme was this: Second Class passengers were forbidden to enter the First Class areas – which included such romantic spots as the Verandah Grill and the Starlight Room – *unless invited by a First Class passenger*. Thus, having mingled anonymously with the throng in, if not the bowels, then the stomach of the ship, and having made one's choice, one could descend on the second night out, wined, dined and dinner-jacketed, to whisk the flushed and eager victim off and up to the ballroom, thence to the Starlight room and so on to the stateroom.

The plan seemed foolproof and I was keen to try it out. My morale was high, for although sadly lacking in self-confidence in the presence of pretty girls – or of anyone else, come to that – I had an asset on which I counted greatly for the success of my mission: a brand new midnight-blue dinner jacket created for me by Anderson and Sheppard.

As with most great works of art, this dinner-jacket had not been achieved without a good deal of conflict, of which it was the triumphant resolution. My coat-cutter, now retired from the company, was Mr Cameron. A difficult man at the best of times, as artists often are, Mr Cameron proved obdurate, if that is the word, in the matter of my dinner-jacket. On the larger themes of the composition – the choice of colour, the weight of the material – we were in complete agreement. It was when we got down to the execution that the whole thing came unstuck. It was a painful scene and I remember it all too well.

The crucial dialogue took place among the flat bolts of worsted, tweed, cheviot and what have you just across the threshold of No. 30 Savile Row.

'I see that some of the chaps have cloth-covered buttons on their evening duds, Mr Cameron.'

'We can cover the buttons if you wish, sir.'

'Then again, I've spotted one or two with cuffs on the jacket. I rather liked the effect.'

'Cuffs, I think, would be acceptable.'

'What really seems to be the big thing though is where the

93

lapels go all the way round the back of your neck.'

'I believe the effect you refer to is the shawl collar, sir.'

'Right! Shawl collar. That's it.'

Mr Cameron fell into a troubled silence, of the kind one imagines overcame Faust when faced with an offer he couldn't refuse but knew he should. I asked him what was on his mind.

'I was merely wondering, sir, whether you will not need a baton to complete the outfit.'

Thus it was that the dinner-jacket that accompanied me to the First Class dining room of the *Queen Mary* on the vital second night out, though undoubtedly a model of its kind, and rightly admired by all, was not the dinner-jacket I had had in mind when I ambled through the portals of Anderson and Sheppard. Still, win a few, lose a few. For the purposes of Project Stobo it would do. If things, as it turned out, did not go according to plan, the fault did not lie in Mr Cameron's art or craft.

There are, it will generally be agreed, few prospects more stimulating to the appetite than a good dinner that has been paid for in advance, and paid for, moreover, by someone else. When I took my place at the Chief Engineer's table, surrounded by ladies in ballgowns of strange pastel shades (except for the Duchess, elegantly slim in black Balenciaga – 'You can never be too rich or too thin' was her motto), I was in fettle of the finest kind.

The poet Burns had something rather penetrating to say about, as he put it, the best laid schemes of mice and men. I don't know how well informed he was about rodents but he knew his fellow-Scotsmen. Philip Stobo's plan, apparently watertight, had overlooked one factor: the steep Atlantick streame, the vasty deep, the cruel sea, as various hands have put it. For it so happens that the time indicated by Project Stobo for pouncing on the unsuspecting girlhood that decked the decks below was also the time that a ship putting out of Southampton reaches that area of the ocean whose frequent storms are generally put by sea-going students of form right at the top of the sea-league.

It was the vastness of the *Queen Mary* that provoked Bea Lillie to demand, 'What time does this place get to New York?' But all this vastness was as nothing when set against the vasty deep previously referred to. In the middle of an Atlantic in vile mood the great ship had as much autonomy as a shirt-button in a washing machine programmed for heavy wash. There was no warning of turbulence to come, there were no seat belts to fasten: that evening, after dinner, suddenly this solid city began to rock and roll, to creak and groan, to heave and fall. If there is one thing you would do well to avoid after a fairly unrestrained dinner of caviare, poached salmon with *sauce hollandaise*, champagne and brandy it is a good old-fashioned seaquake.

I lurched down the drunken corridors of 'A' Deck, my damp fingers feeling for the unfeeling, shiny walnut walls. I passed the Windsors, and their domestics, and their dogs, and found my stateroom. It was not the haven I had hoped to find. When I had left it it had been a perfectly calm, well-mannered stateroom. Now it was heaving about like a roller-coaster. Prudently I lay down on my bed and rang for the steward.

This seasoned salt, his starched jacket about the same shade as my face, had dealt with heaving seas and passengers before. Rapidly analysing the problem, he proposed two solutions: ginger ale or champagne. Given the choice I did not hesitate. For the next few days I lay on my bed, rolling about in concert with the bland neo-*art nouveau* decor, sipping champagne from the bottle in the bedside ice-bucket, while below me desirable girls in the pink of health flirted and jitterbugged and above me stately and robust First Class ladies displayed their first, second and third new long dresses in the ballroom.

On the last night out, which happened to be New Year's Eve, I felt strong enough to essay an asparagus or two, 'white as the arms of debutantes'. Strengthened by the food and inspired by the image I made my way weakly to the First Class lounge, where I knew that my fitter fellow-passengers would be engrossed in the nightly game of lotto (known in Second Class and in the circles from which I came as housey-housey). Although I detest parlour games, card games and other devices for killing time — a commodity, I should have thought, of which one can never have enough – I like to watch people playing them (or doing anything, come to that).

The great swaying hall, garishly festooned for the New Year jollity, was packed and hushed as on the dais a ship's officer called 'Eyes down, look in' and at the tables the gentry concentrated for a win. Ever the celebrity hound, I found a place at a table near my *voisins de palier*, the Windsors.

The Duchess, looking both too thin and too rich, was wearing as usual something simple and black. Matching black hair, pulled tightly back, seemed to draw the chalk-white skin over the harsh bones of the face. She looked like her own death-mask. Across from her, His Royal Highness looked sandily weak, wilful and sallow. The Duchess was at centre stage, her neighbours a chorus, the whole room her audience. (I was nicely placed, orchestra stalls, seventh row, centre aisle.) The Duke, her Fool, sat silent, gazing at his lotto card with the absorption of an archaeologist setting eyes for the first time on the Rosetta Stone.

When the game ended with the thrilled shriek of some dowager who held the winning card, H R H summoned the ship's Entertainment Officer. I leaned closer, not to miss a pearl of the royal wisdom.

'Splendid game tonight.'

'Thank you very much, sir.'

'Absolutely splendid.'

'Very kind of you, sir.'

'Don't know when we've had a better game.'

'Glad you enjoyed it, sir. We do our best.'

'Darling. Didn't you think it was a splendid game?'

'Splendid, darling.'

'There you are, you see. Well *done*.'

'Sir!'

At midnight we all linked arms and sang 'Auld Lang Syne'. Then, as they do every night on the Southampton–New York run, the clocks went back an hour and everybody began to do everything all over again. I had had enough for one year and I returned to my stateroom to profit from the bonus hour of sleep. I would need it to face for the first time the country whose praises Whitman had sung and about which Freud had said simply, 'America is a mistake.'

Chapter 12

Manhattan then, like South Africa now, was White. People – that is, white people – still went up to Harlem at night (and cab drivers were happy to take them): to the shake, rattle and roll of the Apollo Theater or to the bars where whites were welcome under the canopy to hear the black musicians, but black musicians (like Dizzy Gillespie) who came as paying customers were refused entrance. Blacks though, who were still Negroes then and knew their place, did not come downtown, except to work – invisibly it seemed, so naturally menial were their roles – as messenger boys, cleaners and elevator operators. In the Chock Full o' Nuts and the Hamburger Heavens the short-order cook was black but a white man took your money. Even heaven was for whites only.

Manhattan was an enclave carefully contrived and the glamour it possessed, like all glamour, owed much to artifice. Manhattan was as anachronistic, and as clearly doomed, as the ocean liners that snuggled like whelps to the teats that were its piers. The glass towers had not yet come to give Sixth Avenue a shine and that thoroughfare was still plain Sixth and not the Avenue of the Americas. The El amazed the view of fourth-floor residents of Third. Couples danced cheek to cheek then, the women in ballgowns, high in the Rainbow Room, to the Englishman Ray Noble's knowingly American 'The Touch Of Your Lips' or to the piano of Peter Duchin, son of Eddie, on the roof of the St Regis. Cole Porter was living at the Waldorf (where Robert Benchley, dropped there by friends late one night, looked up at light blazing from a hundred windows and sighed with careful audibility, 'Gee, I told Mother not to wait up'). Thurber and Parker and the boys were kidding it up too, around the table at the Algonquin. The Oak Room at the Plaza was closed to women (and to tieless men) at noon but not at night. It was Scott and Zelda country still and the Ritz was as big as a diamond.

Nobody noticed the black clouds gathering over 125th Street, beginning even then to move slowly down toward the lofty Eighties, the cultured Seventies, the smart Sixties and the monied Fifties, past the Harvard Club and the Princeton Club, the Racket Club on Park, the Knickerbocker on Fifth and the more-English-than-the-English Brook. The hatted, brief-cased commuters – all of them white – wore 'authentic' British club or regimental ties with their Brooks Brothers or J. Press Oxford button-down shirts and suits and their heavy-welted, sincere shoes. (On rainy days they added galoshes: America, my newfoundland, where even the shoes wore shoes!) As if by secret signal from some white god, suddenly on the first day of spring, fedoras and grey flannel suits were swapped for club-striped boaters and tan or navy wash-and-wear suits and shirts with short sleeves.

The dry martini – puritanical and cold as the national drink, iced water – had not yet given way to the demand for 'light' whisky (i.e. containing less caramel colouring), although a new drink from England, gin and tonic, was making inroads. The subways were safe and graffiti as an art form awaited the breakdown of the social barriers and the invention of the aerosol spray. People – that is, white people – strolled across Central Park on humid summer nights to dine at the Tavern on the Green, or arrived, like Fred Astaire and Ginger Rogers in the movies, by horse and carriage from the rank in front of the Plaza on 59th. In this season the women carried sweaters at night – to put on, as in no other town in the world, when they went indoors, protection against the cold shock of air conditioning.

There were still Irish bars on Third Avenue, and they were full of real drunks, not whistle-clean young executives with their deodorised girls. They closed Fifth Avenue for the Easter Parade, and for St Patrick's the white line down the middle turned green overnight. So did the beer in the Irish bars. You could pick up the

99

New Yorker, immaculate magazine, thumb through the front pages and stroll West to hear Duke Ellington, Louis Armstrong or Ella Fitzgerald for the price of a drink at the bar of Basin Street. On your way home, at midnight, you could pick up a bedtime book at Doubledays on Fifth. Manhattan was formal, homogenized and rich. It was charged like a new battery. It was the Big Apple, it was a Summer Festival, it was Fun City – for some.

You went to Coney Island and ate soft-shell crabs whole at Nathans and later wished you hadn't when the zooms and swoons of the Big Dipper turned you clammy green. You rode the subway (you must take the A train) up to the Cloisters, an instant seventeenth-century Spanish convent, imported whole. You shushed down to the Village by jumbo cab to eat spaghetti at the San Remo on McDougall and later listen, devoutly, to jazz at the Village Vanguard or watch the young Jason Robards Jr become a star in *The Iceman Cometh* played in the round at The Circle in The Square. (Sitting across from the lovely Mrs Nehru – young then too and brilliantly sari'd – you almost missed the message of the piece: that we can't live without illusions, nor with them either.)

You ate in Chinese, Japanese, French, Greek, German and Kosher restaurants or you settled for a hamburger, the native food, served with three kinds of relish that looked like dog-sick and mustard that squirted from a plastic bottle. You heard the waiter shout to the short-order cook, 'Two on a raft, wreck 'em' and found that the dish was eggs on toast with the centres broken. You learned to order your whisky by brand-name and watched amazed as the barman (Mario, always, it seemed),* dressed, like Lord Raglan at Crimea, in a red, gold-braided monkey-jacket, filled a tall glass with chipped ice, squirted soda from a tap and pushed you a shot glass brimming with scotch that, new switch, you added to the soda and mixed with a plastic stirrer decked in gold with the name '21', or Toots Shors, or El Morocco, or the

* In the interests of uniformity, all headwaiters in New York are called Pierre, just as all barmen are correctly addressed as Mario.

Colony Room. You accepted bland coffee in a cardboard Dixie cup, added Diamond 'when it rains it pours' sugar from a paper sachet and stirred the mixture with a wooden spatula.

You failed, although God knows you tried, to detect the difference between Budweiser and Schlitz, Pabst Blue Ribbon and Michelob, Miller's High Life and Rheingold ('the heartier beer') or the insidious and just as insipid Schaeffers ('the one beer to have when you're having more than one'). You discovered delicatessens and the sandwich in all its declensions: as club or hero, on white or on rye, toasted or open-face. And you discovered the telephone as slave, which would bring food and liquor up to your apartment at all hours – the meal hot, the champagne cold.

When you checked in (back home, you used to register) at a hotel you filled in – no, filled out – a form that asked you, always, everywhere, the name of your corporation, for the business of America, as somebody said, is business. And that was why, all round you, the people said, 'OK, sell me' or 'I'll buy that' or 'It's a deal' and why the news-reader on television could switch without strain from the latest death-roll in Korea to the merits of a roll-on deodorant, and why the title 'executive' was as honoured in America as the title *'écrivain'* in France.

They were singing, then (and even a 'show' was 'business')

> New York, New York, it's a helluva town
> The Bronx is up and the Battery's down
> And the people ride round in a hole in the ground
> New York, New York!

New York, New York was a wonderful town, if you were young, and white, and new in town, and carried, in your Mark Cross wallet, a wad, like holy bread, of neat green dollars.

I knew nobody in this familiar-unfamiliar land, nobody except the girl that I had come to see. I found her, across the customs barrier, a small, pale-cheeked, fur-collared figure.

101

'Happy New Year,' I said and we embraced with awkward unfamiliarity and climbed as in a movie into a waiting yellow cab with a red-and-black-jacketed driver and headed across town through the tall streets to Fifth Avenue and then south down the long hill of Fifth, rising and dipping on the sway-backed surface of the steam-belching road like a yacht heading into waves. We came to where there was sky, went under an arch, into Washington Square, across McDougall, and came to the dark red brick façade, which now I know as brownstone, of the Hotel Earle. Reva, for whom, for official ears, I had been a dentist's appointment, took the cab back to her office – which tomorrow would be my office too – promising to see me again for dinner.

More alone than I had been since my mother had left me on my first day at school, I entered the dark lobby. It was painted in two quarrelling shades of green, kept from open war by a narrow no-man's-land of black. The prevailing odours were of sweet American cigarette smoke, floor polish and boiling radiators. On the left a hand-lettered easel sign, gold on wood, announced that Charley Schultz would be at the piano in the Village Lounge, nitely.

I checked in at the desk and wrote on the line marked 'Corporation', 'Ogilvy Benson & Mather Inc., 589 Fifth Avenue'. The elevator was big enough to use for freight and its flat steel doors, like a jewellery store shut for the night, were opened by the white-gloved hand of a dusty-black woman who said in a warm warble, 'What floor, hon'?'

The room was all right, if what you wanted was a Turkish bath. I opened the window and closed the radiator, in neat opposition. Like the lobby the room was two-toned and dully shiny, like an army barrackroom or the kind of schoolroom small children get to sit in if they are born poor enough. I gazed around the room. It didn't look as if it would ever be home.

I went down and out on to the street. I turned right and then left and walked down Eighth Avenue and noted a building with a lime-green roof and a sign that said 'Howard Johnson'. That would be useful in the morning: the Hotel Earle served no breakfast, in bed or out. I turned left on to Eighth Street and found myself in front of a bookshop. It was called the Eighth Street Bookshop but to me it looked like home. They were pushing the new best-seller, John Malcolm Brinnin's biography of Dylan Thomas. (I could claim acquaintance with Thomas. Once, in White's at Oxford, I had inadvertently squirted soda-water into his cloth cap as it lay on the bar. He had been very good about it.) I went in and bought the book for memory and comfort, shy with the unfamiliar money. I needn't have been. I learned that nobody is a foreigner in New York because everybody is, give or take a generation or two.

Hugging my book like a security blanket, I went back to my room. Somebody had closed the window. In America the buildings do your breathing for you. I lay down on the acid-green cover of the high, hard iron bed and began to browse through Brinnin. It was a good move. The unfamiliar began to become familiar. A few pages into the book there was a letter from Thomas to his wife Caitlin, whom I had also met. It was date-marked 'Hotel Earle, New York' the year before. I read on, feeling better. The next chapter was headed 'O love that hits below the belt'. I knew the line well. It was from a poem by Gavin Ewart.

I put down the book and as dusk fell on Manhattan at what for me had been tea-time and was now the cocktail hour I thought about all these things: about Oxford, and London, and Gavin, and the other poets who were my friends and colleagues too, like John Tessimond and Bernard Gutteridge, and about Reva who was coming to show me her city and her land. I thought about why all that had come to this. And I wondered why I had fled England, and how much farther I would have to travel, and for how many years, before I found safe harbour; not knowing then that it is the journey inwards which is the real long voyage home.

Chapter 13

Whereas the offices of S. H. Benson Ltd had been situated over the heads of the Methodist Church, the offices of Ogilvy, Benson and Mather Inc. were to be found above the premises of the Stetson Hat Company, at 589 Fifth Avenue, between 47th and 48th Streets. The snorting dark green bus had brought me up Fifth – which was then a two-way thoroughfare – from the arch at Washington Square. Breakfast coffee, blindly gulped in Howard Johnson's, swilled about in my nervous stomach and brought on coffee-flavoured eructations: alarums announcing incipient panic. To calm myself, I brooded on this flavour. American coffee, I concluded, was made by throwing away the beans and brewing the package.

Whereas in sepulchral Kingsway Hall I had taken the rickety lift with its crotchety attendant, from the vasty foyer on 48th I rode, for the first time, a smooth and automatic elevator to the ninth floor. The brushed, hushed aluminium doors oozed open on to a neat, fuss-free reception area in which, pert behind a black desk, sat a neat, fuss-free receptionist wearing a smile and that untouched-by-human-hand look often described, for reasons not entirely clear, as band-box.

Behind this blonde guardian, surrounding her on three sides, was a range of black showcases. Framed by the black, and softly lit from behind, was a collection, glowing like gems, of advertisements that were the kissing cousins of those I had admired in the grey corridors of Bensons: advertisements for Schweppes, for Hathaway shirts, for Puerto Rico, for the British Travel Association. The Holy Grail, light shining from it! My quest was ended.

I gave my name to the goddess and gazed, with the kind of fervour you might have spotted in the eyes of stout Cortez when he first glommed the Pacific, at the noble works before me. The reverential silence was pierced by a slow, warm voice that said, using a formula sacred to American corporate life, 'Welcome aboard.'

Beside me, beatifically smiling, stood an alarmingly handsome man of about forty-five, of medium height and sturdy build, with calm blue eyes and thick grey wavy hair brushed back. Clearly only gods and goddesses worked here. His smile stayed fixed, as if it were a contest in which I had thirty seconds to guess the number of teeth on display.

'Hi,' these gleaming beauties said, 'I'm Jud Irish. Copy chief here.'

'Hennessy,' I courteously replied. 'Irish myself, as a matter of fact.' The smile died almost imperceptibly, like the sun going down. Levity is not so much *mal vu* as baffling to the religious believer in American corporate life.

Jud turned and led his chastened novitiate through glass-filled swing doors and left down a gentle carpeted slope into a kind of peopled corridor. On the right was a blank wall; on the left, jutting out at right-angles to the corridor, were desks, each outside the open door of a windowed office. At the desks, facing electric typewriters, sat neat secretaries, *anges gardiens* to the offices' inhabitants, the shirt-sleeved, club-tied, buttoned-down executives.

At the end of this non-corridor (I, the new boy, in shy procession in this so-public place) we came to a corner office, looking out on Fifth Avenue on one side, on 48th on the other. (A corner office, I was to learn, is to the American executive what an outside stateroom was to the ocean-voyager; the ultimate in status was conferred by the placing of a rubber plant in a corner office corner.) This was Jud's office, realm of the Copy Chief, and strung from it like bunting along the 48th Street side of the corridor were the bright red, blue and yellow doors of the copywriters' offices. No secretaries sat outside these rooms, but inside them, on a small castored table in matching grey-green beside each desk, squatted a typewriter. Serious stuff, this, I thought. Very un-Bensons.

In the first office, sitting at her desk and half turned towards her typewriter, grave, business-like, intense, was Reva. From here, through her open doorway, she could see everybody who came down the slope from the glass doors that led to reception, and from beyond where, on the 47th Street side of the building, David Ogilvy had cornered the corner office, the grandest in the agency, with shower and terrace: even his secretary had an office.

Inside the next doorway down Copy Row sat another David, this one of the McCall ilk. You called him Dave; nobody would ever call Ogilvy Dave, even in America. McCall was a young, slim, fresh-faced, clean-cut, crew-cut, buttoned-down Princetonian (he was wearing the Tigers' orange-striped tie) with a bright smile full of milk-fed teeth and, behind round steel-framed John Lennon glasses, the shining, eager, almost inspired eyes one sees in debutant politicians.

McCall was the junior copywriter, and the most ambitious. He had joined OBM from his first agency, where one of his accounts had been White Rock, a soft drink and mixer manufacturer whose logotype, a bare-breasted but puritanically nippleless and somewhat Burnes Jones winged naiad, sat pensively – as well she might, given her unhappily deprived anatomy – on a rock. Even as he took up work in his new agency, some of Dave McCall's prentice work was currently charming, or afflicting, some curmudgeons might have claimed, the ears of the nation on the ever-present radio. The work in question was in the form of a jingle, sung to the tune of 'Down by the Riverside', and repeated some twenty times a day in office, home and taxi. The power of this early work, astounding from the pen of one so young, may be measured by the fact that, after more than twenty years of effort, I have been quite unable to cast it from my mind.

What makes White Rock taste so good?

> True fruit ingredients,
> True fruit ingredients,
> True fruit ingredients,
> What makes White Rock taste so good?
> True fruit ingredients —
> Just ask the White Rock girl!

The unashamed romanticism and vernal freshness of this lyric was in stark contrast to other work then current in the field: for example, the terse, manly, firm-jawed approach of;

> You get a lot to like in a Marlboro —
> Filter, flavour, flip-top box.

or the matey, street-wise:

> Brylcreem!
> Just a dab'll do ya!

Say what you will, this was memorable stuff, and I doubt if the work being done today, good as it is, will hold up as well twenty years from now. *Autres temps, autres* verse, as the French very nearly have it.

Leaving the young poet, past a doorway through which one could hear the naturally slurred voice, like that of a tipsy corncrake, of my wacky and ineffable future friend Ethel Cordner, we arrived at the office, last in the row, of an expatriate Englishman, Clifford Field. While I do not recall any *chef d'oeuvre* by Cliff Field in the genre of the jingle, I have read a great deal of his prose, and always with admiration. If stars could be said to exist in a firmament ruled by the kind of *Roi Soleil* that was Ogilvy, then the star writers (for on Madison Avenue copywriters are thus grandiloquently described) of the agency were undoubtedly Reva Fine and Clifford Field.

It is the profound conviction of all Americans that all Englishmen mumble. If this was so, then in Cliff they had found a rare specimen, a mumbler's mumbler. The English upper- and upper-middle-class accent, which is what Americans mean when they refer, in tones of wonderment and admiration, to the

'English accent', is found now in its pure or fossilized form only in the farthest flung colonies and ex-colonies. Whereas in England the coming of television had encouraged the development of a kind of inbred, 'classless' but self-conscious way of speaking, here in America Cliff's pure public school waffle had been preserved like a plover's egg in aspic.

Physically, Cliff could have been cast as one of those flannelled fools, usually called Reggie or Algy, whose dialogue ran to gems like 'Anyone for tennis?' in English country-house comedies of the thirties. It would, however, have been rotten casting, for Cliff was remarkably intelligent, extremely articulate and wonderfully witty.

He was slim, of tall-to-medium height, with straight and abundant auburn hair that had the kind of parting that looked as if it had been put there for his first communion by a fussy mother and never touched since. As Raymond Chandler said of a character somewhere, had he walked into a wall, his chin would not have been the first feature to make contact. His face had that beardless, uncannily unlined look of men who, like the unfortunate Dorian G., do not seem to age. He wore serious glasses, well-made tweed suits and shirts with tab collars, like the kind of English country doctor who drove a beat-up old Rover down winding lanes to deliver babies in thatched cottages surrounded by hollyhocks and privet hedges. He also wore the surprised and dismayed look of a younger son who had just been advised by a kind but stern father that, what with death duties and the claims of primogenitor, there won't be much left in the kitty for him, so perhaps he should book passage on the next P&O and try his luck in the tea plantations.

Cliff had arrived in America as a British Army officer early in the war to talk to Americans about the British cause. The casting had been right but the script, as I later heard it, was not up to snuff. The trouble, as I see it, lay in the opening lines of his speech. 'July 4th,' he would begin, 'which you I believe call Independence Day but we in England celebrate as Thanksgiving....'

108

Curiously, Cliff subscribed to the American rather than the British work ethic. He arrived early and left late and seemed to be typing all day, including Saturday, which he invariably spent at the office, except in the baseball season, for among his many contradictions was a devotion to this sport which in England is known as rounders and is played exclusively by girls. He was a craftsman and a professional and a writer of elegance and polish. He had once taken a sabbatical year in England with the intention of writing a book, but nothing came of it. So he returned and devoted himself to the advertising craft, becoming rich enough to retire, while still in his fifties, to a cottage in Suffolk, with his second wife, Cathy, who had been an account executive at OBM.

The steady, calm, soft-spoken Jud guided me into the next and last office in the row. My office. I looked around. It was the standard-issue American office, junior executive model. Grey-green metal desk with rounded corners. Behind it, cleverly matched, a plain swivel chair, its back to the venetian-blinded window and the heater/air-conditioning unit which together formed the street wall. The floor was shiny grey linoleum, the walls were sad cream and bare and the ceiling was composed of porridge-coloured squares dotted with holes, like a suspended switchboard. A larger hole contained a flat round light. For late work in winter a metal angle-lamp perched like a small crane on one side of the desk. A typewriter stood challengingly on a castored table beside it. No contest, I thought.

Jud left me and I seated myself, executed a practice swivel or two and tested the desk with my heels for height and distance. These things matter in the long office day. Jud returned with his gentle amble and his firmly shy smile and also with a girl — a word which, though clinically accurate, fails utterly to evoke the creature before me. Brightness fell from the air, as the poet very nearly put it, and probably would have, had he possessed my knack for these things. And talking of poets, this loveliest vision far of all Olympus' faded hierarchy, or something, was, according to Jud, who was well placed to know, for she was his secretary, called Shelley, with Arnesson completing the whole nomenclature. Not Shelley plain, as yet another scribe rather oddly put it, but Shelley beautiful. Her hair glowed with the silver-blond of Swedish birches. Her eyes were as big and blue and cool as northern lakes. She was neat as nylon. Framed by a crimson mouth, her teeth sparkled like fresh snow in the dawn sun. She was a masterpiece carved in ice. If you kissed her you would surely die, but you would have known, in that brief moment, what it was to live, and you would have counted it worthwhile.

This ice-maiden bore with her the standard yellow 'legal' pad, blue-lined, basic recipient for memos, notes, great thoughts and doodles. She also brought typing paper, and the sight of it cheered me, for I had long discovered that for me the throes of literary composition were productive only when the results were bunged down on plain white virgin paper, and only then if the instrument of communication was a pencil. My finest stuff is produced by a 2B pencil. I don't know why, but that's the way it is. Take away my 2B pencil and white unlined paper, hand me a ballpoint pen and a yellow pad, and you'd get better work from a Hottentot.

It was therefore a relieved junior copywriter who next saw the translucent blue-veined hand, like something in marble by Michelangelo (or do I mean Giotto?), proffer a bunch of about fifty new, yellow and fiercely sharp pencils. Now all pencils in America, as if by some great trans-continental decision, are yellow and the blunt ends of these yellow pencils are equipped with what I now call, but unhappily did not then, an eraser.

It so happens that I have an aversion to using this useful little tool of the trade. If I write a wrong word, I strike it out, or start again on another piece of paper. Conjecturing on this foible, and wishing, as it were, to break the ice with this cool goddess, I looked up at the dazzle which was Shelley Arnesson and said, 'Thanks awfully, but I never use a rubber.'

Now you might think, if you happen to be English, that this remark was, though banal, at least blameless: an unremarkable remark, so to speak. You would have been wrong so to think, for Shelley's reaction to it, though baffling at the time, was sharp and clear. She raised, almost imperceptibly, the perfectly drawn arch (Fragonard? Boucher? Greuze perhaps?) of one faint eyebrow and lowered, by an exactly equal distance, the opposing corner of her bow-shaped mouth (Watteau? Marie Laurencin?) as if the information I had conveyed, while not in itself uninteresting, left a great deal to be desired in its timing and appropriateness to the occasion. The shy Jud, meanwhile, had assumed a roseate hue and after one of those silences that seem to last a year the two turned and, avoiding each other's eyes, left me alone. Only after long reflection, during which I passed in review the works of those daring new writers of the *avant-garde*, John O'Hara, Bud Schulberg, Irwin Shaw and so on, did it dawn on me that the word I had used for what Americans call an eraser was in fact the word that Americans used for the most common, and most masculine, of contraceptives. Years later, a young English girl of the wild rose variety, whom I had sent with my commendation to David Ogilvy, told me that in her early days with the firm she had been elbowed rather sharply in a crowded elevator and had squeaked, 'Ouch – that was my diaphragm!' It made me feel better.

Where copywriters' row ended, at my office, art directors' alley began, at first in line, then turning right and right again to form a U-shaped well. In the centre of this well toiled the Production Department in open plan, for in the hierarchy of the advertising business these were a lower grade of employees whose role, nevertheless, was vital: to steer the layouts, copy and artwork into final proof form for the newspapers and magazines.

First of the art directors to my left was Bill Binzen. He had been a cowboy in Montana and looked as if he had been scared out of Marlboro Country by a marauding gang of photographers and creative people from Leo Burnett, the agency which handled that account and whose President was a hero of David Ogilvy's. Bill was a tall, lean, home-on-the-rangy man with the shy firmity and the bred-in-the-bone elegance of Gary Cooper. The chiselled face, under thinning auburn hair, habitually wore an expression of sternness, even gravity. It was the mask of the clown: behind it a

111

jokester lay hidden, waiting, with infinite patience, to spring out with a roar of laughter, to the consternation and discomfiture of whoever had made the error of taking this face, as it were, at face value.

Bill Binzen was working on – among other accounts – the much-talked-about Schweppes campaign. The English Tonic Water had been launched in America by Ogilvy with a strategy built around the personality of the product's advertising manager, a handsome and bearded ex-British Naval officer called Commander Edward Whitehead. The launch (for once an appropriate expression) had taken place in New York and the strategy now demanded that the product infiltrate towards the west. The theme of the new campaign, with a kind of simple pretentiousness not unknown in the advertising world, was labelled 'Americana'. Our hero, Commander Whitehead, would be discovered in typical 'only-in-America' locations, peddling his little yellow-breasted wares.

Bill had prepared one rough illustration which depicted Whitehead seated cross-legged in a tepee, facing a half-circle of costumed Indians, all with glass in hand, a crate of Schweppes between them. Stuck with this inspiration, and no doubt feeling desperate, for here I was a debutant, Bill asked me to provide some suitable wording.

Somewhat nervously, for that is the state in which I invariably approach a major literary challenge, I returned to my little grey home of an office and sketched out a tentative headline or two. One of them, I decided, was not bad. It read 'Navajo hail Big Chief Quinine Water from over the sea.' Although not perhaps in the same league as those immortal lines that used to make the hair stand up on Matthew Arnold's (I think it was) Victorian neck, and thus provided him, by some curious biological process, with 'touchstones' by which all other work might be judged, although, as I say, not perhaps in that class, this effort of mine, in my view, covered the situation fairly well. I took it along to show Bill.

I don't know whether you have ever walked into a room, full of good tidings and great joy, only to have a bucket of icy water fall on your head. It can have a powerful effect on a man's emotional state. This is what happened to me then. Not literally, of course, the perching of buckets of icy water on top of doors being frowned on in the better advertising agencies, but metaphorically, if that's the word. Bill Binzen took the piece of paper on which I had neatly pencilled my first ever headline on American soil, stared at it grimly for a very long time, like one who has received a telegram bearing the message 'FLEE STOP ALL IS KNOWN', and then, his lean frame collapsed in his swivel chair, turned a stricken face up towards me as I stood apprehensively waiting. The piece of paper that carried my first message to the American people, or at least those of them in the A and B social classes, fell from his long fingers and pendulumed to the clay-coloured linoleum. At last, words emerged from the above-mentioned stricken f.

'What devil's mockery is this?'

Somewhat discountenanced, I stood there while his shattered gaze, that of a broken man, stayed fixed upon me. More words emerged.

'My God, man,' he added, rather like the Victorian father in one of those plays when confronted by some bounder who has come to ask for his daughter's hand in marriage.

'My God,' he said again, no doubt for emphasis.

As I was about to mumble something suitable, Binzen suddenly swooped to the floor, picked up the apparently offending piece of paper, leapt to his feet, brandished my *oeuvre* somewhere near the ceiling, and shouted 'Ha!' and then, apparently liking the effect, 'Ha!' again, rather the way that Greek chap Archimedes must have carried on when he hit upon whatever that formula was as he was sitting in the tub.

Then, dumb with disbelief, I heard him say, 'I tell you, man, its great.'

His face cracked open, like an orange hitting a wall, and he doubled up with uncontrollable laughter, now hooting, now wheezing, limbs jerking about like a marionette with St Vitus' dance.

Now although I had already learned that the word 'great' in American English was merely the equivalent of 'good' in English English, I was still pleased by the assessment, such was my relief after the incredible volte-face that I had just witnessed. It was my first experience of the Binzen approach. It was not to be my last, for I shared several adventures with the then bachelor Binzen, before introducing him to his second wife, an English tea-rose with the dew still on, called Gail Longden.

I have had cause to mention this lady before, for it was she who had that most unfortunate experience in the elevator. We had met in London. Returned, a conquering hero, from this first jaunt to America, I had taken up the post of Joint Copy Chief (with my friend John Mellors) of Bensons. A young trainee copywriter at Mather and Crowther, wishing to complete her apprenticeship in New York, had been sent to me as the acknowledged expert on such matters.

Nobody more beautiful had ever entered my office (for, sadly, Mary Hunter had never crossed the threshhold). Gainsborough Films used to have a sort of living logo at the beginning of their productions. You may have seen it. There was this Gainsborough portrait of a lovely lady and suddenly she turned her head and smiled at you. Well, it was like that. Here in my doorway was a walking, smiling, talking (with a charming suggestion of lisp) Gainsborough. She was tall, serene, and, as I think I have mentioned, dewy rose of complexion. It is difficult to be gracious when very young: difficult, but not impossible, for this girl managed it effortlessly. Much taken with the damsel, I invited her to dinner that night, a most unusual occurrence, for such is not my style, inhibited as I am by morbid shyness.

Persuaded, over dinner, that she really intended to go to New York, I wrote to David Ogilvy, who has an eye for beauty, and to Bill Binzen, for I thought the two were suited. Ogilvy immediately engaged her and Bill Binzen almost as immediately became engaged to her.

Bill Binzen became an outstanding photographer (advertising art directors yearn to be photographers in much the same way

114

that clowns want to play Hamlet: in both cases they are usually well advised to stick to their lasts, if you will excuse the rather cobbled up metaphor). His first book was called *Tenth Street*, a record of life on that thoroughfare, east of the Village, where they made their New York home. Before leaving the agency, however, Bill took the picture of Ogilvy which is used on the cover of his bestselling autobiography. The typographer of that book was the remarkable woman whose office, just around the corner from Bill Binzen's, formed the second wall of the Production well.

In most advertising agencies, typography is the sphere of a special department, each typographer assigned, with an art director and a copywriter, to an account or group of accounts. At Ogilvy, Benson and Mather the Typography Department consisted of one woman, a native-born Dane called Ingeborg Baton and universally, for that is the *mot juste* today, known as Borgie. It would be hard to overestimate the role played by this exceptional lady in the creation of that special look which signals, not only to the cognoscenti but to the layman (or consumer), that the advertisement they are looking at is, can only be, the work of Ogilvy.

She sat alone, with a ballpoint pen and a ruler, and her rule was law. Yet in spite of this, or perhaps because of it, not only was she admired and respected, she was loved, and not least by me. It was she who chose and calibrated the typeface for every advertisement that the agency produced – from hectic store sales and Amazing Offers to the august Rolls-Royce and cool Steuben Glass pages tailored for the readers of the *New Yorker*. It was she also who designed the agency's letterhead, labels and documentation; so that it could be said that she, in choosing the typeface, chose also the type of face that the company presented to and on behalf of its clients.

If Borgie said that a headline, in order to be visible, readable and appropriate to the look of the advertisement, needed to be eleven letters (known as characters) long, no more, no less, then it was the copywriter's excruciating task to compose a meaningful headline to that measure. Length of body copy, of subheads and cross-heads was dictated by her, and copy mercilessly cut or invisibly added accordingly. If the first word of the copy (which, to alert the eye that it should start reading here, was always set with a capital letter of three lines in depth) presented a difficult 'dropped cap' − an 'A', for example, which leaves awkward white space between its apex and the next letter − Borgie would courteously but firmly request the copywriter to start the copy with a word that began with a more amenable letter.

It was Borgie, too, who decided which paragraphs in a long piece of copy should be indented, or set in bold face or italic, to give variety. When the copy, to her exigeant eye, needed to be broken up by cross-headings (to encourage the wearying reader to read on) the copywriter produced the required words, in the required number of characters, whether he was the insignificant newcomer from England or the feared and famous Ogilvy himself.

She also kept a watchful eye on widows. 'Widow' was the expression used to designate the one or two words left dangling at the end of a paragraph, leaving the rest of the line blank. Widows aired the copy. The white space left at the end of a paragraph gave the eye, as it were, a breather, and led it by the shortest route to the beginning of the next paragraph. Ogilvy, in his 'Credo', if not mixing his metaphors then giving them a damn good stir, declared that 'widows are the life-blood of copy'. When a widow failed to occur naturally, a widow was induced: the copywriter, suffering but uncomplaining, cut or added the requisite number of characters.

This attention to minutiae, as well as being a good, and humbling, lesson for the writer, contributed hugely to achieving the Ogilvy 'look'. Typographical exigencies imposed upon the copywriter, in an indisputably more trivial field, the kind of discipline imposed upon the poet by verse forms. (Practitioners of both arts, like Tessimond, Ewart or Gutteridge, were better placed than I to measure that.) If there were no prima donnas among the Ogilvy copywriters, not even the Master himself, the universal respect for Borgie Baton's talent and experience may have been largely responsible. There was also the matter of her personality, which was of a rare kind, even outside the feverish world of advertising.

Borgie was, first of all, every em and pica a lady, a word that no more needs defining than love, or grace, or kindness: the higher human qualities break through the barrier of words and pierce the heart. She had that rare form of beauty that ages prettily: round and pale blue eyes smiled eagerly from a round and porcelain face. (Today there are hairline cracks in the porcelain, and silver threads among the flaxen.) Her carriage is serene and queenly. She is slender, as if it would be bad manners not to be. She has a quick wit and a fast brain, and can spot a phoney from a mile away, with or without her lorgnette. A lass unparalleled, as someone said of another queen.

She had been born in Denmark and raised in Paris, where her father was military attaché at the embassy. She had trained as a book designer and typographer in the birth-place and Mecca of the trade, Frankfurt. She married a quiet American, Henry Baton, who had been a military lawyer at Nuremburg and later traded in agricultural machinery. They lived (Borgie for three days of the week) in a hill-top home set in a royal and deer-filled park on the Pennsylvania bank of the Delaware.

You approached Borgie's hidden-away house by a steep, winding and narrow drive. At one blind bend a notice-board carried a warning in two languages. 'Honk', it said to those driving up; 'Hoot', it said to those descending. When the family Volvo approached, the garage doors graciously opened. In the main bedroom stood a spinning wheel, for Borgie wove. She also gardened and I can still taste the young asparagus, of the green and slender kind, fresh from the soil.

The house and its vernal vistas are long since sold, for Henry died suddenly and they became cruel reminders. Retired, Borgie lives now in a cottage in her native Denmark and winters in Majorca. Ogilvy, wise enough to have chosen her (and she him) an age ago, now sends her on missions to his offices world-wide, to show the people there how things might be, if they could aim that high. When she comes to Paris, she calls me, and my heart leaps up.

By circling, as it were, the square in which the Production Department was enclosed one returned, always, in my own case, with a certain libidinous pleasure, to the desk of the unbelievably blonde but curiously unbroachable Shelley Arnesson. In the last few days, another grey-green desk had snuggled up, and who could blame it, to Shelley's desk. Behind it now sat an alarmingly redheaded, drily witty, twangy-voiced Irish Catholic girl from Chicago, who cast around her an alert but sceptical gaze. Her name was Marikay Hartigan and her role among us was to type our copy for presentation, first to our superiors in the agency, next to the clients. An honourable employ, you might assume, for a girl from the sticks, fresh to the Big Apple, and one not without its compensations, for she was daily exposed to some of the finest prosody then being turned out on Madison Avenue. Your assumption, however, would have been wrong, for such was not the view of her task that commended itself to Marikay's inquiring mind and level gaze.

From time to time, now, my copy would be returned with, attached to it, brief notes suggesting how, with a little cut here, a small addition there, and a slight change elsewhere, the stuff might be tightened, gussied up and generally, for that was unmistakably the gist, improved. Not the least unsettling feature of these little homilies was that they were, for impenetrable reasons, invariably signed, 'Crayola Jones, the Mad Monk'.

One day, vivid as ever, Marikay, alias the Mad Monk, shimmered through my doorway, carrying, in her little Chicago hand, some small masterpiece that I had recently given her to type.

'Hey,' she twanged, her voice, like her gaze, as flat as the mid-West plains of home, 'You wanna know what I think of this cahpy?'

'Well, yes,' I lied, fearing, as I usually do, something dreadful, like the truth, for example. 'Go ahead,' I said bravely. 'Shoot.'

'I think this cahpy stinks.'

118

I don't mind admitting, between the two of us, that had I then acquired that facility for thinking in French which I have today I would have riposted with a cutting *'Ah bon?'*, adding perhaps for emphasis an *'Eh bien ...'*, taking as my model here the tight-lipped Gabin just before he hauls off and descends some oily *maquereau* in a too long raincoat and a too thin moustache. Lacking, however, at the time, that *panache* for which I have since become internationally famous, I contented myself with a cutting, 'Well, if you think you can do better, jolly well go and do better.' Not perhaps in the Gabin class, but good enough for my purpose.

That ought to hold her, I thought, and so it seemed for, with a toss of her red head and what sounded like a honk (it was clear to me that she did not give a hoot), she turned on her high heels and left.

It would appear, looking back over the years, that I have a talent, rarely alas called upon these days, for bringing out the best in secretaries. It happened with Joan Kennedy, transformed overnight, almost, from *dactylo* to star woman copywriter at Bensons. It happened again with Marikay Hartigan. Goaded by my taunts, she went right ahead and did do better, or at least as well, for she soon joined Reva on the distaff side of the Ogilvy Copy Department. She then married, though I take no credit for this transformation, another Ogilvy copywriter called Joel Raphaelson, a Harvard man whose father had written *The Jazz Singer*.

Many years after these stirring events, I was sitting in a sidewalk café on the Avenue Victor Hugo, watching the sun shine through the amber *demi* of Kronenbourg before me, thoughtfully savouring the various scents of the 16th Arrondissement's cosseted womanhood as they wafted by, and thinking about not going back to the office, when a twanging noise impinged upon my reverie. In a flash I had placed the alien sound as a human voice and interpreted the twang as the American greeting, 'Hi.'

Looking up, I saw the face, red-halo'd, of Marikay Raphaelson,

119

née Hartigan. She had arrived in Paris the day before, with her three children. Joel would be flying in to take up the post of Creative Director for Ogilvy in the Paris office, with responsibility for the other European branches, for the small firm of three was now a great worldwide concern.

Later, with Joel installed, there was dinner in one of those vast apartments that the canny French keep empty in order to sock the officers of American multinationals for unbelievable rents. Cliff Field came, with his wife Cathy, from England. Borgie was there, from Denmark. For some obscure reason the baked salmon was from Oregon and the beef from Chicago. It was, you might say, just like old times.

Inspired by my meeting with Marikay, I had composed a clerihew and I decided to regale the company with it. This is how the work went:

> The Avenue Foch
> Is for people who are posh;
> The Avenue Victor Hugo
> Is where people like me and you go.

Not altogether displeased with this effort, which had been well received by the assembled *convives*, I was about to take another sip of aged Bordeaux, when I heard Cliff mumble. He too, it seemed, had recently composed a piece in the same verse-form. Happily all of us present were skilled at translating Cliff's gurgle into plain English, and this is what we heard:

> Emilio Pucci
> Calls his wife Gucci:
> It isn't a gag —
> She really is an old bag.

Ah, we were a nest of singing birds, those days, at Ogilvy, Benson and Mather.

120

Chapter 14

For most people, the name of Dr George Gallup is linked inextricably with the notion of 'poll', the word being generally used in a political context. To members of the advertising community, however, the good Doctor is chiefly known as a pioneer in the development of techniques for measuring the 'impact' of printed advertisements.

In its crudest form, such a measurement may be obtained by inviting a 'consumer' to peruse a newspaper or magazine and then asking him (or, more usually, her) what he remembers of his reading. By repeating the process with a number of consumers a score of 'recall' is obtained. In a refinement of the method, the consumer is then reminded of a specific advertisement in the publication he has scanned and asked what he remembers of it. Again, by repeating the process, a score of 'aided recall' is obtained.

Advertising agencies prepared to divert some of their clients' money into the coffers of the Gallup organisation are able to compare the 'impact' and 'recall' scores of their advertisements not only with other advertisements in competing or non-competing fields, but also with the editorial content of the publication – this being, one must assume, the reason for which the reader, or consumer, has purchased it. It is thus possible, in theory, to know how successful an advertisement has been, first, in capturing the reader's attention with its headline and/or illustration (impact) and, second, in conveying the message it was intended to convey (unaided and aided recall).

Brooding on the results of his research, the diligent Dr Gallup drew and, for a small fee, made available to advertising agents, some compelling conclusions. His figures showed, for example, that no advertisement, however enticing, could hope to compete successfully for readership with the adjacent editorial matter in a publication. Since the reader has laid out his own hard-earned money precisely for the purpose of examining the editorial columns of his purchase, the Doctor's conclusion hardly comes as mind-bending news. But, doggedly pursuing his researches, and using the editorial pages as criteria (since, after all, they represented a product successfully sold and it was worth finding out why this was so), Gallup further declared, in effect, that what limited the impact and readership of advertisements was precisely the fact that they were advertisements! For it has long been assumed by advertisers and their agencies that advertisements, by their very nature, must necessarily employ certain verbal and graphic techniques, such as bold black headlines, socko illustrations, catchy slogans, a liberal sprinkling of exclamation marks, 'explosions', balloons and elaborate and arcane symbols know as logotypes ('logos' to initiates). Not so, declared the pollster. An advertisement's impact was in inverse ratio to what, in an unlovely turn of phrase, he called its 'addyness'. The more the techniques used were 'addy', or, to put it another way, the less they resembled those used by the editors, writers, designers and photographers of successful magazines and newspapers, the poorer would be the performance of the advertisement.

The implications of this new thinking (opposed as it was to the beliefs of the Bensons school, where we were encouraged to make our advertisements 'ping out' on the page) were not lost upon a young employee of the above mentioned Dr Gallup, for after rendering sterling service to the Doctor, notably in Hollywood, where his task was to measure the impact of movies, he was now turning over in his mind the idea of starting an advertising agency of his own. And if I have risked boring my reader with so much dry exposition it is because this employee, a handsome, charming, articulate, Irish-Scottish *ancien chef* of the Hotel Majestic in Paris, ex-salesman of stoves, non-graduate of

122

Oxford and former diplomat and secret agent of HM Government, was called David Ogilvy and was furthermore, to employ once again the jargon of the business in which I have spent (some would say wasted) thirty years, of all the people I have known in that trade, the one who made the most impact, and the one of whom I have the highest recall, aided or unaided.

Chapter 15

David Ogilvy had walked, for most of his life, in the long shadow cast by a brilliant older brother. Francis Ogilvy, whom I met only in his decline, was a gifted showman and charmer who had rocketed into the London advertising world to become Managing Director of Mather and Crowther at the age of thirty-four.

It was a time when the advertising business in England had reached its apogee, not only in the quality of its creative output but also in social acceptability. It was therefore natural for David Ogilvy, and for him more so than most, to head for the fresh woods and pastures new in which Francis was cutting such a swathe. He therefore joined Mather and Crowther and, his talent for writing not yet in evidence, became in time head of the Research Department. Anyone who has met David Ogilvy will confirm that, for all his many qualities, the ability to remain for long in a position of subservience was not among them. And yet, always ahead of him, blocking the way to the shining heights, was his brilliant (loved-and-hated, perhaps? Resented but emulated?) brother and rival, Francis.

It was not therefore, one may surmise, entirely by chance that David Ogilvy soon found himself in America, dispatched to garner the latest wrinkles in research; and it was logical that he should find himself (although he tells us that the offer of a job was entirely unexpected) at the feet of the head guru, so to speak, in advertising research – the ineffable Dr Gallup.

After the war, in which he served alongside men like Montgomery Hyde and Jan Fleming, as a Secret Service agent, Ogilvy tried his hand at farming in Pennsylvania. His neighbours

were the Amish people, on whose anachronistic life-style he
became, to hear him tell it, something of an authority: their
industry and frugality appealed, one might surmise, to his deeply
Calvinistic nature. Farming failed, but he had tried, and the
courage to dare was one of Ogilvy's more attractive qualities. He
would need it. Challenges exist perhaps with less in-built promise
of success than that faced by a British subject with an Oxford
accent and manner intending to found an advertising agency in
the concrete jungle of Madison Avenue, but they do not spring
readily to mind.

He started with a partner, an agreeable, if intense, product of
the WASP establishment called Andy Hewitt, and with an office,
a secretary and £20,000 provided by his brother at Mathers and
my old boss Bobby Bevan at Bensons. The fledgling agency was
called Hewitt, Ogilvy, Benson and Mather, this neatly covering all
parties to the hazardous deal.

Without clients, if I may be allowed a truism, an agency does
not exist. Nudged from London, one or two small accounts
arrived, but they were not enough. What the agency badly
needed was a client who would not only bring it money, in the
form of the usual 15 per cent return on the cost of space, but
would also allow it to demonstrate its creative ability and thus
attract more clients. Such a client, happily for the shoe-string
agency, was not long in coming.

Ellerton Jetté was a small manufacturer of good-quality shirts
which were sold in the posher haberdasheries under the brand-
name 'Hathaway'. This name, though perhaps known to a few
men who, with bleary morning eye, had glanced at the label
before it disappeared for the day behind their necks, was totally
unknown on the market place, and this for the very good reason
that it had never been advertised.

Jetté decided that the time had come to make the name famous,
and to this end he set aside in his annual budget the sum of 5000
dollars. Most veterans of Madison Avenue's rightly named
campaigns, inured as they were to handling accounts that billed in
excess of five *million* dollars a year, would have been hugely

125

unimpressed by the proposal. Ogilvy, the unknown, could hardly afford to be so picky. Although the product, compared say to a new model automobile or range of beauty products, was banal in the extreme, he accepted the challenge. He took the money and, as they say, ran with it. Some running. There are other campaigns that have made their mark, in America and then worldwide, in recent years. The Marlboro campaign is one. Volkswagen is another. But I would say that what Ogilvy did with that pittance created, in retrospect, the biggest event, the most clearly defined watershed, in my years in the advertising game. And he did it, in effect, with just one advertisement.

If Ogilvy had taken the classic step of spreading the money through a few selected newspapers (in those days only about 10 per cent of advertising was carried by television: now the ratio is reversed) he could have placed a number of small advertisements with a common theme (or copy-platform) and he would thereby have created a 'campaign'. But because of their smallness and sparseness these advertisements would have fatally lacked what his master, George Gallup, had called − if you remember − 'impact': impact not only for the brand but for Hewitt, Ogilvy, Benson and Mather. Ogilvy decided, daringly, to put all the money instead into one advertisement, in full colour, bleed-page (the illustration running to the edges of the page), in one publication and thus, whatever the content of the advertisement, achieving by its form, its size, its presence, the optimum impact. The vehicle he chose for the do-or-die experiment was the *New Yorker* magazine, and this for two reasons.

The *New Yorker* was read by what the Media Departments of the agencies knew as 'opinion leaders'. They were not only potential purchasers of the goods and services promoted in the magazine: they were also, as captains of industry, of law and of the intellectual pursuits, capable of influencing, by example and by word of mouth, the lesser mortals − that is to say, you and me − who trod timorously beneath their feet. Moreover the mere fact that a product appeared in a magazine of the stature of the *New Yorker* gave it a certain *cachet* in the eyes of the store-buyers whose job it was to choose the season's stocks. A further consideration, in Ogilvy's mind, was that the *New Yorker*, because of its special audience (one's friends and colleagues?) and its internal 'climate', would provide an ideal showcase for the first major work of a new, unknown but ambitious advertising agency.

The medium established, there remained the problem of the message. Ken Tynan once remarked that when you have seen all of Ionesco's plays you have seen one of them. And while, to the caring eye, your run-of-the-mill Arrow isn't a patch, so to speak, on your bespoke Turnbull and Asser job, there is undeniably a certain sameness about shirts. It is, nevertheless, on the look of the thing that the product is chosen. And to show a man what a shirt looks like it is perhaps advisable to show a man wearing it. It is here, however, that dangers loom, as it were.

By employing a professional model the advertiser risks alienating the reader who may have difficulty in putting himself in the shoes, or in our case, the shirt, of a fellow who may be handsomer, slimmer, younger (even though effeter) than he is. Moreover the use of an anonymous model, who may even be glimpsed in some similar role elsewhere in the same publication, destroys credibility, reduces memorability and increases the 'addyness' of the advertisement. On the other, or third, hand, the employment of a 'celebrity' as a model, against a suitable emolument, or free shirts for a lifetime, or something of the sort, courts two possible risks: the celebrity may appeal only to those already susceptible to his charms, and repel the others; and he may, by his presence, charisma or what have you, dominate the advertisement to the virtual exclusion of the product (a situation for which Ogilvy, in another context, has coined the rather gruesome phrase 'vampire video'). The second danger is that the reader may well recall the name of the celebrity but not the name of the shirt, the latter being newer to the game than the former.

What was needed then, for this make-or-break experiment, was a model who was not a model, a somebody who was unknown, a man who had, or who could somehow be given, that memorability, that 'burr' (Ogilvy again), which makes for 'impact' and 'recall'. The problem was put to a photographer called Paul Radkai who, although successful in the commercial field, had started out, like his compatriots the Capas and André Kertesz, as a photographic reporter: a fact which commended him to David Ogilvy.

It happened that Radkai had a friend among the international jetsam of New York by the name of George Wrangel. Wrangel was working as a waiter in a hamburger joint (a fact that was carefully concealed from Ogilvy), but such had not always been his occupation. He was a slim, fine-boned, distinguished-looking man with greying hair and mild blue eyes. He was also an authentic baron, descendant of that famous general familiar to readers of Tolstoy. Wrangel had been, with Cholly Knickerbocker, one of the first of the gossip-columnists, when that dubious trade first saw the dark of night in the New York of the late twenties and early thirties. When the crash came he was assured, like the late Lucius Beebe and others of his kind who had managed to retain a presentable set of evening clothes, of at least one good meal a day by acting as an unpaid *figurant* in the deserted restaurants and night-clubs of the time; anxious owners, in fact, used them as live bait to lure back the smart set by demonstrating in effect that they were already there. Beebe in one of his books declared that he never again ate as well as when he was penniless in a New York where the streets echoed to the thud of falling financiers.

Ogilvy, impressed by Wrangel, or anyway by his title and provenance, proposed to Radkai that he should be photographed (in shirt-sleeves of course) taking breakfast on a villa balcony. Radkai has since told me that he found this suggestion not only banal but lacking in those intimations of class, quality and easy assurance that the picture should bring to the shirt and its wearer. He had another friend, tailor to gentlemen, whose fitting-rooms were richly panelled and deeply carpeted. A man who has his suits made to measure would be a man of taste and means, attributes which by a kind of osmosis would be conferred also on

128

his ready made shirt. The situation was also one in which even the most patrician of chaps would expect to be discovered coatless. Persuaded by the Hungarian (Hungarians being, as everybody knows, people capable of entering a revolving door after you and coming out in front) Ogilvy gave his approval of the setting.

But that decision resolved only one of the problems. For all practical purposes the Creative Department of HOBM was David Ogilvy. He would supervise the shooting. He would also write the copy. Already he thought he had the headline – if, that is, the illustration turned out to be strong enough to justify a somewhat prosaic line. I have often wondered if Ogilvy was influenced, consciously or unconsciously, by the title of a best-seller of the time: *The Man in the Grey Flannel Suit*. There have been precursors ('The Girl in the Alice Blue Gown') and followers (*The Spy Who Came in from the Cold*). Some rhythm that calls to that collective unconscious old Jung told us about? Nursery rhyme memories? Who knows. Ogilvy's version was 'The Man in the Hathaway Shirt' and, although lacking a verb, it did contain, like every Ogilvy headline since, the name of the product – for, as he later in his wisdom put it, if you haven't said it in your headline, you haven't said it at all.

But it was not the problem of the headline that exercised Ogilvy. In a 'Credo' circulated among his small staff, Ogilvy had written that they should not be content merely to score a hit with each creative effort: they should strive to 'bunt the ball out of the park every time'. Had he achieved this kind of strike with the first and only Hathaway advertisement? Would the combination of a top photographer, a handsome aristocrat, an oak-lined room and a headline with archetypal reverberations be enough to make the advertisement noticed, talked about, nay, unforgettable?

Far away in England that week the American ambassador, Lewis Douglas had gone fishing. Casting for trout, he caught the hook in his eye. An operation followed and he was photographed for the newspapers as he emerged from the hospital. He was wearing a plucky smile, and a black eye-patch. Ever a scourer of

129

newspapers and magazines, Ogilvy had not missed these photos of the brave plenipotentiary. They had, for some reason, 'impact'. On his way to the shooting, Ogilvy recalled them and stopped at a drugstore, or wherever you go to buy such things, bought a black eye-patch and put it in his pocket.

At the studio, all was ready: setting, lighting, background, model and stern but fawning tailor with his tape. When Ogilvy arrived, shooting had already started, with Radkai well into his mad Hungarian genius number (it was Radkai who gave me the authentic recipe for making Hungarian goulash: 'First, steal a cow ...'). He has told me since that although he knew the pictures he was taking were technically impeccable, and as good as he could make them with the material available, they lacked pizzaz, that little extra something that made the difference between a good photograph and an unforgettable one. He could not think what to do about it and was feeling vaguely at fault (When you meet a Hungarian in the street, punch him in the nose: he'll know why).

It was at this point that Ogilvy, actor *manqué*, master of timing, Mr Unforgettable himself, reached in his pocket for the eye-patch and said, with his usual courteous authority, 'Could we try one with this?'

It is possible that Kraft-Ebbing, author of that gripping tome, *Psychopathologia Marginalis*, and general whizz on the more *recherché* aberrations, might have made a better stab at explaining the impact that the resulting photo had on the unsuspecting readers of the *New Yorker* (and, indeed, the unconscious motivation that had led Ogilvy to his startling choice), but for Ogilvy the appeal of the eye-patch was clear. It gave the wearer an interesting past, a history. He looked like someone who had bravely suffered great hardship. He looked like a hero.

Under the four-colour, bleed-page picture of Baron Wrangel (so named in the advertisement), grey-templed, Eton-tied, gazing out autocratically with his one good eye, appeared in bold but softly spoken type the headline: 'The Man In The Hathaway

Shirt'. Underneath that were three short columns of type chosen by Borgie Baton: it was the same typeface as that used in the adjacent columns of the magazine. There were no vulgar incitements to buy, no 'addy' expressions, none of the usual clichés that Ogilvy has labelled 'bromides'. The 'image' had been, in one stroke, forever stamped upon the 'brand', could never be copied or taken away, would serve for a lifetime of variations (and does so still, after several changes of agency).

What Ogilvy had in fact achieved was the sort of advertisement that the staff of the *New Yorker* might itself have designed had it been responsible for the contents of the advertising pages. It was simple, literate, well mannered. It had class. It set the tone for all future Ogilvy advertising – and for a great deal that was not created by him. (It also, single-handed, or anyway single-paged, started the trend that made the *New Yorker* fat, as first Ogilvy with other clients, and then other agencies, saw the possibilities of this medium, both for advertising and for self-advertising.)

The man in the Hathaway shirt became famous, if not overnight, then overweek. And so in turn did his onlie begetter, the suavely brash, acceptably impossible *enfant terrible*, David Ogilvy, and with him, his infant British-born agency.

Chapter 16

There are in the advertising business, as there are no doubt in other fields, men and women who reveal extraordinary capacities for, say, leadership, or management, or future planning, or clear exposition, or creative inspiration, or spell-binding presentation. What was unique, in my experience, about David Ogilvy, was that he contrived to combine all these qualities in one undeniably attractive, though not to everyone desirable, package.

This apparent paragon was the man who ruled, in his split-level corner office, in the airy, girl-lined corridors, or in the claustrophobic, windowless boardroom, the advertising agency that was now Ogilvy, Benson and Mather. (Andy Hewitt, rather against the wishes of Bobby Bevan and Francis Ogilvy, had been squeezed out like a pip after a bitter internecine, me-or-him battle: Ogilvy told me later, with obvious glee, that now, alone with his power, he felt like a child with the nursery to himself at last – no usurping big brother? – and all those lovely toys to play with.)

In his *Confessions* Ogilvy compared himself to a *chef de cuisine*. I would compare him also to a master tailor. Both métiers demand the combined qualities of the artist, the leader, the psychologist and the diplomat. Both, like the advertising agent, depend finally on the approval of the client. And both require the finest raw materials, be it *matière première* or men.

When I arrived at OBM I was immediately conscious of joining an élite. Of course, those who are strangers to the inner workings of the advertising business, which they may well regard as a rascally trade at best, may find this hard to swallow: but here I found an instantly sympathetic and universal suspicion of, and

132

scorn for, all that was scamped, shoddy, make-shift or make-weight. There was a horror of the false note and hence in these corridors it was rarely heard. Like chooses like and deep calls to deep, and so on, and people who were not well mannered, or sensitive to others, or quietly spoken, tended not to be hired by those who were, and who had been there, almost, from the beginning. And they had been hired, and first of all attracted, by (since it takes two to make a deal) the man who set, and still sets, the tone for those who consider themselves to be privileged members of his *atelier*, or whatever.

The first impression, for those not too impressed, is that of an actor: not your flamboyant, sock-it-to-them style, but the watchful, underplayed theatricality of a man who, having at last found the perfect role, by dint of playing it had become it. It is possible that nobody has ever seen David Ogilvy off-stage. It is possible that nobody will ever be allowed close enough to see the man beneath the make-up. He was something under six feet tall, slim, boyish in looks and movement, firm in stance, and no more relaxed, but no more tense either, than a boxer in the ring taking the measure of his opponent while not missing a sound from the audience that is always there. The hair, a fighting-Irish auburn-to-red, never ruffled, was brushed in shallow waves back and sideways from a high parting. A red-head's inevitable freckles dotted here and there a healthily clear pink Anglo-Saxon skin. Clean cheekbones lent shadow to the hollowed cheeks and above the well-cut chin a large, generous mouth seemed always to be repressing a smile, like that of a small boy who has just set up a practical joke and is trying not to give the game away. He wore, often, the kind of dark-rimmed serious glasses that Cary Grant affected when required to play the handsome young academic. A pipe gave a stagey seniority to his boyishness.

Beneath this face, which was redolent always of aftershave or cologne, discreet ties cohabited with striped shirts. In winter the suits were of subdued, English-gentleman-abroad tweed; in summer, tan or navy wash-and-wear, bought from Sears Roebuck − who later reciprocated by becoming his client. But

133

winter or summer, the lower half of the suit was supported by wide braces of a startling red colour. (Why do firemen wear red braces? To keep their pants up. But Ogilvy's, as we shall see, had another function too.)

The walk was spring-heeled and eager, the regard attentive, the reactions fast, the understanding subtle. Ogilvy possessed that nice mixture of masculine, man-of-action strength and feminine, *à fleur de peau* sensitivity which seems to be irresistible to women and yet acceptable to men. (In the cinema, Cooper, Fonda, Gabin would be types of this.) He seemed both active and reflective, spontaneous and measured. Deploying an 'Oxford' accent and a soothing timbre, he could, as they say, talk a dog off a meat wagon.

It seemed to be for him a matter of deep urgency that no interlocutor, however obscure, should leave his presence without being stamped with an inerasable image, without the profound conviction that he had just been talking to The Most Unforgettable Character He Had Ever Met. I have seen people leave his office after such an imprinting: their expressions were not unlike those I had seen, as an unwilling altar boy, on the faces of communicants returning, rapt, purged, blessed and wafered to their pews.

About such striking characters, stories are told by lesser men (I am using the world's measurements, not, necessarily, mine) and if some are apocryphal it matters little: if their hero had not existed, they would not exist either. The first important publication of Ogilvy was a paper entitled 'The Image and the Brand'. In it he argued – what in the Hathaway campaign he had demonstrated – that in the long term the facts about a product are less important than its aura, the impressions that stick in peoples' minds. Thus the feeling was created, or reinforced, that the Volkswagen was an endearing, ugly, chic and dependable 'Bug' or 'Beetle' while the Rolls-Royce was august but not too much so, acceptably snobbish, a wise investment. If one accepts Ogilvy's thesis, and if one considers him, to use his own term, as a brand, then it may be possible to see his life as an attempt, not unsuccessful, to create a lasting image.

His style from the beginning was one of calculated daring, of acceptable outrage. One of his account executives who accompanied him to a first meeting with a prospective client (the intimidating board, I believe, of the Morgan Guaranty Trust) later told me about one such example of image-creation. It was winter and the two men wore overcoats. The conference room, like all rooms in America in winter, was overheated, and its occupants, sensibly, discarded not only their overcoats but, as is normal practice in the States, their jackets as well. All, that is, except Ogilvy, who retained not only his jacket but his overcoat, which happened to be a long, black, theatrical job with a Diaghilev astrakhan collar. Too polite, perhaps, to comment, the others continued the meeting. On leaving the building the account executive, to whom the question had become more burningly vital as the meeting wore on, inquired solicitously of the muffled Ogilvy if perhaps he suffered from a cold. No, replied his president, why do you ask? Well, pursued the account man, weren't you a bit hot in there? Yes, confessed Ogilvy. Then why, insisted his colleague, by now understandably exasperated, didn't you take your coat off? Ogilvy fixed him, over his glasses, with a pale blue eye, and said in measured tones, 'I'll tell you why. Because by tomorrow none of those people in there will be able to remember your name. But they'll never, ever forget that madman with you who sat in that heat with his overcoat on!'

It was partly by playing the lead in such mini-dramas that Ogilvy, propelled now by the success of Hathaway, began to acquire more valuable accounts, accounts which provided him not only with income but with further opportunities to demonstrate his agency's skill in producing advertising that not even enemies of that trade (and some of them are my best friends) could accuse of shoddiness, banality or bathos. Shrewdly, wherever possible Ogilvy selected clients who suited his style, clients who could provide those heroes, or heroines, about whom literate fantasies could be created and brand images invented: Helena Rubinstein, genius of fards, white-coated in her laboratory; Margaret Rudkin, sort of Irish colleen made good on

135

her Pepperidge Farm (an American brand of bread that had the unheard-of quality of tasting like bread), Albert Dimes, the grizzled English tea-taster, in shorts and topee, selecting the tiny teabuds for Tetley; a whole (fictitious) family of little Lords and Hons. for Viyella; Eleanor Roosevelt, no less, to promote Good Luck margarine on television (when asked how he had managed to persuade the First of First Ladies to perform this task Ogilvy replied simply, 'It's surprising what people will do if you only ask them nicely').

It did not escape the notice of many observers, including gleeful rivals of the upstart, that when, on the other hand, Ogilvy was presented with the problem of advertising products that were humdrum, banal, inextricably linked to kitchen, washboard or daily use – Rinso, Franco-American spaghetti, Saccony women's wear – he was less successful. Where he could find no intrinsic nobility, he stumbled. But give him the chance to manufacture a hero, and watch his dust. Such an opportunity soon arose with the arrival in America of Schweppes Tonic Water, on the face of it an ordinary enough product but, to Ogilvy, one that was to give him his second great opportunity to show that as an image-builder he was unsurpassed in a nation that had invented the genre.

As is usual when a new product comes on the market, several agencies – most of them big guns – were invited to pitch (in the jargon) for the Schweppes account. The Chairman of Schweppes, Sir Frederick Hooper, had also been head of the British Travel Association, whose account was already handled by Ogilvy ('London's heart beats faster as the Horse Guards clatter by'), and it was through this connection that David was invited to join battle with the Goliaths.

As was also usual in such cases – but is no longer – it was the advertising agency that, win or lose, bore the cost of such speculative presentations, and the cost, in man-hours and material, could be painfully high, particularly for a small and still struggling agency. Dozens of glossy layouts, with specially taken photos and typeset copy, are mounted on boards and covered with cellophane. Their purpose is to demonstrate the kind of campaign the agency proposes to run if the agency is fortunate enough to land the business. Along with these layouts go elaborate easel-mounted research and media charts whose function is to explain and justify the tone and theme of the advertising and the choice of media it is proposed to use. Each agency in competition is allotted a fixed time (agencies prefer to be first or last to present) to introduce itself, its people, its past, its potential and to explain, as convincingly as possible, why, out of all the agencies in America, the prospective client would be well advised to choose this particular one. These are unenjoyable occasions – some would say debasing ones – but that, as they say in such circles, is the name of the game.

At the beginning, Ogilvy's presentation can have looked little different from the others. His efficient, grey-suited (and doubtless grey-faced, for these are tense occasions) lieutenants had prepared the easels, the screen, the projector, the batons, the Magic Markers, had stacked the impeccable layouts with their surfaces hidden from the row of Schweppes directors seated around the table in front of them. As it happened, this lavish material, lovingly prepared, was never to be used, for one of those company officers had at that moment caught the waiting Ogilvy's attentive eye and lo! what he saw before him was, not a director of Schweppes Inc. (USA), but, yes, another hero!

Edward Whitehead (who died recently in England) was Advertising Manager of Schweppes in America. He was also tall, slim, handsome, blue-eyed and russet-bearded, like a more aristocratic sea-dog off an old packet of Player's Navy Cut. The comparison is not all that far-fetched, for Whitehead was also entitled to the rank of Lieutenant Commander in Her Majesty's Royal Navy. When, from the gingery shrubbery, a voice emerged, there were heard in the room those plummy tones, distorted vowels and mangled consonants that for Americans, blandly ignoring the nuances of region and class, comprise the 'English accent'.

The hour for do-or-die having struck, Ogilvy stepped forward, shucked his jacket − thus riveting the gaze of his fustian-clad audience on the startling sight, in America, of trousers held up by braces, and fire-engine-red braces at that − and instead of, as the programme demanded, introducing self and cohorts, began calmly, carefully and wordlessly, before the horrified stares of the latter, to tear up, one by one, the lavish layouts stacked beside him. Spell-binding, might be the word.

There was more to come. His actor's sense of timing telling him that the moment for the *dénouement*, or clincher, had come, Ogilvy ceased his destructive work, drew himself up, pointed a finger of one sandy, freckled hand towards the pop-eyed Whitehead and spoke the words that, true or false, have become part of the legend of Madison Avenue: 'Gentlemen, give me that man and I will sell your product throughout the United States!'

It was, of course, straight out of a B-feature costume drama − but it worked. For while the brilliant layouts of his competitors survived the presentations intact, they were now worth less, much less, than the spoiled fragments lying at Ogilvy's feet. The new account, an unbelieving Madison Avenue soon heard, had been awarded to the johnny-come-lately Ogilvy, Benson and Mather. There had been another flash in the pan.

Once again, Ogilvy had got his hands on a man whose presence suggested a 'past', a hero around whom he could create an 'image' for the 'brand': two words which he seemed now to have pre-empted (although the notion had been more crudely expressed in an earlier advertising dictum, 'Sell the sizzle, not the steak'). Once again, Ogilvy used the technique of creating a market with a limited budget in New York, starting a trend among the cognoscenti in the metropolis that would then spread outwards to the hicks in the sticks. Once again, Ogilvy eschewed the then-prevalent mode which would have called for a large picture of the product looking appetising ('appetite-appeal' was the catchphrase) above a headline that blared, 'AMAZING NEW DRINK SENSATION FROM BRITAIN'.

Instead, what the readers of (again) the *New Yorker* discovered was a full-colour '*reportage*' photograph of an elegant, smiling,

138

bearded, briefcased VIP descending the steps from a BOAC jet towards a red carpet that led down to a quiet caption-headline that read, 'Schweppes' Ambassador Extraordinary arrives in the USA.' It was an invitation to read the by now familiar three short columns of type that described the pleasures that the English had long enjoyed from the 'beady little bubbles' that 'last the whole drink through'. The man who was charged with bringing these delights to the grateful American palate was none other than 'Commander Edward Whitehead' of the Royal Navy.

From that moment, it was this same Whitehead, in press, on radio, on television, in personal appearances across the States, who carried the tonic message to a grateful nation. If he had not been a hero before, he was something like one now. He became a famous figure, the image of the brand. He became President of Schweppes in America and owner of a white Rolls-Royce. He also became a firm friend of his 'creator', David Ogilvy, who himself was now off and running. He has not stopped running since.

Chapter 17

The lawns below the technicolor-blue sky were dollar-green and the table-cloths on the patio flamingo-pink. So was the writing paper in my room. The telephone was movie-white and when I picked it up to make a call a girl's voice said, 'Good afternoon, Mr Hennessy. Welcome to the Beverly Hills Hotel.'

A group of my colleagues from the Copy and Television Departments of OBM had preceded me to Hollywood. At that time (the mid-fifties) most television commercials were shot there, on sound stages and backlots deserted by the moribund film industry, employing the talents of directors, actors, sound and camera men who had spent their lives in the business. Our New York team, here to supervise production of commercials that they had written, was composed of two men and a woman (I, the newcomer from England, had tagged along as acolyte, dogsbody and free-loader). The two men posed no problem, but the woman was Ethel Cordner, the lady whom we briefly glimpsed on our tour of Copywriters' Row.

If, attending the smarter kind of cocktail party in Manhattan at that time, you had approached the most animated group in the room, forcing your way through the mesmerised crowd you would have discovered a small, teetering, animated woman conducting a witty, if surrealist, *tour d'horizon*. If it wasn't Dorothy Parker, it would be Ethel Cordner. If she was wearing a hat, as women did in New York in those days, it would have been of the most fashionable kind but it would have become tilted tipsily over one round outraged eye. A tuft of her expensively set hair would have detached itself from the main mass and be sticking out at an angle from her small head. Her make-up would have become smudged, lending her face that smeared look that Francis Bacon has caught so well in his paintings of ecclesiastics. If you left Bette Davis out in the rain overnight, what you would have in the morning would be Ethel Cordner.

She spoke with a Tallulah Bankhead slur. What she said was always funny, in a zany, Perelman way. She stood, as Forster said of Cavafy, at a slight angle to the universe. She was married, in an absent-minded sort of way, to a pleasant, quiet man called Carter Cordner, a copywriter in a rival agency. In a resigned tribute to the force of his wife's personality he occasionally referred to himself as founder-member of the Hi-Carter-How's-Ethel Club. It was Ethel Cordner who had arranged my flight to what smart New Yorkers called 'The Coast'.

It was my first flight ever, and I was terrified. (In case the word should seem too strong I ought to mention that I am pretty scared most of the time, just walking around.) I had been told to report to the West Side Air Terminal at 6 a.m., an hour at which what courage I have has not reached its peak. From there a limousine would take me to La Guardia, the airport for domestic flights. I cheered myself up with the thought that once in the air, with the sun coming up and the refreshments going down, I would feel better – not less ill and scared perhaps, but learning to live with it. I had reckoned without Ethel Cordner.

I suppose the greatest achievement of the image-makers is the air hostess. By this I mean that if, for example, you hear the word 'Paris' your mind streaks off to a world of gaiety, chic and general ooh-la-la; see the word 'Oxford' and pictures form of dreaming spires and golden youth. So it has become with the words 'air hostess': today they instantly evoke feminine desirability at its most femininely desirable.

Reality, as so often, explodes this myth. On American Airlines Flight 127 to Los Angeles it did not stand up to the thin light of dawn. The hostess whose smile loomed through my panic like a homing boomerang, while no doubt a credit to her uniform, was far from being an oil painting. Her behaviour, moreover, was

141

distinctly odd. Having bosomed eagerly down the aisle towards me, she now proffered a cup with one hand, pointed elaborately to it with the other and with great care pronounced, or rather mouthed, like a professor of elocution, the word 'tea'. It was as if, experienced hostess that she was, she had decided that with me she had to deal not only with a cretin but with an illiterate cretin.

This unnerving behaviour, which continued throughout the seven-hour flight, persuaded me that not only was I incarcerated in the claustrophobic rumbling belly of a DC7, I was locked in there with a raving lunatic. The steady all-American voice of our captain confirmed that below us flowed, in back projection, the russet gash of the Grand Canyon, the blonde acres of Iowa, the white peaks of the Rockies. To me they were one long blur. All I wanted, in my new-found idiom, was out. I wanted back to New York. Or better, to London, home, where the big slow, safe, red buses had no constraining doors and the conductresses were sane. Flying, I decided, was strictly for the birds.

It was, it will be understood, a shadow of the man who had left Manhattan that morning who checked into the Beverly Hills Hotel. When I picked up the phone in my room, to be greeted unnervingly by name, it was to call Ethel Cordner, already installed in the hotel. She proposed that we meet in the Polo Lounge, and I changed into the kind of clothes I would have worn for an evening on the terrace of the Carlton in Cannes and went to the bar to straighten out my psyche and await Ethel. When she had found me in the green gloom she peered at my costume and said, 'Gee – you've gone Hollywood already!' We had a couple of Whiskey Sours, the modish drink, and walked out into the light of the lobby and the waiting rented Cadillac convertible ('incontrovertible', Dylan Thomas would have said).

As we entered Ciro's the band swung into 'Mr Wonderful', a nice touch, I thought, if exaggerated: the drinks and the sultry Californian night were getting to me. Over dinner I told Ethel about the weird happenings on my flight. As I talked there stole over her features a look of secret and pleasurable triumph, such as you might surprise on the face of a girl picking out her

142

engagement ring at Cartier. Over coffee she confessed all. Before leaving New York she had called American Airlines to tell them that a passenger named Hennessy, travelling on Flight 127 to Los Angeles, should be given special attention. Not only was this his first flight; not only was he highly neurotic; but further, he was a foreigner who understood not a word of English.

Back in New York − I pleasantly conjectured − bitter winds would be whipping the ears and ankles of pedestrians trapped at intersections by the DON'T WALK signs. Avenues and cross-town streets had become giant wind-tunnels. All over town, under the medieval canopies of the ritzier apartment blocks, foot-stamping, ear-muffed doormen were piping without conviction at the deaf drivers of cruising cabs. But here on the patio of the Beverly Hills Hotel all that was cold was the chipped ice in the silver bowls that cradled the cherry-nippled grapefruit and those stern glasses of iced water that cast their puritanical chill over even the most festive tables in America. The expensive sun beamed on jacaranda and on flamingo-pink table-cloth. It beamed on Ethel Cordner and on me. But it did not beam on our client, who would soon be heading for his desk in the glassy Lever Brothers building to make the money to pay the bills we were running up.

The Lever product we were here to work on was called Good Luck Margarine. The campaign strategy, as it is grandly called in the trade, had been devised by the New York agency and was, like most campaign strategies, of stunning simplicity. Margarine was failed butter. If margarine could, it would be butter. What people really liked was butter, but margarine was cheaper. Therefore we would assert that there was no detectable difference between Good Luck and butter − except, of course, the price, which was to our advantage. One flaw in this otherwise beguiling strategy was that by an inconvenient quirk of American law, concerned no doubt to protect the consumer from just such claims, we were forbidden to name the product to which our product was to be so favourably compared.

143

However, as that excellent magazine the *New Yorker* has observed, there'll always be an adman. Heeding Wordsworth's sensible advice, the agency contrived to turn its necessity to glorious gain. Digging deep, it unearthed a weasel. For the profane, or suckers, as they are sometimes called, it should be explained that a 'weasel' is Madison Avenue jargon for a linguistic device that allows the advertiser apparently to state a fact while leaving himself an opening to wriggle through should the statement ever be challenged. Thus the forbidden 'butter' became 'the expensive spread' or, in a further refinement that might be called a weasel's weasel, 'you-know-what'.

In the press campaign with which the new product was launched – in full-page newspaper advertisements known to the trade as block-busters – readers were chummily buttonholed by headlines like, 'Bet you can't tell Good Luck from you-know-what', followed by subheads in which, for the slower-witted, the qualifier 'expensive spread' was employed. Well-remunerated spontaneous testimonials declared: 'I can't tell the difference between Good Luck and you-know-what.' And in a masterly touch, the authors of these declarations were revealed as farmers and their wives – or purportedly so, which, in advertising, may amount to the same thing.

The task of our small 'creative' group had been to translate this winning theme into television terms: into, that is, the space of ten, twenty or sixty seconds of screen time. Conventional wisdom in the trade has it that the viewer in such a short time can absorb only one idea. Even the maximum time of a minute does not provide licence to say more things: it merely provides more time to say one thing more forcefully, or more often, and thus to increase the 'impact' of the spot.

The hero, or perhaps anti-hero, of our commercials was to be Joe E. Brown. Brown's wall-to-wall grin had helped to make him, for a while in the thirties, the biggest box-office attraction in Hollywood. (He made a notable comeback in the film *Some Like It Hot*, with Marilyn Monroe: he played the amorous millionaire, so besotted that when at the last his inamorata protests that she is a man, he says with loving forgiveness 'Nobody's perfect.')

Joe's role in our spots was simple. He would be cast, for example, as a plumber. His task finished, refreshment would be due. An unctuous voice-over (VO) would address him thus:

VO: Gee, Joey, been quite a day, huh? *(Joe shuffles feet, nods modestly)*

VO: Now Joey, how's about a little snack? *(Joe looks surprised but pleased at the attention paid him)*

VO: There you go, Joey. Good Luck Margarine! *(A hand appears, offers him a cracker on which a creamy substance has been spread. In CU (close-up) Joe takes a bite (SFX – sound effects – 'crunch'), manifests surprised pleasure)*

VO: Mmm ... better than You-know-what, eh Joey? *(Joe, though willing, looks blankly bewildered)*

VO *(helpfully):* You know, Joey – the expensive spread! *(Joe gives this a second's reflection, than beams in slow recognition, clearly pleased not only by his discovery of delicious Good Luck Margarine but with the intellectual grasp he has displayed. He continues to munch the cracker, then gives his famous wrap-around grin)*

VO and SUPER *(text superimposed on the screen image of the Good Luck pack):* Get Good Luck Margarine – better than you-know-what.

This modest *chef d'oeuvre* was filmed on a huge sound-stage in the Paramount Studios and directed by Mark Stevens, a B-feature and soap-opera actor turned independent producer. Stevens, it became clear as shooting progressed, was not Ethel's favourite.

'He's going bald,' Ethel whispered during shooting one day, 'and I'm *glad*.'

The production manager was a Hollywood old-timer called Manny Cohen. We learned a lot about film-making from him. A call used sometimes before takes had baffled us. We hesitated to expose our East Coast greenhorn ignorance before Stevens and we asked Manny what MOS meant in the expression 'This is a take – MOS'. He looked at us with mild surprise, raised his hands palms upwards and said, 'Mit-out sound, what else?'

Joe E. Brown adopted me during my Hollywood stay. He was a short, trim man of great energy, warmth and kindness. He had followed James Stewart in the West End run of the play *Harvey* and had been very happy in England. He admired the English and for his purpose I was English, although I am Irish. He also chose to believe that I was an aristocrat, although I am of verifiable peasant stock. Whenever he introduced me to his friends, who seemed to compose the entire population of Hollywood, it was as 'my friend Sir Charles, from England'. Any protest I might make was interpreted by Joe as yet more evidence of English – aristocratic English – modesty.

The old stand-up comic had found in the shy, or withdrawn, young visitor a new straight man and our act went on the road, to Romanoff's (the owner, another phoney aristocrat), to Chasen's, to the Brown Derby – and to a Chinese restaurant whose name, for good reasons, I failed to note.

In one of the variants of our Good Luck spot Joe wore a dinner jacket. When the morning's shooting ended Joe decided to take me to a Chinese restaurant for lunch. The restaurant was crowded and people paused in their unequal struggle with chopsticks to cast looks of humorous admiration at Joe. There was anticipation in their looks, as well there might be. The premise that he had chosen for his Chinese act was that his guest, Sir Charles from England, never having been to America before, had never eaten Chinese food. The premise was false, but I seem to remember someone saying somewhere that it is by carefully selected lies that art expresses truth.

Seated, our artist took the menu and looking alternatively anxious (brow furrowed like a field in winter, mouth set in a grim line, the corners turned down at 45° angles) and triumphant (eyes popped, mouth spread in a smile like the radiator grille of our rented Cadillac) guided me through the selection, translating helpfully from the Chinese by the simple device of, as it were, Peking at the English version printed alongside. When the food arrived he carefully explained that what appeared to be shrimps

146

were in fact shrimps and that the soup was Chinese soup and therefore eaten with a spoon, while the shrimps were eaten with two pieces of bamboo known, curiously enough, as chopsticks. He not only showed me how they worked. He fed me with them.

One of the characteristics of Chinese restaurants, in London, Paris and New York, is that they are the quietest of eating places. Waiters arrive and leave silently, rarely pausing for a chat. Customers, conscious perhaps of the respect due to the founders of gastronomy, speak softly, even in France. But on this sunny afternoon on Sunset Boulevard the clientele were presented with the unexpected floor-show of Joe E. Brown, star of stage and screen, force-feeding his stooge, an English toff, and they responded magnificently. There was even restrained applause. They were what we troupers call a wonderful audience. For myself, I felt a sudden kinship with that anonymous author whose desperate note was found, replacing the habitual motto, in a Chinese fortune cookie: 'Help, I'm a prisoner in a Chinese fortune cookie factory!'

I recovered from this ordeal next day beside the palm-fringed pool of the hotel. The sun, a Californian orange, hung above water that looked like something surgical instruments are kept in. We were working on script changes, waiting to be hailed, impressively, to one of the pool-side phones to take a call from the client or our New York office.

I looked about for Marilyn Monroe, and saw only her husband, Joe diMaggio, a man of indisputable charm, modesty and dignity, but not what I had in mind that hot afternoon. I fantasised staying on here as a highly paid scriptwriter, working on my crowning triumph, the life of Christ, with Garbo playing the lead.

Today few stars will drag me out on to the cold streets. Garbo (now *there's* an aristocrat born of peasants), Astaire, Gabin, Raimu, Monroe, Bardot, early Bette Davis, Chaplin, the Marx Brothers, Brando. And I regard few directors as true authors: Renoir, now silent, Bunuel, Bergman, Antonioni perhaps, Truffaut – and Satyajit Ray who, while I was goofing around in

147

the Beverly Hills Hotel, was laying out advertisements in the Calcutta office of S. H. Benson.

Almost all the films that had helped to form my youth, in twice-weekly visits to the High Street Odeon and subscriptions to *Picturegoer*, had been made here, and the stars on whom I had modelled my persona had lounged, like me now, around this pool in the brief days of their glory. I did not want to become like them now though. All I wanted to become was myself, and it might take a lifetime to do that.

Chapter 18

My Achilles' heel is my stomach – psychosomatically speaking, that is. Others may have stomachs that growl or rumble: mine screams silently for help. In those dreaded situations – meeting new people, going to new places, assuming new responsibilities – that add to the psyche's normal crushing load, I usually expect to be nobbled by the gastric gremlins. So was it when I was a boy. 'Specialists' to whom my anxious mother took me could find nothing wrong. I could have told them that. They were the wrong kind of specialists: what I needed was someone whose inner ear was attuned to a cry for attention, for affection, for the kind of love you didn't have to merit. So is it now I am a man. So shall it be, no doubt, when I grow old, for as the old mountain sheep who penned that line concluded, the child is father to the man.

So that in what the reader might have taken to be those jolly, whoopdedo days at OBM New York, always there, behind my devil-may-care insouciance, stress was at its destructive work. Maybe everybody is a bit like this. I don't know, and maybe you don't either. A story someone once told me is one of the few that I haven't been able to forget. A man goes to see his doctor, complaining that he hasn't been quite up to snuff these last few days. The doc asks him to describe his daily routine, hoping to spot therein some clue to what ails him. Well, says the chap, let's see, I get up, shower, shave, have breakfast, vomit, go to the office. ... Hang on there, says the startled medico, I want your *everyday* routine. Yeah, well like I said, I get up, shower, ... etc. Hold on, says the doctor – you mean you vomit every morning? Why yes, says the fellow, vaguely surprised, doesn't everybody?

149

Now those of you who are up on the vogue words might call that a little parable about human isolation, or alienation, or whatever. And you might be right. Maybe that's why I remember it, being, as it happens, only human myself. Anyway, in those first weeks at Ogilvy, Benson and Mather the old tummy, as is its wont, acted up and Reva, ever solicitous, sent me to her doctor. This doctor (who, operated, as it were, not in a surgery but in an office – America being, as we have noted, business-minded in all things) suggested, among other things, that I stop drinking. This rather offended me, for in those days I had hardly started drinking.

But I did stop drinking, and after six months on Canada Dry Ginger Ale started a notebook in which I jotted Great Thoughts. I have since glanced through this tome and think, on the whole, I would have been better off drinking. The good doctor also prescribed some tablets to aid digestion (I can eat everything: everything gives me indigestion) and I had these made up downstairs from his office in the pleasingly named Wickersham Apothecary. The love potion worked so well that I became hooked on it and panicked at the thought of a meal without it.

The Wickersham Apothecary was handy for fixes, for I had now moved uptown from the institutional paintwork of the Hotel Earle to the gothic brick of the Hotel Winslow – a style of building that would have represented the *dernier cri* in New York opulence in the Hollywood films of my youth. For five dollars a day what you got was a large television set furnished with a tiny room. Becoming claustrophobic after a while, and with my first fears and nausea calmed by the ministrations of Wickersham, I bravely answered an advertisement for a furnished apartment in the lean columns of the fat *New York Times*.

It's a curious fact, but it so happens that wherever I have lived, in London, Paris and New York, I have paid, or, let's face it, sometimes owed, my rent, not to a landlord, but to a landlady, in every case divorced or widowed and of quite outstanding beauty. Mrs Stuyvesant, who concerns us now, was, as they say, something else again.

I met her, by appointment, outside an apartment on 72nd between Madison and Fifth. She was the classic New York beauty, as advertised. Slim, sober-suited, seamless. Tanned as a lifeguard, blond as butter on brown bread. Under those groomed nails no grime would ever gather, on that svelte skin no sweat would every surface. She was, as the expression then went, a living doll. And she had, I discovered, that easy equalness with men, that give-and-take wit that American women share with Shakespeare's heroines; they come on like boys, but you know damn well they're not.

She led me into an elevator in which anyone accustomed to spending time in a two-man submarine would have felt instantly at home. Belly to flat belly with this cosmopolitan stunner I stared in front of me like a sentry as we sighed towards the tenth floor. Halfway there she gently nasalled, like an upper class Mae West, 'You know, they have these things in Paris. By the time you get to the top you have to marry the girl.' Cool stuff, I thought hotly, as I stepped into the airy apartment, like a Finn lurching from the sauna for a bracing roll in the snow.

In the middle of the bright, sparely − indeed scarcely −- furnished room a blind television stood, like a murky aquarium. The kitchen was refined by a bar with stools, empty as a Glasgow pub on Sunday. There was a bathroom with a shower − America's great contribution to clean living, and a standing rebuke to the bidet. There was also a narrow cot which, as my landlady-to-be deftly demonstrated, converted into a double bed. 'For when you have company,' she explained, thoughtfully. I liked the place. It didn't impinge. It was a space to get away to. I liked being with people, but I liked not being with people too, maybe more. I have measured out my life in furnished rooms. It would be a base, like any other.

Now when I left the office I would walk straight as a guided missile up Madison from 48th to 72nd, carrying out groceries in brown paper kit-bags from the cold green morgue of the supermarket, picking up my shirts from the Chinese laundry or my cleaning on those wire hangers that, in the closets of

Manhattan, breed like rabbits. Back in the new apartment, almost always alone, I felt almost at peace, for the first time since I was twenty-one, and almost for the last time. I felt that all things were possible, as of course they always are. I could float free of advertising, do scripts in Hollywood, write a book. Brave thoughts, for a devoted coward.

I began, untypically, to write long letters home (if home was the word), to family, to friends. Startled no doubt, John Tessimond, Gavin Ewart, Bernard Gutteridge wrote dutifully back. In my new serenity, with the authority of one who has no need of it, I wrote at length to Philip Stobo, recounting my experiences, proposing the excellent John Mellors as Copy Chief of Bensons. It was as if unconsciously I had, sea-changed, already left that world. I even, for a brief moment, glimpsed that state that Tessimond had described:

> ... Grow, be tall, yet reconciled
> To yourself, the weeping child.

> Love; be easy, and be warm.
> Find the fire beyond the form.
> Laugh. Forgive yourself; forgive
> Sins long dead, and learn to live.

Evenings not spent here would begin at Reva's place, a two-room floor-through, as they say, with a pull-out kitchen that would suddenly appear, the way places do in those pop-up books. The whole was packaged in one of those endearingly ugly brownstones (so-called, but they were the colour of dried blood) that disappeared before the advance of the newer, lavatory-tile school of New York architects.

Over the aperitif, accompanied by a little something on the phonograph from the latest Broadway hits: *Damn Yankees*, *Pajama Game* or the hot new album, *My Fair Lady*, we would glance through the front pages of the *New Yorker* (always available *chez* an OBM copywriter, for there would almost always be one or more of our works in it) and choose a handy mid-town

152

restaurant, invariably one proposing a foreign cuisine, for an American cuisine does not exist (although I note that my Oxford contemporary the journalist Robert Robinson maintains that it does: it is the American menu.)

It was the habit then of gipsies, housed, by city tradition, in vacant store fronts, to make the rounds of restaurants, offering for a far from token sum to tell the fortunes of the clientele. Whether such intrusions were welcome or otherwise depended largely on how well the victim had dined. One night, in a restaurant of Arabic orientation, our table was approached by such a mendiant – but one, I perceived, of a rather unusual kind. No *gitane*, she was elegantly garbed and of apparent cultivation. Flown with loucoum and gritty Turkish coffee, I offered her – this being, as I have noted, an Arab joint – a palm. Taking my hand in her well-manicured ditto (already worth the money, this, I thought libidinously) she launched into her dialogue.

'You're a rider,' she said unhesitatingly.

'Eh?' I said, ever courteous, but somewhat baffled.

'Yep. A born rider.'

I looked at Reva. She spoke the language. 'Writer,' she said, clearing things up.

'Oh. Ah,' I said, for I had forgotten the American way with the letter T. 'Spot on,' I said, conceding a point. 'I am a writer – in an advertising agency. So's she,' I added, waving the free hand towards Reva and thus graciously getting her in on the act.

'That's not what I mean,' said the clairvoyant lady. 'You ought to be tapping away at your own typerider.'

'Ha,' I said, quickly spotting a flaw in her argument. 'But I can't type.'

'No excuse,' replied the stern witch. 'You ought to be home nights, riding away.'

'Well, right-ho,' I said, thinking it best to play along with this *Folle de Chaillot*. 'But what makes you think that?'

'I don't think it, I know,' she said, tracing the lines on my careworn hand with a dainty finger. 'This is what we call a rider's hand.'

153

'Well, well,' I murmured thoughtfully, smiling inwardly the while, for Reva looked glum.

It is the illusion of most copywriters that inside them a 'real' writer is signalling wildly to be let out. (Understandable, since every advertisement aspires to be a best-seller.) Fortune tellers, who deal in illusion, have perhaps a true gift, the gift of insight, of instant psychology. Flattery follows easily. We left the restaurant, I somewhat elated, Reva subdued. The moment of make-believe was worth the money and it was some time before I returned to what that other soothsayer, Krishnamurti, calls the state of 'conditioning', the state of almost all of us, almost all our lives. Writing is concerned with the truth, and telling the truth requires courage and strength. If I have a weakness it is weakness.

Chapter 19

Meanwhile, back at the OBM Ranch, I wrote copy religiously for the Christian Brothers of California (the 'hero' this time was the Cellarmaster, the photogenic Brother Timothy) whose wines and brandies were distributed, in the finest ecumenical spirit, as it were, by a canny Jewish partnership. I learned what I could from Cliff Field and Reva Fine, the two undisputed stars, though both would have deferred unhesitatingly to the man often referred to around the shop as the Leader.

I saw him occasionally at meetings and at the bizarre, Byzantine lunches that took place monthly in the Conference Room. These, like the tea and biscuits served to him every afternoon by a uniformed Irish maid called Bridie, were part of the cultivated ambiance that Ogilvy, well, cultivated in the offices. It may have been culture at a *Reader's Digest* level, but it was culture of a kind, the *Digest* being for him 'a force for good in the world'.

Formal invitations to these *festschrifts* were sent to senior, or junior but deserving, members of the staff, predictably arousing jealousy, worse, anxiety, among non-recipients. On the fateful day of the fête, place-cards would be set on the sawn-off oval table: a newly-elected vice-president or some such hero-of-the-day would sit at Ogilvy's left hand, a guest of honour from the real world, perhaps, at his right.

What the genial Wodehouse has called the 'browsing and sluicing' at these functions was usually good, for the better restaurants of Manhattan were invited to prepare and serve their specialities, and to provide a description of the provenance of the dish. This would be read out before the feasting started by a nominated *invité* and Ogilvy, the once and future *chef*, would embroider on the theme. The chosen wines were subjected to like comment.

This monthly and universally detested rite stopped suddenly when some ill-advised (or possibly self-sacrificing) executive took it upon himself to invite a Chinese restaurateur to provide the fare. Ogilvy, never perhaps having had occasion to study the world's other great cuisine in a Peking hotel kitchen, was scandalised and sat grim-faced and silent through the meal. That black afternoon a memo shot out from Ogilvy's office to the members of the catering committee. It said, simply enough, MESSAGE FROM D.O. (he was sometimes referred to by the staff as D. O. Gratias): 'The meal served at luncheon today was revolting. Never again must Chinese food be served in these offices.'

He was in fact a master of the memo as a device to keep people on their toes, or to keep them guessing, or both. The astounded Cliff Field received one attached to an advertisement already in proof form, and therefore universally approved, which he had innocently prepared to encourage American industry to invest in Puerto Rico. 'If you run this advertisement,' it read, 'you will be doing the Puerto Rican people the greatest disservice in their long and difficult history.' It gave Cliff pause. Another, addressed to All Staff, said engagingly, 'The other day I went to the zoo and saw bear cubs. I have always adored teddy bears. They are warm and cuddly. Could we not introduce baby bears into our advertising?'

These apparently irrational *idées fixes* of Ogilvy were a source of worry to those requested to act on them, but one such hang-up was to lead me to a certain glory and perhaps – who knows – immortality. It was the conviction of Ogilvy, often expressed, that the phrase, 'Last night I had the most extraordinary experience ...', if used in a headline, would compel the reader to read on. He may well have been right. The problem for his minions was to sell that notion to a client. (He had had luck in disposing of another of his obsessions, the phrase 'something wonderful', which was at last unloaded on to a new cigarette with the unfortunate name of 'Spud'. Thanks to its miracle ingredient, menthol, it was claimed, Spud 'freshens your smoke something wonderful'. The American consumers, unfortunately, choked either on the smoke or on the unwonted anglicism and dropped Spud like a hot potato, thus proving that, when they put their minds to it, human beings can reverse the usual process and kill cigarettes.)

Playing their part in that unceasing search for ways to improve the quality of life which is the special contribution of big business to civilisation, Lever Brothers, already creators of the substitute butter, Good Luck Margarine, had recently invented the first anti-soap, or detergent bar. They called the thing 'Dove' and confided the launch of the new product to Ogilvy, Benson and Mather. In their brief to the agency the Brothers Lever had noted, among other 'consumer benefits', that their product contained one-quarter cleansing cream. This news was received by the researchers and copywriters about as phlegmatically as would a Wandering Jew who has been handed a sack of guaranteed 100 per cent proof manna. Since women traditionally were reluctant to use soap on their faces, and because a claim of cosmetic benefit could well counter any negative reaction to the discovery that the product was, in fact, detergent in soap form, Dove was launched, successfully, as a product for use on the face. The headline was: 'Suddenly Dove makes soap old-fashioned'; 'Dove creams your skin as you wash,' it continued, because it contained 'one-quarter cleansing cream'.

The cakes of this first-ever non-soap sold like – er – hot cakes, and hot cakes were selling well that year. The trouble was, they didn't go on selling: there were alarmingly few 'repeat orders'. What had happened, as surveys in 'the field' soon showed, was that women, only too willing to be persuaded by the Dove claim, had reserved the marvellous new product for washing their faces while continuing to lavish upon their other desirable surfaces the vilified, but much cheaper, old-fashioned soap.

The urgent problem now, therefore, was how to re-position Dove so as to get the stuff off the over-crowded supermarket shelves and into the bathroom where it belonged. That was the problem, and it was so put to the copywriter, who was Reva Fine. Reva's immediate response was to re-position the product by re-positioning its potential user. She placed her in a bath-tub, and not only in a bath-tub, but on the telephone. And this is where true copywriting talent showed through. For what this pretty, and of course naked, consumer was made to say was, 'Darling, I'm having the most extraordinary experience....' Turning, as Wordsworth neatly put it, her necessity to glorious gain, Reva had taken the club bore's opening sentence, so long plugged by Ogilvy, and converted it into an infinitely suggestive 'True Romance' headline. The only thing lacking in this otherwise compelling piece of prose was the name of the product, an Ogilvy imperative. The solution was to include the missing word in a subhead immediately following the thrilling exclamation.

This line of copy is described in Ogilvy's memoirs as one of the great ones of all time, and who am I to disagree, being merely its author? Taking my simple yellow 2B pencil with the, ah, eraser on the end, I wrote, '... I'm head-over-heels in Dove!' Game and set, I rather think.

It was my last contribution to advertising history during my first stint with Ogilvy, Benson and Mather and, after an exquisite lunch with the Master at Henri Soulé's Côte Basque, it was, therefore, to cite the old Lakeland sage again, trailing clouds of glory, and one or two streamers, that I sailed on the *Liberté* out of New York harbour on 4 July, the English Thanksgiving Day. Bill Binzen drove me to the pier. The ship had been well named, for free was what I felt, the best feeling there is. I quit the shores of America knowing that I was not the same person who had set foot on them, and knowing that this other person, sooner or later, would be back.

158

Amble III

Chapter 20

With that devil-may-care attitude to the merely practical which is the despair of my friends I had made absolutely no plans for my return. It is my wont in such circumstances to exploit one or other of the above-mentioned buddies. I therefore sent a dispatch which said 'ARRIVING LONDON STOP NO ROOF OVER MOUTH STOP CAN YOU HELP'. The recipient, or victim, of this message was good ole Robin Jacques, who has a heart as big as his sister, Hattie. He offered to share his house (a cleft palais?) with me while I looked around.

Robin lived, like everybody else in those days, in Ebury Street and this allowed me to return to the same world that I, the other I as it seemed to me, had left an age ago. Faithful to its public as a soap-opera, the Prince of Wales pub had not changed, its cast of characters reassuringly the same. Charlie, the landlord, told me of a flat available around the corner in Chester Square, stony heart of Belgravia, and I went, inevitably, to meet London's answer to Mrs Stuyvesant. This cool and beautiful lady quickly sized me up as one of them, a mistake they all make, and offered me the use of a two-room furnished flat on the top floor of her house. There was just one snag, she pointed out: I must be there clandestinely, for it was a condition of the Grosvenor Estate that leasors of houses in Chester Square should not divide them into flats.

No name at the entrance, no name on my door, must reveal my presence there. For one who has always seen himself as Musil's *Man Without Qualities* and whose personal dynamic was perfectly described by Keats in his phrase 'negative capability', the situation was most congenial, and I settled happily into my new non-existence.

At Robin Jacques', where pretty girls were packed wall to wall, thick as autumnal leaves that strow the brooks in Vallombrosa, I met one who, as they will do, changed my life, or more accurately, since my life is steered by some drunken automatic pilot from within, confirmed the direction in which I was already moving. This presager of Paris was what might be called, with some accuracy, a designing woman. She had won *Vogue's* Bianca Mosca prize, and as a successful *modeliste* now sold her *toiles* and drawings to dress manufacturers on both sides of the Channel. Her name was Marianne Spottiswoode and she was small, with Monroe-blond hair that could, you felt, given time, become brunette. She had large, alert eyes and a full Leslie Caron mouth that flashed one of those too vivid smiles that should not be taken, as it were, on face value, for the eyes may be saying something else. What attracted me most in this neat *garçon manqué* was her unmistakable chic, the chic of the *petite Parisienne*. It was not, I knew, couldn't be, the real thing, but it would do to start with.

John Mellors and I were now Joint Copy Chiefs at Bensons, each with his own secretary, groups of copywriters and powers of hiring and firing. We were dangerously near the top of the heap. I was threatened, not for the first time, with success. Time to cut and run again? But who would be running, them or me? Or to put it another way, which is what, as it happens, T. S. Eliot chose to do, wasn't it possible that 'in a world of fugitives, the person taking the opposite direction will appear to run away'?

As a kind of dress rehearsal for escape, I went with Gavin Ewart to Ischia and Capri. In the toilet of the international express a notice said 'To obtain water, turn the tap indifferently to the left or right': easy – I didn't care either way. At the *pensione* Gavin ordered, in slow, pedantic Italian, chicken, veal, pasta and salad (thus running the whole gamut of Italian cuisine) and ate it, as is his way, slowly and pedantically. Overambitiously, we tried to walk around the perimeter of Ischia, Gavin in the knee-length khaki shorts he had worn in the Italian campaign. They must have greatly distracted the enemy and probably did a great deal to hasten final victory. On the silver-grey sand of the, literally, for we circumambulated the island, endless beaches, silver-grey sanded children knelt at play. 'They look like shrimps,' said Gavin. Fast on the draw with a simile, these poets. Like me at Monte Carlo, Gavin was waiting for a message from an American girl. It never came. It was closing time in the gardens of the west.

My weekends now were often spent in Paris, where Marianne was based. One day, in a Viscount, I sat next to a Lord. Edward Montague had been at Eton with Digby Neave and Anthony Blond, in the Guards with Alan Cooke, at Oxford with all of us. He suggested we dine that night and as I embraced Marianne I said, like a fool, 'Would you like to have dinner with me, or with me and Lord Montague of Beaulieu?' 'With you and Lord Montague, darling,' she cooed with unengaging frankness. Everybody hates a lord.

Back in London, I drew up a list of the top French agencies and sent off a letter to all of them, together with what the Americans call a *résumé*, but the French, with typical perverseness, don't. Most of them agreed to see me. I stayed with Digby Neave, now an insurance broker, in the Ile St Louis for a week, while I was interviewed. Four of the leading agencies − Publicis, Synergie, Agence Française de Propagande and R. L. Dupuy − offered me retainers of 100,000 francs a month as a *concepteur*. I was, as they used to say on Madison Avenue, in like Flynn.

I resigned, for the second time, from Bensons. This time it took. Bobbie Bevan bought me a drink. I asked for ginger ale. 'Don't know what a chap's doing going to Paris who doesn't drink,' he muttered into his gin and tonic. 'Going to write a book, I suppose?' he ventured. He ruminated on this grave thought. 'Trouble with a book,' said the grizzled old copy man, 'you have to write the bloody thing yourself.'

I had a farewell lunch with the Tynans, at the Ritz, the Frenchest building in London, to get acclimatized. They thought I looked tired. I said I had been up late, saying goodbye to a chap I liked but whose wife never stopped talking. 'The trouble is,' I said, no doubt light-headed, 'he's suffering from an incurable *diseuse*.' 'Who said that?' asked Tynan, quick as a flash, for like most writers, he is a snapper-up of unconsidered trifles, as one of them put it. It was a reasonable question, for most of my best stuff is attributed to Dorothy Parker, Perelman or Benchley. This one, I told him, was freshly minted, hot from the press, stamped with guarantee of origin. He looked thoughtful. Years later, I bought an *Observer* at St Germain des Près and read, in the middle of a Tynan theatre review, 'But by this time the hero, to lift a phrase, is suffering from an incurable *diseuse*.' There is honour among thieves.

I wrote to Dr Partridge at St George's Psychiatric Unit to inform him of my imminent translation and asked him if he thought that I should consult a fellow practitioner, or shrink, in Paris. 'I doubt it,' he replied. 'In any case, there are no good psychiatrists in France.'

On my last day at work I left the office with Gavin and we strolled, as we had through many dusks, down to the Strand and the No. 11 bus stop. As we approached the stop a truck braked suddenly. The tailboard crashed open and the contents, which happened to be a load of table-lamps, fell out on to the asphalt. 'The shades of night are falling fast, Gavin,' I said. Ah, I had genius then.

Chapter 21

When you first live in Paris it is spring the whole year round. A twelve-month holiday. A sensuous sabbatical. A moveable feast (to put it the Hemingway). And if you are young and happen to live, chestnut-screened, river-wrapped, on a *quai* of the Ile St Louis – soft heart of this hard, bright city – you will know, at least for a moment, what it is to be in a state of grace.

Digby Neave lived in a ground-floor apartment on the southern, sunny side of the island. His neighbours to the left included Helena Rubinstein and an obscure schoolmaster-turned-banker called Georges Pompidou. To the right lived the novelist James Jones and a lady called Madame Milinaire who is now the Duchess of Bedford. On the prow of the island the Princess Bibesco, patron of Picasso and such, still carried some cultural clout. Around the bend, on the shady side where the great *hôtels* sat dankly, lived Marc Chagall and Michele Morgan. Directly across the river from the Quai de Béthune, a bow-shot from Neave's bower-eaves, so to speak, the Tour d'Argent looked snootily down as it served its umpteen thousandth numbered duck (*specialité*). You might say that Digby's apartment had, in spades, what my New York friends would call a nice location.

It was his *bonne à tout faire*, Marguerite, who let me in. Not everyone perhaps, on hearing the expression 'French maid', would find forming in his mind the image of a stooped, wizened, crotchety, faintly-moustached old woman with a wooden leg, but that was the vision that greeted me (the word is perhaps an exaggeration) at the Neave threshold. This Marguerite, however, for all her only too apparent inadequacies, possessed in the eyes of her fellow-citizens, I discovered, two indisputable merits: she was a cook of genius in a city where talent in that art may be found by walking a hundred yards in any direction and turning into the nearest doorway; and she spoke a French that ravished the ear with its purity. (The French believe in their hearts that there is, always attainable, a pure, accentless French, even if, at the moment, it is spoken only by Madeleine Renaud and three old ladies in a remote village of the Touraine.) So people came from all over Paris to the Neave apartment for the incomparable pleasure of eating Marguerite's food and the comparable pleasure of hearing her speak, which she would do only if provoked. There were rumours, never confirmed, for her life was a mystery, that Marguerite had once been a member of the Comédie Française. For those of you who have not had the experience I can report that it is an eerie feeling, as the soup is served, to hear behind you the step-thump-step of an ill-favoured crone softly complaining in the mellifluous tones of, say, an Edwige Feuillère.

The reason that I had been welcomed, if that is the word, by Marguerite, was that my host was not at home. There had been a vague plan – the only sort you tended to get with Digby Neave – that I should accompany him to his *moulin*, but he had left a note to say that perhaps another weekend would be better, and to make myself at home. *Cherchez la femme*, I murmured to myself, almost without an accent. Little did I guess, as they say in the sort of book where they say that sort of thing, how right I was, and how close to home.

Brooding on such deep stuff, I sat on the window-seat and looked out across the sun-warmed cobbles at the chestnut trees, their young-leaf green dappled with yellow blobs of light. As I was thus kibbitzing on Mother Nature's works, like a dark cloud coming between me and the golden apples of the sun, a head appeared at the open window. It was not just any old head. It was the head, large, sad and saturnine, of Sam White, Beaverbrook's man in Paris.

I had met Sam once before when, sent by Robin Jacques, I had called at his apartment late one Sunday morning during one of

165

my Paris recce trips. After a long pause, punctuated by sounds of the kind that might be made by a large body bumping into heavy furniture and cursing devoutly, the door opened suspiciously, like a door that fears the worse, having seen it all before. In the doorway appeared the face of a man who, dwelling on old, unhappy far-off things, had little hope left for the human species, and none at all for the example of it that he saw before him. It was the sad, wise, time-and-weather-ravaged face of Geronimo.

The Western image was confirmed, if confused, when this heavy set man led me, with courteously concealed reluctance, into his living-room. Now he was John Wayne, broodingly walking before me, toes turned slightly in, arms curved and akimbo as if to avoid the bulk of low slung six-guns, the gait slightly rolling from the hips. At high noon he was wearing, over striped pyjamas, a dressing gown to which was attached, by means of a safety pin, a large box of kitchen matches. This arrangement was, he thoughtfully explained, lighting an acrid Gauloise, a precautionary measure. It had been a roughish, if not stormy, night at the Elephant Blanc and he was in no shape for hunting around for things, entailing, as the search might, delicate manoeuvres like, for example, bending over.

This same Sam was saying now, in his slow, gravelly yet nasal Australian voice, a kind of strine whine (Sam White, incidentally, speaks French with more accent than anybody I know and his ability to communicate meaningfully in that language is a triumph of will over syntax), that the next day, Sunday morning, there was a party, along the *quai* in the Notre Dame direction, given by a lady called Virginia Vernon, Paris correspondent of the *Daily Mirror*. There would be other such members of the intelligentsia there. Why didn't I come along?

On Sunday morning, light with the euphoria of the traveller just arrived, I floated down-river, across the Rue des Deux Ponts and on down the Quai d'Orléans to the bend where the sharp black spire of Notre Dame moves, like the foresight of a rifle, to a point midway between its two blunt towers. On target now, I wheeled right into the narrow Rue le Regrattier (a street easier to find than to pronounce: the well-dined Anglo-Saxon is advised to direct the taxi-driver to the Quai d'Orléans). I turned into the *port-cochère* of No. 1 and climbed the shoe-smoothed stone steps of the curved front staircase to the *entre-sol*.

Somebody opened the door. The long, low-ceilinged room was full of people, noisy on the parquet floor, dark forms against the spring sunshine that filtered through the pointilliste trees outside and the daffodils inside on the Louis XVI escritoire. Light, reflected from the Seine below, shimmered on the gently sway-backed ceiling. As is my habit in such settings, I sidled in and tried to melt into the crowd: the effect I aim for is that of always having been there, like the Louis whatsit writing-desk. The dark, watchful eyes of Sam White, however, had spotted my arrival and he bear-walked over to me, took my arm and led me back to the doorway.

'You can't get away with that,' he ground out. 'You're in France now, *mon vieux*.' He towed me around the room for formal introductions and ritual handshakes. When we reached the small, blonde figure of Virginia Vernon, my hostess, I said, for something to say but also because it was true, 'What a beautiful apartment you have.'

'Oh – do you like it? Then why don't you have it? I'm going back to England.'*

What inspiration is to application, chance is to persistence. People tend to acclaim the result and not the effect, putting it down to 'genius' in the one case and 'luck' in the other. Living in this apartment would be, as I later confirmed, like being on vacation all the time, but it wouldn't be acquired without industry, cunning and a fair amount of the ready. My income from my various retainers would be 400,000 francs a month. The

---

* 'A year or two later Hennessy left the Agency and went to work in Paris. He acquired a magnificent flat on the *Ile St Louis*: it was like a good but much more spacious set of rooms in an Oxford college. It was furnished as elegantly as Hennessy himself was dressed. He had always liked the dandy's life. In London he had preferred champagne cocktails at the *Ritz* to beer or gin in pubs ...' (John Mellors, *Memoirs of an Advertising Man*, London Magazine Editions, 1976).

rent of the apartment, if the landlady didn't sneakily increase it, as they do at the drop of a latch-key, would be 90,000. It gave one pause. But not for long. On his return from the country that evening I asked Digby, an insurance man and hence a prudent fellow, what he would do if he were me. You could see from the expression on his face that he was throwing the whole power of his considerable intellect into the problem.

'Well,' he said, after a good bit of pacing about, 'if I were you, I wouldn't take it. But if I were you being me, I would. If you see what I mean.'

There were two obstacles to be overcome. It became clear, after her spontaneous and no doubt champagne-primed offer, that in fact Miss Vernon, ace reporter, was not in a position to pass the enviable apartment on to me. All she could do was recommend me to its owner. Then it would be for me to persuade my potential landlady, who lived in the flat above, that I was a suitable tenant. Sharing a trait with the rest of humanity, neither of them knew me except, in Miss Vernon's case, as a freeloader.

Digby assured me, however, that this same Miss Vernon had a soft spot for him, as I believe the expression goes. What he proposed was that we take her out to dinner and work her over a bit, with a special one-two to the above-mentioned spot. We chose Quasimodo ('I have a hunch she'll like that,' I said), a restaurant that looks askance at Notre Dame. Flanked by two eligible, if you didn't inquire too closely, and not unattractive bachelors – Digby tending towards the younger Gabin in looks, I to something between Tyrone Power and Cary Grant – and with a few glasses of a modest but well-rounded Morgon under the belt, Miss Vernon slowly came to the view that I would be the perfect tenant. Any friend of Digby's was a friend of hers. Would I like to borrow some sheets, perhaps? Would Miss Vernon like a little *digestif*? A calva? Poire Williams? Cheers Miss Vernon.

The next day I returned to the mysteriously named Rue le Regrattier and climbed the smooth-worn stairs, past the *entre-sol* entrance to the coveted flat and on up to the floor above. I rang and the door of the apartment – the kind of old-lady's door that has heavy, brown-turning-orange velvet curtains hanging from elephantine rings behind it – was opened by a middle-aged, rather masculine, chain-smoking, Women's Voluntary Service Englishwoman of the sort whose upper-class accent reaches you before the words, the way a Frenchwoman's perfume reaches you before her body. Madame Salle's paid companion showed me into one of those tapestry-hung, furniture-crammed French salons which somehow contrive to be dark and musty in spite of having an abundance of ceiling-to-floor – well, French windows.

Sitting in a tall-backed, unbending Louis Quinze chair, side-lit by one of the windows, between the bright yellow-green of the *quai* and the glum dun of the room, was a small, white-haired woman dressed in a black sweater and skirt, the ensemble simply *égayée* by a string of softly spoken pearls. She looked both eighteen and eighty, as if, in the same trim body, a spirited girl lived under the watchful gaze of a serene and indulgent matriarch. She was pretty, bright of eye, poised and flirtatious. If you took a large dollop of feminity and reduced it like a sauce, this is what you would be left with.

French women have fingers the way other women have hands. You can observe this innate distinction even in little girls: as they arrange a curl each finger plays a separate part, like instruments in a quintet. You can see it too in a *midinette* in an haute-couture *atelier* or in a shop-girl tying a parcel on the Faubourg St Honoré (like all confection and decoration an art that is specially French). Although I had come, as we admen say, to sell myself, I became instead, as we also say, a captive audience. She was witty, malicious, quick, and a past-mistress of nuance. ('The subtle-witted French', Shakespeare called them, getting it, as is Will's wont, just about right.) She had lived a great deal, this little lady and, at eighty, looked all set to live a great deal more.

She had been married, she told me with simple pride, seven times. Her first husband was the son of Gustave Eiffel and the first night of their marriage had been spent, just the two of them alone, in the gently swaying apartment that Eiffel had built for himself on the top platform of his tower ('An erector set that made it,' some wag has said). The husband was gone but she kept a free pass to the Tower for life and was always nipping up there. She looked out at the Tower now, across the Seine, and across sixty years.

Another husband had withdrawn, defeated and speechless, to a Trappist monastery from which, from time to time, he visited her, for the orgy of a chat.

Yet another fellow, a wealthy Argentinian sportsman, with a title, had gone down for the count, as it were, because of a little episode – *'C'était parfaitement ridicule!'* – in England while he was off playing polo in South America. Burdened at the time by a baby and eager not to miss the hunt, she had solved the problem with French practicality, not to say *verve* and *sangfroid*, by riding to hounds with the baby bouncing in front of her. When, on his return, the fiery hidalgo heard about this innovative contribution to the English hunting scene he was, greatly to her surprise, less than enchanted. She was quick to point out, she told me, that the English were not at all scandalised by the affair, but not at all. *La preuve*: they had printed a big picture of the horse with mother and child, both, as it were, in the pink, on the front page of a respected newspaper, the *Daily Mirror*, for which Mademoiselle Vernon, *voyons*, worked, *n'est-ce pas?* To prove her point, she showed him the newspaper. *'Il était furieux!'* she said, in the tone of one amazed, after all these years and husbands, at the stupidity of men.

Thus it was with the kind collusion of Virginia Vernon, of the *Daily Mirror*, and Madame Salle, of *Daily Mirror* fame, that I moved into my first Paris apartment.

With the move from London to Paris – less a leap in the dark than a hop in the sun – I found my life translated. From being a nine-to-five bus-queueing wage-slave with a numbered slot in the pecking-order of a large enterprise I had become (heady phrase!) a freelance, a kind of high-class layabout or bum. After the survival training of living in bed-sits, I was now the tenant of a seventeenth-century showplace. Once a member of the faceless gang on the No. 11 double-decker, I was now the owner of a spanking new sky-blue Renault Dauphine with authentic red plastic seats. From buying Normandy butter at nine shillings a pound at Cullens in Ebury Street to sex up my London cuisine, I now slowly realised, rather like that chap in Molière who discovered that all his life he had been talking prose, that everything I ate was genuine French food.

Each morning, happily unaware that even then some fellow was inventing the electric grinder, I ground my breakfast coffee by hand in the small kitchen looking down on the cobbled courtyard and its *porte-cochère*, using one of those wooden box affairs with a little drawer to catch the grounds. The rich, dark, sensuous coffee smell, the rich, deep morning burps of the barges easing past the *passerelle*, the domestic rite of the *'Bonjour madame'*, *'Bonjour monsieur'*, of *facteur* and *concierge*, the iceman coming with my sack-wrapped daily cube to cool the slam-door *glacière*, the archaic bathtub with its moulded splayed feet, the suggestive promise of the bidet, the wood-leather-velvet of the furniture with its patina, acquired through the years, of Gauloise and Caporal – all these conspired to make me feel quite other, like, perhaps, (for my fantasies tend towards the corny) some young, romantic bohemian painter or poet waiting to be tapped for a vital role in *An American in Paris*.

171

Chapter 22

When you are next lunching under the crimson-and-gold awnings and among the tailored green shrubs of Fouquet's (you will, of course, have directed the taxi-driver '*au* Fouquet's' and not '*chez* Fouquet's', pronouncing the 't' – these things separate the bounders from the rest of us), look up for a moment and glance across the Avenue George V. There begins a totally undistinguished street called the Rue Vernet. It runs, or rather sidles, parallel to the Champs-Elysées up towards the Etoile and peters out at Publicis, the only drug store in the world to have its own advertising agency. A convenient – for me – fifty yards down from the back door of Publicis a plaque announced the presence of D. S. Neave et Cie, Insurance Brokers. What it did not announce, but what anybody who was anybody knew, was that these were also the offices of the fledgling *Paris Review*, lately founded by Messrs George Plimpton, Peter Mathiesson and Bob Silvers. These premises, or more accurately the bar next door, became my launching pad for the night's activities.

The bar was that of the Stockholm, a hotel which runs through from the Rue Vernet to the Champs-Elysées, with a revolving door at one end and a Volvo in a showroom window at the other. In those days it was a neutral, dull and mostly deserted place, staffed by quiet, underworked and self-effacing waiters. It had the attraction of a club without a club's self-aggrandising, coterie exclusiveness. I generally managed so to arrange my round of agencies as to end at Publicis around 6 o'clock and from there, the conscience clear, or as clear as it ever gets, I sloped towards the Stockholm bar.

It being a Swedish bar in a French city, what one drank was Scotch. Whereas in England, in order to get a measure of the stuff discernible to the eye, you were obliged to order a double, in France, in order not to get squiffy too fast, you ordered a small whisky. You did this, hard though it may be to believe, by saying, *'Donnez-moi un baby, s'il vous plait.'* Not, *marquez-vous, 'un bébé'*, and not, *signallons, 'un baby whisky'*. Don't ask me why. But it separated the men from the boys.

In the Stockholm, then, and anywhere else, before dinner we drank babies, with Perrier, and with ice, of which, in France, there is never a shortage. (The two great social changes of my time have been the American discovery of oral sex and the English discovery of ice.) There was lots of time before dinner. For one thing it was considered chic to dine late in Paris – *'en ville'*, that is – the lateness being circumscribed only by the fact that in any serious restaurant the kitchens would close at 9.30. For another, anyone who has lived in France for a while learns to combine a clear idea of what restaurants are acceptable with a total distrust of anybody else's views on the subject. It will be seen that a consensus in these circumstances is not readily arrived at and during the lengthy process several babies find their life-expectancy shortened. (The reader should not deduce from this that your reporter is an alcoholic. More of a drunk really: an alcoholic being someone who needs a drink in order to get to the office, while a drunk is someone who needs a drink because he has been to the office.)

Now in this crucial matter of choosing a restaurant I have evolved two basic rules which I happily pass on to you. The first is that I refuse to eat in any restaurant I have not eaten in before. This is merely prudent and needs no further comment. The second is that any restaurant that is any good will be listed in the *Guide Michelin*. I tend to be so unhappy in any other establishment that it really isn't worth inviting me. The *Guide Michelin* is, in my opinion, the greatest work of collective authorship since the St James' version of the Bible, and you know how that caught on. If you were to ask me what was my greatest

173

pleasure in life, I would reply that it was driving, in a suitably elegant car, with the right companion by my side, in any direction (or in all directions, as the natives so kindly invite us to do) in France, heading towards a tranquil inn and a starred restaurant, both chosen, with the blind faith of which great religions are made, from my red-coated catechism, the *Michelin Guide*.

My first rule, on second thoughts, perhaps needs justifying. It is my conclusion, painfully arrived at, that great cooking (which I take to be, like great tailoring, an art) shares with poetry the distinction of being created by the very few for the appreciation of the very few. And while I place in my friends my total trust (a trust rarely, alas, reciprocated) in matters of money or of business, there is not one of them whose judgement on restaurants I will accept unreservedly. This is stern stuff, but there it is. I will trust my friends with my life, but not with my food.

The incomparable French cuisine being a daily and riveting subject of conversation in Paris, I experienced great difficulties in getting my companions of the Stockholm bar on the road for the practical, as opposed to the theoretical, part of the night's curriculum. This, however, was no great hardship for they were, though hardly a crew and far from motley, as varied a bunch as you are likely to meet in a long day's night.

George Plimpton was good looking, long legged and well heeled, a combination hard to beat, especially if you add talent, guts and a Harvard degree. I knew him only briefly in Paris but to give you the measure of the man, there was this girl that I was courting in New York, and that Digby was after too, and who got the girl? Ask Mrs Plimpton. (I was cooling anyway. This girl, a Miss Espy who had the rather worrying given name of Freddy, gave cause for concern in another way, perfection as she was in most of the important sectors. She never blinked. Never. Imagine a reclining girl, gazing ceilingwards with those great big orbs and never closing them. Off-putting. And in grimy New York you got to fearing that dust, which was reported to have done Helen in, would finally close Freddy's eyes. Hasn't though, I'm happy to say.)

174

Having got the *Paris Review* going, Plimpton returned to New York and simply invented a new literary form. All you have to do is to get in the ring with a world champion heavyweight like Archie Moore, box a few rounds, and then, if you live, write a book about it.

The man who followed Plimpton as editor of the *Paris Review*, and therefore took his place in the Stockholm bar, was cast from another mould, if I've got the right cliché. Nelson Aldrich was a slight, charming, some would say fey young man, fresh from Harvard. His eponymous uncle was called Rockefeller, which may have done no harm, for the *Paris Review*, like most little magazines, paid little if at all. Like many an East Coast, Ivy League, establishment toff, Nelson looked almost, but not quite, like an English undergraduate: button-down Oxford shirts were not worn at Oxford and there would have been reservations, so to speak, about Red Indian moccasins. He had long (for those days) lank blond hair that fell over one eye in the style perfected by Yehudi Menuhin and he would push it back from time to time, revealing a complete set of blue eyes, with a gesture that charmed, or anyway was meant to. When Nelson was not editing the magazine or sitting in the Stockholm bar – the two activities not being mutually exclusive – his chief function in society seemed to be to escort the stunningly pretty Jill (*née* Pretty) Goldsmith to those plays or parties that her husband Teddy, older brother of Jimmy, did not wish to attend, which was quite a lot of plays and parties.

When Nelson was not escorting Jill he was escorting Joan, a tall, dark beauty who rejoiced, as married or divorced American women do, in two surnames, which were, in this instance and in chronological order Dillon and, *plus loin*, Mosley. She was assistant editor of the *Paris Review* and, it was rumoured, though the one did not follow from the other, a good deal of the money behind it. If so there was more where that came from, for Joan's daddy, to whom her heart indubitably belonged, was a certain C. Douglas Dillon, founder of a prestigious Wall Street firm of brokers, ex-US Ambassador to Paris and, though naturally a

175

Republican (*richesse oblige*), Secretary of the Treasury to John Kennedy, whom Joan called Jack. Heavy stuff, but there was more. For the Dillons were, and are, proprietors of one of the three *grands crus* of Bordeaux: Château Haut Brion. The Dillons, apart from the desirable residence in the Gironde, and of course a town house in the Faubourg St Germain, possessed, as one must if one is ever going to get away from it all, crash pads in Far Hills, New Jersey, Palm Beach, the Riviera and so on; I do not include in this inventory the apartment next to Nelson Rockefeller's on Fifth Avenue, for I regard that as a purely functional necessity for a New York businessman and in any case, having seen a mere five rooms of it, I am hardly qualified to speak. But it was none of this evidence of ready bread, not even the promise of Haut Brion in abundance that drew me to Joan Dillon Mosley. While I go along with the practical French view that, on the whole, and all things considered, it is better to be rich and beautiful than to be poor and ugly, I have a respect for the deeper values and it was for this reason that I refused to allow Joan's enormous wealth to stand in the way of true friendship. Although the Hennessy family background runs rather less to the château and villa than to the terrace house with outdoor privy, I found myself drawn to this displaced heiress, an attraction explained in part by the fact that her hair was polished chestnut, her skin porcelain where it wasn't alabaster, her eyes summer's day blue and her smile, later used as a model by Geraldine Chaplin, a benediction.

Joan was tall, but taller than Joan, and indeed than almost anybody, was another American *habitué* of the Stockholm bar. Topping off a six-foot-something frame was a finely carved, early Gary Cooper head, bent permanently and courteously to lesser people like myself. And topping that was a thick thatch of straight, black-going-prematurely-grey hair through which, from time to time, the hand that was not holding a glass of beer would run worriedly, as might run the hand of Rodin's 'Thinker' were it not fully occupied in holding his head up. Eddie Morgan ran an organisation, within the Neave–*Paris Review* complex, that financed the purchase of cars for American soldiers in Europe.

176

Except on days of urgent business, when he leapt out of bed at noon, the languid Eddie was rarely seen until late in the day, for, unlike the French, who claim to be *matinales*, Eddie's energies grew to their peak as the day progressed.

At around 3 o'clock in the morning this steady development began to produce startling results, if you happened still to be around, for it was at this hour that Eddie revealed himself as the kind of candidate in a quiz show who could win any prize, as long as the subject was history. I never discovered whether his knowledge in this field was exhaustible, for I tend to be exhaustible myself in the smaller hours, and Sam White, one of the few in our crowd capable of staying the history course, was usually unable, next day at the bar of the Crillon, to give a satisfactory report of Eddie's thesis at the Village or the Nuage or the Calavados, in the last of which Sam's attention would gradually stray (*'Remarkably* pretty girl, *mon vieux'*) to the *vestiaire*, who had the amazing attribute of growing more desirable as the evening, or morning, progressed.

Peter Lyon, who worked with Digby, was married to a Belgian called Ninette, a writer of cookery books. Peter had the russet moon-face and crinkly black hair of Hore-Belisha in a cartoon by Low. Though a good-hearted fellow, he had nevertheless an unnerving way of confiding, with great authority, some calamitous event that had recently befallen his listener, this air of authority being quite unshaken by the said listener's refuting with hard fact his latest fiction. Thus life would be going swimmingly, at some jolly function, when you would spot Peter approaching, with little sideways movements, like a slick dance-instructor demonstrating the basic steps of the fox-trot; beaming benevolently always, he would remark agreeably, 'So your wife's run off with the chauffeur' or 'Been fired from J. Walter Thompson then?' Unnerving, particularly for one to whom catastrophe must always seem imminent, since the dread that precedes it is always present.

Then there were what you might call fringe or country members of the group. Thierry van Zuylen, known as Teddy,

177

was a Belgian count with Rothschild connections who owned racehorses and magazines, including *Femme d'Aujourdhui*, the offices of which were just around the corner. He was a swarthily handsome man, in the Omar Sharif mould, a trifle humourless and more than a trifle rich. One of the nicer things about seeing Teddy was that you might see his wife too, the stunning Spanish-looking American, Gaby. Paid-up members of the jetset, these two.

So was Saddrudin Khan, another Harvard man, and not yet roly-poly. He had the pleasant charm and a little of the look of Perry Como and was married to the mysterious Nina Dyer, an ex-model who later committed suicide. Saddry's big brother, the dashing Aly Khan, was the patron of the *Paris Review* and there was an annual bash at the *pavillon* near the Bois that he shared with another ex-model, Bettina, to announce the winner of the magazine's prize for humorous writing. *Le tout Paris* of 'Anglo-Saxon' literature would be there (and a few free-loaders like me): the ruddy-faced, warm and courteous Irwin Shaw, still plugging away, though the mere title of *The Girls In Their Summer Dresses* is enough to ensure him immortality; the fey black sprite James Baldwin, a frivolous and deeply serious man and a master of polemical prose, accompanied usually by his mentor, the Paris-based Chicago novelist Richard Wright; Tom Keogh, whose fluently angular drawings brought jazz and other subjects to the magazine's early issues; and the gang from the Stockholm bar.

In my first year there a young man called Philip Roth won the prize with an extract from *Goodbye Columbus*. Joan Dillon gave a lunch for him in the family *hôtel particulier* in the Rue Barbet de Jouy. I sat next to Roth, pleased, as I always am, and as any copywriter ought to be, to break bread with what was indisputably a Real Writer. Grateful for the opportunity, I sat quietly beside the author – a sensitive and reserved fellow, I thought – as intellectual banter and literary chit-chat flew around the table on wings of Haut Brion, the home brew, served in two attractive shades. But throughout the formal, butlered and waitered meal, the *victor ludorum* said not a word. Silent Roth.

178

Observing, I decided. Taking notes, to be the source of some future *oeuvre*. Then, towards the end of the meal, there were signs that the great man was about to speak. Ever the snapper up of unconsidered trifles, I leaned towards my right in order not to miss a word.

'Do you,' said Roth, 'know any place not far from here where I could just go and lie on the grass?'

As I was saying, the first problem, in those *folles nuits*, was to get the show on the road. The rest was easier then than now, for Paris was still a village and where you were going was where you parked your car. Some of the creative daring of the Parisian parker rubbed off on the newly arrived and places were usually found, with the *trottoir* replacing the road as the chosen field of battle between motorist and pedestrian. Honking, or hooting, had been developed into a fine melodic art, a concerto on the move, a full symphonic blast at traffic lights, those major irritants.

The feast, then, was a moveable one and if you happened to be on the Right Bank, where it moved to was the Left Bank. You headed first for the Village, scouting. The Village, carefully hidden from tourists and almost everybody else, lurks in the short and narrow Rue Gozelin, which runs from the Rue Bonaparte to a little *place*, where it is stopped dead, no doubt by the brooding aspect of Diderot's statue. The decor of the Village may best be described as indescribable. On the left, in a sort of defeated fresco above the dun-coloured walls, are drawings that resemble visual ravings, the work of a regular who, though clearly having had enough to drink, wished in this way to pay for more. Across the room, over the bar, hangs an elongated, blue-tinted double nude, like an erotic pre-Raphaelite night scene laid flat and viewed at eye-level. After a couple of drinks at the bar an almost irresistible impulse comes over one to stand it up and see the distorted forms flesh out.

What got the Village off the ground, so to speak, was the buzz that Francoise Sagan drank her baby whiskeys there. Sartre and Beauvoir had cornered the Deux Magots across the *place*

179

('*Rendezvous des intellectuels*', assert their table cards), but the Deux Magots had been *dans le vent* ever since the heavy thinking crowd, squeezed out of Montparnasse by the bourgeois who had come to see them, moved down Raspail and the Rue de Rennes to the fresh woods and pastors new of the church of St Germain. But what the mob found when they came, bashing open the saloon-type swing doors of the Village, was not Sagan, who was over the road at Lipp, but Sam White, Eddie Morgan, Teddy Goldsmith, Peter Lyon and me. Not, perhaps, the absolute top team in the celebrity league. Hardly *le tout Paris*. But not without a certain interest, one might claim, for the sociologist, the psychologist (and even the future memoirist). For if you set aside the obvious motivations (as such thinkers say) for the presence in this city of this group, like the twice-a-day arrival of the best bread in the world, baked just around the corner, warm as the arms of the girl who carries it, in swollen sheaves, to the restaurant counters, or the wine-as-a-matter-of-course, or the food-that-can-be-discussed, or the sitting-outside climate, or the beauty of a city that cherishes the green and blue of tree and sky, or the femininity-in-essence that pervades all like perfume, or the this-is-it sureness of fashion and of taste – if you set aside such diurnal treats, you might still ask yourself what forces combined to persuade such a disparate group to leave their own countries and to live in Paris.

What deep unease at home – whatever that may be – has driven or drawn them here? And what succour do they find in this city? The anonymity of the stranger, left to be himself? The absence of class, for the outsider has none? Sensual relief from puritanical restraints, the repressed transplanted and born again? And if, or rather when, they find that their salvation is not to be found here, or anywhere outside themselves, where do they go then?

For those who lived there know that Paris spoils you for living anywhere else. The senses are better served here. If New York is designed as a machine for producing money, Paris is designed as a machine for producing pleasure. And while it may be true, as Colette wrote somewhere, that 'devoting oneself to sensual

180

pleasure is not a career for a respectable man', I have never claimed respectability (though I do a nice line in faking it, for peace and quiet's sake). But what is certain is that the word 'career' might be applied with much more credibility to my pursuit of pleasure, or of pleasurable inactivity, than to my life in advertising, which has served me as an aid, though sometimes an obstacle, to that pursuit. I may also, half-known to myself, have been pursuing other things.

In the poet David Gascoyne's *Journal 1937–1939*, he writes about what he sought during those years in Paris:

> Coherence: a gathering-together of the dispersed powers of one's personality. Such a state could not be lasting, but might, nevertheless, permanently alter the *level* of one's life. Attainment to a lasting deliverance from the trivial and the unmeaning: from the quicksands.

Well, while not, to my grief, a poet, I know what he's talking about. And when Philip Toynbee, reviewing the book, describes the outer trappings of that life, bells ring in the memory:

> But what was he *doing* during those 27 months? He was doing the sort of thing which that archetypal poet is always doing ... drifting about Paris in a state of penury and isolation; ricocheting off minor literary acquaintances, both French and English; sometimes meeting, or at least seeing, such major figures as Auden and Stravinsky; going to concerts when he can raise the money or sponge a ticket ... and to picture exhibitions if they are free; falling in and out of love, and bed; communicating with editors, kind and cruel; thinking of suicide and madness; then suddenly describing some scene or person with a brilliant and percipient clarity which reminds us, if we happen to need the reminder, that this is a writer of outstanding talent....

Well, that gave me the old Wilsonian shock of recognition, except of course, for that last bit, for in the literary game you could put me down as the non-writer's non-writer, although I sometimes suspect that I may have *seen* persons and places with more clarity than some, and not only through being soberer at the time. For I have had reason to think that I observe people and events with a heavier emotional baggage than some, seeing them as others remember them, with a kind of instant nostalgia and also with a sort of hopeless hope. And this has made my life, in a way, a series of possibilities unfulfilled.

Chapter 23

Weekends in town – in a town that, after all, people from all over the place came to for weekends – were loafed through (and a French loaf, as we have noted, is the world's best) between the Ile St Louis and St Germain des Près: an agreeable stroll, with a stop at the eccentric American bookshop on the *quai*, or an easy, traffic-free drive. Outside the Deux Magots a makeshift kiosk proposed the English Sunday papers and the lone French Sunday, the *Journal du Dimanche* (typographically an improvement, though slight, on the French dailies, which are a visual blight).

In a city where nothing much is delivered, including the papers, the purchase of the Sundays was a pretext, if one were needed, for what the French persist in calling the Anglo-Saxons to gather at the mottled-marble, metal-edged round tables of the café, blond-woven chairs facing the street where the action was. As a youth, a grief or two ago, I had admired the work of Man Ray in that extraordinary magazine, too good for the English, too good to last, Stefan Lorant's *Lilliput*. I had seen his unforgettable blue *baguette* and the iron with the nails in its base, like an inverted fakir's bed (and those are the worst kind of fakir) at the Museum of Modern Art in New York. Now, on those weekends, I rubbed elbows with the old Surrealist, a small, white-haired (with a neo-Fouija fringe), black-bereted man with surprised round eyes and the mild-and-bitter look of one who would nurse a grudge with gentle devotion. I last saw him, a couple of years before his death, leaving the painters' restaurant, *chez* Alexandre or Les Trois Canettes, walking with terrible slowness on the arm of his gentle and devoted wife. He was curved by age and illness

183

into a kind of self-consuming *cedilla*, face strained forward almost at waist-height, like a man eaten up by bitterness.

Not all my weekends were spent in the graceful city. There was also the country, and the country meant the Neave *moulin*. *Moulins* were coming in just then, in France (where they were just discovering the pleasures of *'le* weekend' and of the *résidence secondaire*) as in England. Digby's, however, was no run-of-the-mill mill. It was a *moulin's moulin*, a mill to make lesser mills grind their wheels in frustration.

This first among *moulins* stood, or rather crouched, on the wooded fringe of the vast park of the Château de Maillebois, a village itself on the fringe of Normandy, about half-way between Dreux and Chartres. The red-brick, slate-turreted château was the property of a family called Armand de Lille. The Armand de Lilles are Protestants of Hugenot origin who speak impeccable French and English with, for some reason, a guttural German accent which the family's traditional Harvard education has failed to eradicate. Dr Armand de Lille, the late chatelain, was a man revered in the village and loathed throughout the rest of France: revered because he had the habit of treating the impecunious without fee, and loathed because it had been his inexplicable folly to import, in the name of science, the malady of myxomatosis into France, thus depriving the nation of two of its favourite sports – shooting rabbits, and eating them.

In was *moulin* country all around and the same stream, the prettily-named Blaise, which turned the mill-wheel of Digby's house turned the more functional wheel of another in the nearby village of Blevy. This converted eighteenth-century tannery was inhabited by an American who had married Ariane, gracious, kind and cultivated daughter of the château.

Bill Murray was a ruggedly-built, Calder kind of man whose white hair was turning into a tonsure as his weather-burned, freckled skin inexorably expanded its territorial possession. He had, quite naturally, that persona of the sensitive outdoorsman that Robert Frost cultivated, with more or less success. Before he began building walls, or raising turkeys for Christmas or

Thanksgiving, or tethering sheep to mow the lawn by natural means while waiting to be converted into *gigôts* to turn on the outdoor spit, Bill had spent his life as a cameraman for Gaumont News, starting in the days when you turned the camera by hand. A drop-out from Princeton (when he gets around to writing his memoirs, he assures me, the title will be, 'Don't bother me with a college education'), he had found with unerring aim a métier that neatly combined a need for the keen, observant eye and the hardiness of an infantryman.

He was an inspired *bricoleur* to whom his friends and tenants (who were usually the same people) turned whenever mechanical disaster struck. His credo was a simple one: 'If something doesn't work, fix it; if you can't fix it, throw it out.' He was also a registered silversmith, with a nice line in cream-jugs, bowls, ash-trays and, for specially adored girls, rough-beaten rings that glowed with the bright rugged honesty of the man. His finest achievement, it was generally felt, was the harnessing of the gentle Blaise to provide, through the mill-wheel and a turbine, electricity not only to warm and illumine his house but to floodlight the screen of trees at the end of the lawn: a Blaise of light, so to speak. A fan placed in a side wall of his walk-in fireplace drove warm air through a cluster of pipes into the living-room – an impressive artifact that might have been the world's first jet fireplace, had not the Romans thought of it first.

During the frequent *pannes d'électricité* that occured in winter, when the entire village was blacked out and frozen in, Bill's *moulin* shone like a good deed in a naughty world, this latter being represented by the officials of the EDF, or Electricité De France, whose contention, fiercely opposed by the libertarian Bill, innocently seeking opportunities to apply the good ol' Yankee know-how, was that citizens or residents who felt a need for electricity ought to pay for it. These faceless fellows have retired hurt from countless skirmishes over the years and, though the battle continues, those who are, as it were, *au courant* say that of recent years they seem to have lost heart and that their ritual raids now are desultory and lack conviction.

It was, naturally, Bill Murray who helped Digby Neave to get his *moulin* going. There are certain places that, visited for the first time, seem somehow to have been known before, in some other but parallel existence. This one would have been known to anyone who has ever been a child: it was a house that sprang into view as magically as those forest-buried cottages lifted to delight the innocent eye in pop-up editions of the works of the Brothers Grimm.

You approached the house from a country road that turned into a steeply descending and winding dirt track. Below you the tops of the trees in the Parc de Maillebois stretched out like a carpet. Easing slowly down, braking all the way, you felt like a jet pilot circling and descending from the untouched blue through the cloud-layer to the unseen airport. Suddenly a slim wind-sock of smoke, the colour of blue-rinsed silver hair, stretched above the tree line, announcing life, though its source remained invisible almost until the car nosed an aged gate. As the land fell back like the pages of a book in this Hansel and Gretel glade, the house rose slowly up.

It was a faded dusty-pink L against the deep green bower of lawns and gardens lightened by the willows that swooned over the maundering stream. Against the right wall of the house – the top of the L – a mill-wheel of warped and blackening wood gave that sinister touch that pins fairy tales to reality. There had been strange and sudden deaths associated with this place. There would be two more in my time.

Lawns, fresh back from the cleaners, stretched on either side of the Blaise to dry. Beyond the house a herb and vegetable garden thrived and scented the air with promise, and along the mill-race flowers gently bloomed. The small and rock-strewn pool below the seeping *vannes* had been known, even in mid-August, to turn strong men to stone. Uninhabited hammocks were slung, convenient lifeboats, between trees. They would be needed, for below them a disused mill-stone, reluctantly supported by groaning wood piles and threatening to knee-cap anyone foolish enough to sit at it, was beginning to bear the additional weight of food and drink. Through the open window of the kitchen the clatter of pots announced that Digby Neave, a graduate of the Cordon Bleu, was *dans ses oeuvres*. And outside, in the warm and rosemary-scented summer air, I cooled the Ricard and the gin with chips off the old block of ice I had brought, Figaro-wrapped, from the *glacière* of the Ile St Louis.

It was this bow'r that I had failed to check in at on my first weekend in the city of light, a note from Digby having *décommandé* our rendezvous. On that same occasion I had, with that nose for these things that has made the clan brandy what it is today, smelled, if not a rat, then what the French would call a *souris*, the English a bird and the Americans a chick. Well, I was right. For now, while making use of the bathroom, my eyes wandered to the back of the door. Pinned thereon was a sketch of the handsome Digby, left profile, I rather think. It was dated as of the previous weekend. And it was signed Marianne Spottiswoode.

Now I suppose that a girl selecting a suitable companion in London and a ditto in Paris, the two to run in tandem, and having no reason, *a priori* and *ab initio* and so on, to believe that the two chaps in question might be buddies from way back, could hardly be expected to envisage a situation, as the happy arrangement continued through the months, where the party of the second part would chuck job, country and everything else and move in with the party of the first part. That however, if my reading of the art-work was correct, was how the cookie, or in this case perhaps, the sandwich, crumbled.

Unable, after prolonged discussion, to decide who had priority in the affair or, as it would seem, affairs, Digby and I, while congratulating each other on our admirable taste in girls, decided mutually, reluctantly but nobly, to renounce our common soul-mate. Stern decision, but we saw no other way.

(It was this same Marianne, always heavily into seers and such, who had dragged me to consult a peer among his seer peers called Maurice Woodruffe, star-gazer to the stars. This chap had taken one look into his crystal ball, which seemed to be moving pretty fast that day, and said, in a rather lilting voice, 'My goodness, why aren't you writing?' I would have stayed for more of this interesting stuff but he wanted to move on to another theme, which was concerned with the vulnerable parts of the body, and as he stood and advanced towards me, healing hands outstretched, I made, as they say, my excuses and fled into the street and the arms of Marianne, who was rather more in my line.)

Well, nature, as is well known, abhorring a vacuum, it was not long before two other girls, one a Dane (by way of Rio de Janeiro), the other an American (but also, curiously, by way of Rio) moved into our lives with gifts of tenderness, and beauty, and gaiety and fun – at least, that is, for a while. But then, as Mr Ayckbourn has somewhere said, and he should know, what is comedy but tragedy interrupted?

Chapter 24

My advertising life, if that is not a contradiction in terms, had become as near as you can get to not working without actually staying in bed. Like all good things, it couldn't last. My contracts had been for three months, and not all of them, my instinct (infallible as an early warning system when the old heave-ho threatened) told me, would be renewed. The French agencies were, well, very French: Chauvin was, after all, a Frenchman. All very well for me to arrive among them like Shane riding into the plain out of the foothills. I wouldn't be there to stay, and I wasn't necessarily a force for good either.

This raised a vital question. The younger reader may not believe this, but in those days, before the liberation of women, such was the appalling socio-economic inequality between the sexes that it was almost impossible to meet a girl without having a bit of the ready to hand. And, as one who was soon up to his neck in millionairesses, my need for a steady source of moolah was greater than that of your ordinary breadwinner in the A–B socio-economic group.

Another reason I needed a job was so that I could have a vacation. Not that I needed a holiday: my whole life was a holiday. But my observation had established that in France, unlike other countries, there are only two seasons: *avant les vacances*, and *après les vacances*, sometimes referred to as *avant les départs* and *à la rentrée*. Whereas, for example, in your average London or New York office the arrival of the vacation period, calculated at two weeks out of the year, was signalled only by the occasional postcards of palm-fringed places pinned up on departmental wall-boards, your average Paris office, I discovered, was either dead, and for a whole month, or so near to being dead you'd want a second opinion to be sure.

And not only were the offices closed. So were the restaurants and the laundries and the bakeries. So were vast tracts of Renault and Citroen and Schlumberger and Rhône-Poulenc. The whole country was closed. Everybody was altogether elsewhere. In my own case, I had been invited by the hospitable Joan Dillon to the villa she had rented for the summer at Villefranche-sur-Mer. In order to take a vacation I needed a job. Confident that they would understand my need, I wrote to the Paris office of the world's largest advertising agency, J. Walter Thompson. A man by the name of Kevin Farrell kindly invited me to go and see him.

On the same side of the Rue de la Paix as Roberts and Cartier, but a little closer to the Opéra (which resembles nothing so much as an opera house), an obscure passage ran between two store-fronts, like a tradesman's entrance. On the right hand wall, among a plethora of plaques, one, more sober than the rest, announced in institutional gold on black that J. WALTER THOMPSON (FRANCE) SA found itself on the *6-ième étage*. It was the right location for a *Société Anonyme*. On the left, a little farther down the passage, stood the familiar wooden door with a window in it that revealed the diamond shapes of another, concertina door, reluctant entry to one of those contrary Paris elevators that, complaining all the way, contrive to stop slightly above, or slightly below, the floor of your choice, but never quite at it. (Relieved to be anywhere in the proximity of your destination, you accept the compromise and stumble out, swearing softly; and you remember that to return a favour, in demotic French, is *'renvoyer l'ascenseur'* − further support for those who hold that the French don't like each other very much.)

I rode the elevator to the sixth floor, give or take an inch or two, and fell out into an area that had a desk but no receptionist in it, giving a new meaning to the phrase 'mixed reception'. A corridor led off the lobby and the offices on either side of it were glass-walled down to waist level. In the last one on the right (the

190

corner one: this was an American agency, and knew the form) a face behind a desk smiled a greeting. I knocked and entered.

The tall spare man hitching his belt over no belly at all was one of those quiet Americans. His face was the face of a man who had done some boxing but stayed pretty, like Mohammed Ali: gentlemanly, amateur boxing it would have been, at a good prep school. His eyes which were blue-grey and gave nothing away except their anxiety to give nothing away, were slightly hooded, the nose faintly, elegantly broken, the smile toothily-sweet (the eyes twinkled 'charm' in practised unison). There wasn't much not nice about him. When he talked about advertising Kevin Farrell had that barely concealed missionary zeal that Americans have about their jobs. He was here to spread the good word and convert the natives. (He did a good job: the French trained here could be found, ten years later, in top posts in the best French agencies.)

He liked my stuff. He could use me. When I proposed, with desperate courage, that I start work with a month's paid vacation he laughed out loud, but the laugh was one of those throw-the-head-back-and-study-the-ceiling laughs that people use to cover shock and gain time for thought. He knew I was a rare bird in Paris. Top creative people with any sense would be in New York. The laugh died to a sincere frown. There was a pause as long as a minute's silence in church. (This was a man, I was to discover, who was the longest pauser in the pausing business.) Then he stood and buttoned the jacket over the no-belly and the deep voice said, 'OK,' and the quick charmer's smile broke out like sun from behind a cloud and we shook hands.

I had a job again. Boo. But I was salaried again. Hooray. 400,000 francs then would be worth 10,000 francs now, and with free board and lodging you could have a nice vacation with that and still be able to tip the servants. So I said goodbye until *la rentrée* and like 40,000,000 Frenchmen took my car for a last check-up before the garages closed for ever and before it faced the mortal dangers of the long black poisonous snake they called the Nationale Sept.

191

You can hit the Autoroute du Sud in Paris today at 8 a.m. and be sipping your first Ricard on the terrace of the Carlton in Cannes, all fresh and agreeably *dépaysé*, by 6 o'clock in the evening. Not then, though. Not, anyway, in the first days of August, when the July vacationers, basted for weeks with Ambre Solaire and now done to a turn, were crawling like *escargot* unwillingly to Paris, and when the blithe *aoûtiens*, in furious counter-march, were snarling down to their marine *marinade*.

It was close combat all the way, with fear, my old travelling companion, in the passenger seat. They hadn't rolled up the landscape and taken it away yet, but you hardly noticed as the white Charolais turned to ginger Limousin, the dusty-mauve grapes of Macon gave way to the chewy nougat from the stalls that lined the road at Montélimar, the stench of the oil refineries of Lyon changed to the musk-heavy, sickly-sweet smell of those fragrant green cannonballs, the melons of Cavaillon. You hardly noticed these things because your eyes were set on a non-collision course and the odds were stacked against you.

They came in wave after kamikaze wave and the élite troops were the Belgians. For the Belgians then were not required to pass a driving test and to celebrate this unique liberty they chose the narrow roads of France and the fat cars of America. Next came the French, on their own ground, more skilled, knowing what they were doing, taking a Cartesian positon in the centre, suicide, lane and choosing as their weapon the deadly black Citroen *traction avant*. Perfidious, the English forayed in pairs, GB, GB, with not a car's length between them, so that to overtake these self-righteous slow-coaches was to dice with death, for a Frenchman would be there, lying in wait, out of sight over the crest of the hill, face contorted in rage and hate behind the low-browed windscreen and the silver inverted chevrons of the Citroen.

The back of your shirt and the backs of your legs were soaked with sweat long before you glimpsed the first haze-blurred orange roofs and serene cypresses of Provence. You were used now to feeling frightened all the time but when you got to Aix-en-

Provence, if you got to Aix-en-Provence, common sense or panic told you to pull into the haven that was the front court of the Roy René and take a cool room in which to lie until the shaking stopped. Then you gathered your strength and your courage for the morning's start (rather later than you had planned, for a French breakfast in bed, warm sun on the shutters, is something to be savoured and, if you are two, celebrated), out of Aix on to the now two-laned road, past the hot shrub plains below the Mistral foothills down to the matey Englishness of Nice or the white-flannelled snobbishness of Cannes or, by vertiginous winding mountain road, up, up, up to La Croix Valmer and down, down, down to the chic bohemia of St Tropez, where you would meet all the people you would meet any other month at the Deux Magots, the Village or *chez* Lipp – that is, if you didn't mind all the other people who had come to see them.

The villa lay, flat-roofed and functional, silvered by moonlight, on the right side of the tracks, looking down on its own private patch of lawn and rocks and coast and feeling good about it. The gravel in the drive scrunched obsequiously, fooled by the tyres of the plebeian Renault. I drove between silhouetted laurel and muted bougainvillea, the way they do in novels, and parked near four or five better-bred cars whose '75' plates sneered 'Paris' at the passing peasant.

Lights were on in the house but nobody was in it. I took my case from the car and walked in through the fraught-iron-and-glass door. The living-room had that unfurnished look you get in furnished houses and that sits well on summer places where cosiness is not what you're there for. There was still nobody home but from the direction of the soft and silent sea came the knock and pluck of a guitar. Accompanying it, in that devout tone that nicely brought-up American girls employ when singing folk-songs, but folk don't, were the voices of several nicely brought-up American girls. This would be the place. That was the year that folk-songs and the guitar were invented.

I saw them, in silhouette against the sea and sky, as I came out

193

on to the back terrace and stumbled against cane furniture. They were gently patronising 'Down by the River-Side' down by the low wall at the foot of the lawn, overlooking rocks and a small wooden jetty to the south and overlooking me to the north. The moon, such is the power of money, had made a white highway on the black sea, direct to where they sat singing. And beyond their bare shoulders and groomed hair the lights of cars on the Basse Corniche swung up and around the Cap to swoop on an invisible and unsuspecting Nice. There are a hundred places called Villefranche in France. This one would do for me.

I had been here before, in what seemed like another life because it was another life. We were three boys and a mother, in steerage on a troopship heading for Egypt and the Bay of Aboukir, where Napoleon lost a fleet and my father, a lesser military figure, wasn't doing too well either. The ship, in its uniform of white, blue band, yellow funnel, had anchored, as the troopships of Empire did in peacetime, in this bay of Villefranche, to recover from the bruises of Biscay and prepare for the doldrums of the Indian Ocean. I had looked from the deck past the serene yachts and the grim bad taste of the Royal Navy to the white, ochre and rose villas that clung like wallflowers to the slope of the hill, punctuated here and there by the exclamation marks of cypresses, and to me it seemed a homeland. On the day excursion ashore, up and over the brow to Nice, I saw French bread for the first time, and aubergines, and olives, and I smelt oil cooking and the tang of garlic and I felt *chez moi*. I wouldn't have to change to fit in here. All that would be needed would be a certain narrowing of the socio-economic gap between me, mere mortal, and the gods who surely inhabited this place. It might mean a life's work. There were worse goals.

You could say that I had made it, and you would be right, and wrong. Here I was, legitimately there, part of the lush landscape seen from that bleak ship, part of the life, sharer in the wealth that had brought the two together. Well, yes. But these people crooning now in graceful silhouette had made me part of them because they took me already as being part of them. But what they were doing here for pleasure, they had been doing all their lives. After dinner, which was the name we gave to lunch on the troopship, one played cards, or games, or, this year, the guitar. One always had. One's parents had. I hadn't. My parents hadn't. Yet what I was doing I had been doing all my life too. I was watching them, and maybe that was my pleasure: the melancholy exultation of the outsider inside, properly in, because invited, inalterably out, because born that way.

There was lunch at one, dinner at eight, but mostly, we bombed along the coast: 'bombed' was the buzz word that year and the song they were playing in the places we bombed to was 'Volare'. We bombed to the Hôtel de Paris at Monte Carlo, and drank among the *grandes dames* of this place and another time while the gorgeous gigolos of indeterminate sex and nationality danced in attendance round the old host bodies. We bombed up the mountain road in hectic convoy to Le Pirate where the rich went to rough it under the neutral stars and eat barbecued lobster served by saucy waiters stripped to the waist and wearing gold medallions and head scarves. We bombed to Cap Ferrat and the votive shrine of Eden Roc where the richest flesh on the Côte offered itself to the expensive sun, on the rocks or around the Roc pool. And, slumming a little, we bombed to St Tropez. You didn't stay in St Tropez, you visited it, especially if you owned a boat, or knew someone who owned a boat.

For there were the Boat People, the Villa People and the Hotel People (any of them could be *all right*). The three groups intermingled, swirled throughout the season, in a kind of permanent floating bombing. The Hotel People lured guests back to the hotel or out to restaurants. The Boat People, more desperate for guests, for the ownership or rental of a boat had to be socially, as it were, amortized in a short season, made raids to shanghai guests from hotels and villas, often without success, for these people had learned that there is no escape from a boat at sea, and who knows what one might be missing ashore? The Villa People solved their social problem and fulfilled their obligations by

195

giving a party. They gave the same party, catered by the same firm, musicked by the same band, for the same guests. And the swankier ones gave it twice: early in July, and late in August. That way you had everybody covered.

When the late-August party reached our place it brought a girl who, being Villa People, immediately asked me to her house. The invitation was flattering and tempting. She was slim, dark, very pretty, bright, American and cosmopolitan, with twang-free French. She looked both tremulous and determined, like the young Judy Garland, with the same fear-flecked eyes, the same vulnerable mouth and that capacity for disturbing that the disturbed have. She had the same name too. Judy Douglas was the adopted daughter of James Douglas, millionaire brother of that Lewis Douglas, Ambassador to the Court of St James, whose adoption of an eye-patch had given David Ogilvy the idea that made him famous.

I told her that though I would love to bomb over to her villa I was driving back to Paris, and to work, the next morning (I felt it better not to add injury to insult by reporting late to the company that was financing my hols). Come to breakfast then, she said gamely. It's on your way. But, bombed out now, I said I'd call her in Paris, *à la rentrée*. And I did, but that was in another country, and besides, the wench is dead.

196

Chapter 25

If you have to come back to a city after time-out from reality, Paris is the city to come back to. September comes with a gentle tread, autumn with, well, a dying fall. And soon there would be Judy. It was therefore a tanned, reposed and chirpy *concepteur-redacteur* who wheeled in from the Rue de la Paix to report for work. Everyone else in the offices of J. Walter Thompson was sun-tanned too.

The No. 2 man, Pierre Bourdin, was one of those people whose tan seems to be there for life, strange considering that much of his life had been spent in a BBC studio, broadcasting for the Free French. He had the flat dark hair of the heroes of pre-war French films and the half-closed smoky eyes of Boyer, which he got by never removing his Gauloise from his lower lip. No. 3, the money man, who was probably still figuring out how he had paid an employee a month's salary before he'd joined the company, was called Anstedt, and the reason for that is that he came from Alsace. His hair was short and blond and so was he. He managed to be just not so Germanic as not to be French.

Huguette Leforestier, quick, bright, dark, had ambitions, one felt, that would not be contained by this small stage. Indeed, this lady, a kind of gallic Margaret Thatcher with none of the 'feminine' weaknesses and many of the 'masculine' strengths (myself I'm a heady blend of both), was last seen running for the Senate. I do hope she made it.

Dick Morgan, another account executive (and now highly effective International Advertising Manager of that admirable newspaper, the *Herald Tribune*), was a big, wise-owlish, kindly old-Etonian (contemporary of Digby Neave), son of an American father who had served in the Canadian Flying Corps and of an American francophile mother. Thanks to his variegated background and education, the amiable Dick spoke three languages impeccably: American English, English English and French French, depending on the company. Maybe by now he knows who he is.

Jacques Sorbac was another of the perfectly bi-lingual account executives, a tall, handsome man with a nose broken in the paratroopers. (Any Frenchman who had not been a *résistant* during the war had been a paratrooper.) He was a man whose suavity and *savoir faire* seemed to mask some inner unease, like that of a man who knows something about himself, not necessarily to his discredit, that nobody else knows or will ever know.

There was an English art director, called Rigby. There is an English art director today. Rigby. Same chap. Unhappily married to a Frenchwoman, he divorced her and married an Indian, with whom he lived happily ever after. Better safe than sari.

Next to this reticent Englishman in the studio on the top floor worked a volatile Frenchman, Bob Lescaut, short, bearded, vital, twinkling. He was both maniacal caricaturist and serious painter (today he exhibits frequently). He was given to quick, euphoric enthusiasms followed by sudden and bottomless black depressions. There was no mood in between, no autumn and no spring. During my time there it pleased him to draw hundreds of cartoons of me (these may be seen, by appointment), whom he saw, for some impenetrably gallic reason, as essentially a comic figure, whereas I, taking a calmer, more Anglo-Saxon view, saw myself as more of a tragic figure. (Well, just read on, then see.)

Nicely rounding out the cosmopolitan studio was an American of great charm. Lee Barton was a slim, rangy, dark and handsome man, with an almost winsome, sudden-life smile. He and his wife Pat, a pretty, marmalade-haired model who became a successful naïf painter – a sort of *Grandmère* Moses – were old friends of my London friend, the artist Robin Jacques, who had worked in this same studio.

Philippe Saalburg, last of this small group of art directors, was both French and American. His father was that Leslie Saalburg who did those water-colour illustrations in the old *Esquire* of terribly British men in co-respondent shoes and pipes beside cloche-hatted, twin-setted women leaning on Hispano-Suizas at Henley. Philippe, though inwardly a warm, sensitive and kindly man, was painfully reticent and found difficulty in communicating easily with others. He was the kind of man who wore his heart up his sleeve. An innate courtesy did much to make up for a brusqueness in manner.

As is always the case, at the heart – faint or stout – of an agency is the Copy Department. They don't order these things differently in France. This civilized enclave, its tone no doubt set by the honourable Kevin Farrell (to whom I introduced you, if you remember, before my hols), was to be my cage for the next year or two. I have known worse.

Bernard Galmiche looked and acted like a failed clergyman of Presbyterian leanings. He was a slim, bony man with a long neck and a head of hair in a constant state of shock. He had a quick dry laugh and a quick dry wit. Like most French people, except of course in August, he had that conscientiousness which goes with the high sense of métier. His political views were far, as they say, to the left. He should have been, in the real world, an intellectual contributing brainy think-pieces to the front pages of little magazines. He was one of those admirable sore thumbs of rectitude that were to be found – one of the few compensations – in the creative departments of agencies. We were to work again together, in less happy circumstances.

A newcomer arrived among us, a junior copywriter who was not only pretty but kind, patient and understanding: just the sort of material that asks to be leaned on by one of nature's exploiters like yours truly. She was called Lorraine and inevitably I became known as '*La croix de Lorraine*'. Her other name was Davidovici and her parents had come from Rumania to Paris, which was a mistake, for they were Jewish. She had only one parent now, for the French police, co-operating courteously with the German visitors, had come to her home near that symbol of liberty, the Bastille, and taken her father to that symbol of shame, the stadium known as the Vel d'Hiver, where the Germans, doing their bit, issued him with a ticket, one way, to Auschwitz.

Lorraine and I shared an office at J W T and since we went in the same direction I often drove her home. This sometimes took a little time, for you work late in Paris, and you get peckish towards the end of the day. It was with Lorraine that I did my more profound researches into the French cuisine. She was a willing assistant.

She was small, dark-haired, a little plump, with hands that featured often in our campaigns for Lux soap. She had the face, sorrowful but gallantly gay, of Jeanne Moreau on the body of the young Elizabeth Taylor. She married (I never get the girl) a few years ago. Her husband, the sportive and gentle Alexandre, is the son of Polish Catholic immigrants, sound trenchermen and connoisseurs of vodka. He was born, as it happens, and no doubt Maurice Woodruffe would have had something to say about this, on the same day as me, 24 September (though he has the advantage of me by twenty years). It has long been our custom to meet *chez* Lipp on our anniversary, to drink a toast to Scott Fitzgerald, who has the distinction of sharing our birthday. We drink to him, that is, until midnight, when we raise our glasses to William Faulkner, who was born on 25 September. It makes a pleasant literary evening.

At J. Walter Thompson I managed to leave my mark on several accounts: LU, those splendid *petits beurres*, Lux, Mobil, Ford, Burroughs. And more important to me, I contrived to work with photographers who, like Elliott Erwitt in New York, became my friends. Marc Riboud, who had been little used, perhaps to his credit, by advertisers, went off on safari with Galmiche and Lescaut to photograph the filling stations of France (the results, in double page spreads in *Paris Match*, were worthy of the editorial pages of that magazine). I met and worked with people of the calibre of Eric Lessing (who later spent years photographing the

Bible: *après moi le déluge*), Eric Hartmann, the quiet master of still life, Rene Burri, the Swiss, who married the widow of Werner Bischof, killed on assignment for Magnum, and Inge Morath, who became Mrs Arthur Miller when Marilyn Monroe withdrew from the role.

I also tried, unwisely some would say, to spread the gospel I had learned at the feet, or right hand, or some such member, of David Ogilvy. In one way this spreading of the good word fell on fertile ground, if I've got the right cliché, for J W T New York, the least addy of advertising agencies, had over the years evolved a classic, distinguished (by advertising standards) look based on bookish typography and layout and supported by thorough research and by, uniquely, a formula called, for impenetrable (i.e. not known to your reporter) reasons, the 'T-square'.

This device was a kind of questionnaire or checklist and was intended solely for internal use. By responding to the standard questions the account executive, and after him, the creative group head, could isolate and define such disparate elements as: (a) what the product had to offer that the consumer might possibly need, or anyway, want; (b) by what devices the advertisement or campaign might embody and convey, verbally and visually, the selected benefit or promise.

The completed 'T-squares' were formally submitted to two 'Review Boards'. At the first of these the account executive presented to a panel of his peers the amazing discoveries that led inexorably to the last entry, the 'consumer proposition', which was the bedrock and sounding board and bellwether of the whole show. This *trouvaille* would be along the lines of, 'XYZ toilet soap contains more ingredients to give you a beautiful skin. That is why 9 out of 10 film stars use it.' (I'd like to be able to tell you where and how they got that last fact, but I didn't get on in advertising by asking damn-fool questions.) If this proposition was not deemed by the First Review Board to be well founded, its author was given the old thumbs down and told to think again, or simply to think. If it was found acceptable after scrutiny and questioning, which could be sharp, for the Review Board was a

201

show-place for the ambitious, the creative group working on the account would be invited to exploit it in various ways in copy and layout form and to present the results, with cogent justification, in, say, two weeks' time, to the Second Review Board, which would check them against the imperatives of the First Review Board and accept them, with or without emendation, or reject them.

These presentations, splendidly equipped as I was to make them, gave me the heeby-jeebies, because having to address a gaggle of colleagues throws me into the kind of emotional lather that others might get into if suddenly asked to deliver the Pope's Easter address to that mob in St Peter's Square without being given the script. Now this *faiblesse* in the Hennessy make-up may well have prevented me, though some might say saved me, from reaching the very summit of my profession.

But if these ordinary Review Boards gave me cold sweats and sleepless nights, the annual Big Productions made me ill for weeks beforehand. These were the dreadful occasions when we were called upon (I tried not to be home when they called) to present our work in progress to one or both of those *monstres sacrés* of the huckster's trade, the men who had, in tandem, developed from small beginnings the biggest agency in the world, an American institution whose very name was a symbol of a way of life, like *Time*, *Life*, Ford and *Reader's Digest* – all of them, as it happened, clients of J. Walter Thompson.

The No. 2 man of this daunting duo was Sam Meek, International Director and roving supervisor of every JWT office in the world (there were about as many JWT offices as there were CIA offices, and that's all I'm saying here). He had opened the London office and, an anglophile, had stayed on to see it become the largest, and most English, of the London agencies. With less than impeccable timing he opened the Paris office in 1938. Its archives (and I don't know what else) were hidden during the war, thus denying to the Germans the secrets of the 'T-square' and almost certainly shortening the war.

Sam Meek's visits (*'Frappez-moi cerise, ici vient le grand*

202

fromage,' Rigby would mutter drolly) were, as state visits go, comparatively relaxed, for he was a man of great human warmth and in his presence I was able to keep what would have been a visible shake down to a barely perceptible tremble. Sam Meek was over six feet tall, or seemed so to me, in his grey flannel suit, plain tie, button-down Oxford shirt and solid-citizen shoes. In the easy-going American way, he managed to stand erect while giving the impression that he was lounging. He was nearing sixty-five then and his straight, firmly parted hair was clubman grey. His eyes were round and blue and bright and his mouth curved upwards towards the corners but downwards there, like the mouth of Charlie McCarthy, as if a smile was on its mark and set to go. His look was humorously watchful, that of the kind of man who would be shy with everyone but his close family and all children.

He talked without moving his lips much, in a Mr M'Goo-like continuous mumble, a gently babbling brook into which you had to dive from time to time to fish out a meaning. Everything he said seemed to be in the form of a courteous, tentative suggestion. He neither smoked nor drank. He was irrevocably decent, the very model of the deep-dyed puritanical American WASP of the nicest kind. He had been a friend at Yale of Britten, who with Luce founded *Time*, and was on the board of that enterprise.

Then there was Mr Resor. There was no conclusive proof that he was God, but if Mr Resor hadn't existed it would have been necessary for Madison Avenue to invent him. He was the undisputed Grand Old Man of advertising. He had taken over the agency from its founder, a Commodore Thompson, and built it up to a position where its name could be mentioned in the same reverential breath as such other bastions of the American establishment as Morgan Guaranty, General Motors and Standard Oil of New Jersey. He had brought, or attempted to bring, Ethics, Morality and even, heaven help us, Truth into advertising. Almost single handed he had made advertising, and not only in America, as respectable, if you can call them respectable, as banking, broking and the law.

He eschewed razzmatazz. He refused to accept any liquor or cigarette advertising, though such accounts are among the jumbo budgets in the trade. If sex played any part in Thompson advertising it was at the wholesome level of titled ladies in riding habits recommending Ponds Cold Cream to those less fortunate and fortuned. The house-style of JWT under Mr Resor, who was never called, in or out of his presence, anything but Mr Resor, was one of Dick Stover decency, high quality, self-effacement and service.

Stanley (God forgive me) Resor was a refined, distinguished Judge Hardy of an American lawyer. He was slim, tall, erect, ascetic, shy, courteous and piercingly intelligent. Next to this straight man Sam Meek came on like a jolly jester. If nobody, as I have noted, ever called him anything but Mr Resor, that looked as if it was perfectly all right with Mr Resor.

On the last night of the only visit he made during my time at the Paris office (he was kind enough to describe my Mobil campaign as 'beautiful', but when the snapshots are by Marc Riboud how could it be anything else?) Kevin Farrell had planned a dinner for him, as is standard practice on such occasions. A private room had been reserved (and for Mr Resor, no room could be too reserved) at the St James and Albany, which runs between the Faubourg St Honoré and the Rue de Rivoli, and at which, it being as handy for the office as the Ritz but more austere, the great man was staying. As is also the custom, a menu had been chosen. It wouldn't be Maxim's but it would be all right.

We sat at a round table that filled most of one of those Louis the something grey-green panelled rooms with gold trimmings and fashion show chairs you find in the older Paris hotels. Things started well enough. I was on Mr Resor's left, Kevin Farrell on his right. Across from us, flanked appropriately by a couple drawn from the next echelon down in the Paris office's pecking order, Sam Meek was burbling courteously.

Waiters shimmered in from secret entrances with the first course: the usual sort of thing, an oyster here, a spot of smoked salmon there, a modest little sancerre to help the conversation along. In France, when the food is on the table, you don't hang around. You pitch in. Relic of all those wars, no doubt. Eat while the going's good. You never know. So I pitched in. Kevin Farrell pitched in. Likewise Dick Morgan, Lorraine Davidovici, Philippe Saalburg. Also Sam Meek, except, of course, for the sancerre.

Not Mr Resor, though. Not only no wine, but no oysters and no salmon too. Mr Resor sat there, picture of quiet dignity, spurning all offers, with an empty plate before him.

The oysters and stuff slipped down with what looked like record speed and before you could say fish-knife, there was the *turbotin poché* and next to it the *hollandaise*. Not next to me, though. Courteously but firmly Mr Resor declined. Gamely, *solidaire* to a man, the *collaborateurs* of J. Walter Thompson (France) SA pitched in once more. I glanced past the aged guest at our leader. He looked like a man who, having been under the impression that he had scooped up a forkful of juvenile turbot, found himself with a mouthful of ashes instead. He chewed on bravely, but the strain was beginning to show.

I looked around the table. Eyes everywhere were glued to plates as if they were bingo cards and this was the big prize of the evening. Ever sensitive to the stickier moments of the social round, I sought to engage the saintly Mr Resor in conversation. This was not easy, however, for Mr Resor, sensibly perhaps in retrospect, having said what he had to say, tended to shut up. And since through shyness or perhaps wisdom he failed to introduce one of those hot topics that could be counted on to produce some dazzling cut and thrust, I was forced to leap in and plug the gaps with topics of my own, only to see them die a horrible death, twitching and jerking like a turbot on a hook.

In came the *filet de boeuf en croûte, sauce marchand de vin*, accompanied by one of those crusty Bordeaux that have become so old and fragile they have to be carried about in baskets. None of these goodies, however, tempted Mr Resor. Nor did *la suite*. No *brie*, no *bleu d'auvergne*, no *munster*, no *chèvre*. And to follow, no strawberries with no cream. The room had got smaller and far too hot.

By the time coffee came around, Kevin Farrell, convinced no doubt that his days with the Thompson organisation were numbered, and in single digits at that, now that the financial and culinary excesses of the Paris office had been revealed by the evening's browsing and sluicing, flung all caution to the wind. With a recklessness born of despair, he offered Mr Resor a cigar. The whole room held its collective breath.

'Why that would be very nice,' said Mr Resor, lighting up a Monte Cristo and inhaling with apparent pleasure. The whole room exhaled.

'You know,' said Mr Resor, as a dozen pairs of eyes watched him fervently, 'nobody told me this was for dinner, so I had a little something in my room.'

He paused, savouring the cigar, or something.

'I'd have mentioned it before,' he said, with a shy smile, 'only I didn't want to spoil your meal.'

Chapter 26

Work, for me in Paris, was mostly something you did before lunch and dinner in order to be able to live in Paris and enjoy those meals. I hated to leave the Ile St Louis in the morning and I returned to it with pleasure in the evening and earlier when I could. I had new neighbours now, a few doors up the *quai*, called James and Gloria Jones.

Students of the literary scene will no doubt wish me to record, for the sake of history, my first encounter with the famous novelist. As Thurber said about the disapproving doorman helping him on with his coat, he didn't exactly throw me, but I took a pretty good tossing around. There I was, recently brought to his flat by someone or other, standing and looking thoughtfully about in an attempt to locate the source of an odd, squeaky, high-pitched noise when POW! suddenly, like Auden's herds of reindeer, I was altogether elsewhere, silently and very fast. For Jones, a more acute, softer hearted and more practical man than I, had perceived what I had not, which was that I was standing on the tail of his cat. And having been a boxer of some renown in his army days, and his right hand having lost none of its cunning, he had decided in a flash that the way to remove a 147-pound male from a cat's appendage was to haul off and sock him one, in the friendliest possible way of course, for he was an affectionate fellow. From these propitious beginnings a friendship, not close, for we rarely seemed to be in the same cities at the same time, naturally developed.

Jones was a shortish, stocky man with thinning, greying sandy hair and slit-like, brow-dominated, steady blue eyes above a nose

207

of no importance in a square, squat, lean and thin-lipped face that was faintly concave, like one of those Leonardo caricatures of a warrior. Jones looked at people as if he was trying to learn something not just about them but from them. His were eyes that yearned for better things. He spoke softly and slowly in a voice that managed to be both grating and gentle. He was a vulnerable man whose vulnerability went deeper than a disadvantaged social background could account for. There were those who found Jones coarse, brash and vulgar but to me this outer roughness was unconvincing. In all essential matters, the caring for loved ones, for literature and for art, I found him exquisitely refined. He had a reverence for the best, in people and their works.

He loved Paris and he loved his wife, Gloria, a tall, slim, well-mouthed (as Rabelais put it) near-beauty with silvery-blonde hair. She liked to give and take parties and you had the feeling that she saw people and things just about the way they were. Sunday nights at the Joneses was a kind of open house: the hosts supplied the food and drink and the guests cooked a mountain of easy-to-dish-up food like couscous or spaghetti. A lot of people who hadn't eaten too much all week came and ate too much on Sundays.

War, obviously, was Jones's subject, or rather the field and frame for his subject, which was, like that of any writer, the human heart. Like Hemingway, one couldn't help feeling, Jones tried to conceal what he really was, as if being simply an artist was not justification enough for a life and that it was necessary to be, as well and above all, a man – even if you had to create a myth to prove it. And yet – you could see it in that softly eager look – the artist yearned for recognition.

You couldn't say Jim Jones wasn't a man of action though.

Outside my windows, a tree-screened, cobbled space, with its slope down to the barge-loud, fish-teeming Seine, was much favoured in spring by lovers. Stylised courting, more public than pubic, was still a rite in France, and an aesthetic backdrop was felt to improve the performance. For similar reasons, throughout the year, fashion photographers, directors of publicity films for the cinema (for advertising had not yet spread its blight over the home screen) and the makers of feature films were attracted to my forecourt. Framed by my shutters, there was always action on the *quai*, a kind of feastable movie.

One day in winter my gaze was attracted by the intriguing sight of a squad of men, in green overalls printed with the letters MGM in white, engaged in sticking leaves on to the bare boughs of the trees. Other men were setting up lights that sent what appeared to be a beam of moonlight across the water from Notre Dame. Romantic turn-of-the-century lamp-posts sprang up on the pavement. Folding chairs unfolded and announced, in capital letters, that they were destined to bear the backsides of no lesser persons than Yvette Mimieux and Glenn Ford.

Below me a man was bellowing officiously through a megaphone. He wasn't wearing riding boots, but he had a lot of style. I leaned out of the window, my head two feet into the cold air above the peaked pill-box of a cop, there, as usual, to control the crowd that gathers always in Paris to turn the dullest happening into an exciting social event, half-theatre, half-debate. The *flic*, saluting as they always do before reaching for the cosh, informed me, somewhat superfluously, that they were shooting a scene for a film, adding that the director was Vincente Minelli, a name well-known to the citizens as that of the man who had made *An American in Paris*. This movie would be called *The Four Horsemen of the Apocalypse*, a re-make of the silent success. (They should have re-made the title too, I thought. Any advertising agency could have told them you can't peddle a product with a word like 'apocalypse' in the headline.)

It was after work and the crowd was thickening now. The French, though not notorious for being fresh-air fiends, are street people. Lost in the country without a café terrace, they picnic by the roadside, faces to the traffic, backs to what you and I would call the view. The everyday incidents of Paris life − a traffic accident, a painter with his easel, a man beating his wife − are democratically assumed to be public spectacles, open to all. A hundred or so people had gathered now, ready and willing to offer careful and reasoned advice, as one free citizen to another.

And through the crowd towards me threaded the figures of James Jones, in brown sheepskin coat and matching cheroot, and Gloria, in simple mink set off by a wall-to-wall grin. They looked up and saw me. Night was falling. That would be why they'd been working on the moonlight. It was drink time. It always was in Paris. I waved to the Joneses to come up.

They had been to one of those late lunches, the only kind, *chez* Lipp, and it showed. Other people's drinking always does. But as everybody except Sam Meek and Mr Resor knows, there's only one thing you want when you've had enough to drink, and that's another drink.

I poured some non-babies and chipped some ice in a sink that looked as pitted as an old actor's face. The Joneses moved over to the window. People always did in this apartment. When you have a view you get to know the backs of your friends.

'What's the movie?' asked the World-Famous Author, hitching his shoulders the way boxers do. I told him.

'Oh yeah? Who's directing?'

I told him that too. He spun round as if I'd rung the bell for the first round.

'Minelli?' he almost screamed. 'Minelli! That sonofabitch owes me money!'

Enlarging on this theme between gulps of whisky, Jones explained that when he had sold the film rights of his novel, *Some Came Running*, he had settled for what is known in the trade as a piece of the action – a percentage of the profit. He would start to get his cut when the film had grossed, as they elegantly put it, over a million dollars. The trouble was, according to Jones, that the film never reached that figure, for whenever it threatened to, new and previously unsuspected expenses would be discovered to set off against the gross. And Jones, for some reason, blamed the director of the film, the very same Minelli who was outside my window now. I wished he was back in Hollywood.

Below, a coach and horses had joined the actors (Ford in top hat and opera cloak). The wooden prop street lamps flickered with prop propane gas. A thousand watts of MGM moonlight beat a path across the beaujolais-dark Seine. The director called for silence with a ferocity that hushed even this French crowd. Then, 'Hey, Minelli! Move the lamp-post, Minelli! That's all wrong!'

The startled and internationally celebrated director lowered his megaphone and glared across the *quai*. He could not, however, see who was addressing him in this over-familiar manner for, as they say in his métier, the three-shot was back-lit and it was night out now. Frustrated, he shrugged and turned to his work again.

'This is a take,' he said. 'Roll 'em!'

The camera tracked slowly forward out of the spaghetti of cables.

'Hey, Minelli! You can't leave that lamp-post there. C'mon, move it! You never make a movie before, Minelli?'

Warming to his role, applauded by the glorious Gloria, our author took another swig of scotch. His combative profile became more concave and his chin jutted out like Epstein's 'Adam'.

'Hey, Minelli!' he bellowed, beaming at the subtlety of his own wit. 'You'll never make a movie director, Minelli!'

This prognosis, based, as perhaps he felt, on an inaccurate diagnosis, seemed to get in among Minelli. The set was stilled, like a freeze-frame. The crowd was hushed, a hundred connoisseurs in rapturous silence. Now this was something like a movie. *C'était du cinema, quoi!*

'Cut!' screamed Minelli, on the *quai*.

'Roll 'em!' shouted Jones, *chez moi*.

The actors were looking up at us now. The cameraman had unsqueegeed his eye from the rubber viewer and peered towards the lighted windows. Several thousand watts of moonlight vanished from the Seine. From over our heads a frail but girlish voice cried: *'Mais qu'est-ce qu'il se passe en bàs?'*

It was the voice of my landlady, Madame Salle. Things, never exactly in hand, were now getting out.

Minelli spoke to his assistant. The assistant spoke to the production manager. The production manager talked to the scriptgirl and *la script*, bi-lingual as they always are in France, put down her board and pencil and spoke to the *flic*. This worthy, heavy now with the responsibility that the *entente cordiale* between Metro-Goldwyn-Mayer and the Ville de Paris placed upon his caped shoulders, took a purposeful step towards us, saluted and asked us sonorously if we would well wish to keep the silence during the turning of the film, which would be kind on our part; if not he would be well obliged....

'Wassee say?' asked Jones, who, in those early days of residence, had not yet acquired that uncertain grasp of the French language that was his in later years.

I translated freely, adding that, for my part, welcome as he was to stay in my apartment, it might not be my apartment for much longer if he didn't stop squaring his accounts with Hollywood in public.

Jones gave his gentle, wry pug's grin, early-Cagney model, and said, in his crooning voice, 'Aw, what the hell....'

Turning towards the river, he raised an arm and called 'Night, Minelli,' and, pleased with his evening's work, retreated into the room.

'He's a nice guy, really,' he said.

As I closed the window against the cold night air a voice rose again from the *quai*.

'Take one,' said Minelli, gamely.

Chapter 27

'Like everybody else,' said Jill Goldsmith, 'I was the first to know.'

Along the *quai*, past the Joneses, Digby Neave was letting it be known that he was about to marry. He had returned one day from a trip to London with a small, slim, dark-blonde Danish girl called Ulla. He had known her years before when she had been an art student at the Slade, evacuated to Oxford during the war and in no great rush, it seemed, to return. From the Slade, Ulla had disappeared to Rio de Janeiro, where her father, a Mr Schmidt, was something vital with Shell. This sojourn, during which she found congenial employment as an interior decorator, left her with that almost sallow tan that blonde people acquire in the tropics. Her hair was straight and she had about as much fat on her as a four-minute miler. She had one of those boyish figures that French girls have and for which the bikini was invented.

She had a dread of crowds and strangers and claimed to have no higher an opinion of children than she had of adults, preferring the company, she said of dogs, and in particular of whippets. She acquired a batch of these hounds and when you saw four or five of them doing a lap of the Ile St Louis with her you had your work cut out to tell which one was Ulla. Since these dogs, under the infinitely tolerant eye of their mistress, regarded the Neave flat as simply an indoor track, to be used in inclement weather to keep their muscle tone up to par, Digby soon discovered who his real friends were. Even I, a lover of order and harmony in all things, found our long friendship severely tested.

A more restful activity of Ulla's was painting and since Chagall had cornered, as it were, the other side of the island, she moved her easel into my flat for a while. The resulting work, my view immortalised by the all too mortal Ulla, may be seen, for reasons which I will explain later, still on its easel, in the greenhouse of the house of Alexandre Dumas at Marly le Roi.

Although, as I have said, timorous with people, Ulla seemed to be physically fearless. That winter the Neaves had gone to Gstaad, the Swiss ski resort patronised by Irwin Shaw, Galbraith, Jimmy Goldsmith and that crowd, while I, preferring not to leave France, was being patronised by Megeve, the St Tropez of the Alps, frequented by Vadim, Bardot, Sagan and that gang.

Tearing myself away one morning from my balcony at the Mont d'Arbois, the splendid hotel owned by the Rothschilds and at which only a Rothschild would be able to afford to stay for more than a week, I descended to buy a paper and scan the headlines over a refreshing *champagne-orange*. In the lobby I found Digby and Ulla who, unable to stand Gstaad and its denizens, had moved on here, not knowing that I had preceded them. It was good to see them, especially since their whippets had chosed to winter in Paris.

For most of each day Ulla, a skilled and intrepid skier (she had skied to school in Denmark), vanished to the higher *pistes*, leaving Digby and me on the nursery slopes. It must be assumed that the two met up again at night, for on her return to Paris Ulla was pregnant.

Weakened by jaundice, she gave birth prematurely to a girl. I got the news at dawn when, the French telephone for once working, Digby called from a clinic with the cute name of La Cigale, across from the American Hospital in Neuilly.

'Got to come over straight away, old boy,' he burbled, with that, as far as I was concerned, uninfectious enthusiasm which is his strongest trait. Though never at my best before taking on board the old *croissant* and *café-crème*, not wishing to be a wet blanket I climbed out of the sheets, dived into a Washington Tremlett, threw on an Anderson and Sheppard, laced up the Lobbs and zoomed off to greet the precipitous Miss Neave.

214

New babies look like rather angry oranges – to start with anyway, because later they turn into North Koreans, then South Koreans, then Eisenhower, then Churchill, before becoming recognisable as ordinary human infants. This one was at the angry orange stage, which made it hard to see why its father was tickled pink. A couple of years later I went through the whole scene again, with roughly the same cast of characters, which means that, apart from the doctor and papa, I was the first chap the Neave girls met, and God knows what that did to their psyches.

They took Victoria away in an incubator to the Salpetrière, the Paris children's hospital. They gave her a 50-50 chance, rotten odds for your first draw in life's lottery. They wouldn't give information by telephone. Parents had to go there every day and be told what the latest score was. There were two snags about this arrangement. One was that you wouldn't get Neave into a hospital – conscious, that is – without using a straitjacket: he is the only man ever known to have fainted in bed, while reading a restful detective story, through unexpectedly coming across the word 'blood'. The other snag was that Ulla didn't drive.

So every day for two weeks I had the job of driving Ulla, who gave every indication of caring at least as much about babies as whippets, to the hospital for a distant squint at Victoria, if she was alive. It was April in Paris again. April is the cruellest month.

Victoria lived. Philippa, second child, lived. Ulla, though, died, suddenly, brutally, pointlessly, before they could really know her. That was in another country too.

The problem about going to an office is that it uses up time that could be spent on living. Agreeable as the company was in the J. Walter Thompson Company, I decided that I was meant, if not for better, then for other things. Trying to impose a philosophy – well, anyway, a technique – of advertising on an organisation which seemed quite happy, and successful, with the one it had cost too much in energy and friendships put at risk. That was the rationalisation, anyway, and the desperate can't be too picky in

215

these matters. What I wanted was out, where I thought freedom might be, not knowing then that it lay, if anywhere, in the opposite direction. So I quit JWT in order to carry out a plan that had that simplicity which is the mark of great ideas and idiotic ones. I decided to start my own agency.

Being no one, I would need as a partner someone who was someone. Two such would be even better. So I wrote to Philip Stobo, of S. H. Benson Ltd, and to David Ogilvy, of Ogilvy, Benson and Mather Inc., sketching in my sketchy plan. You see the beauty of the thing. Bensons, handy across the Channel, would provide the ante; Ogilvy, the most famous name in advertising, would provide the prestige. And I, profiting from both, would have an instant international agency. Hard to see where the thing could go wrong.

In fact, it kicked off rather well. Bensons were interested in foreign fields: already, through Ogilvy, they were in America, and they had long been in Canada, South Africa, Australia and India. Ogilvy, who had strong ties with France, would sooner or later need to have a presence in Europe. He wrote encouragingly. (The last sentence of his letter asked, 'Did you know that Rue le Regrattier means "Huckster Street"?' Well, I lived there, but I didn't. Be memorable, said the Ogilvy credo. You bet.)

Stobo invited me to come and talk to him and Bobbie Bevan and their newly appointed international director. That seemed to go well, and then Stobo came to see me. I gathered together a team, the nucleus of an agency, and paraded them in my flat for Stobo's inspection: Lorraine Davidovici, copywriter, Bob Lescaut, art director, Philip Levet, account executive. I was ransacking JWT. They were heady days.

I flew to New York to see Ogilvy. I took the new *Michelin* and handed it to him in the sunny corner office high above Fifth.

'Has anything happened?' Ogilvy asked, involved immediately.

I told him there was grave news. One of the long-standing three-star restaurants had lost a star.

'I'll bet it's La Mère Brezier down at Lyon,' Ogilvy mused. 'She's had it coming to her.'

Right. Make it memorable. You have to hand it to the man.

Back in Paris, hunting around for accounts to open the business with, I went to see Ogilvy's New York client, Helena Rubinstein. I walked from the Rue le Regrattier along the *quai*, past the Milinaire apartment, past the Joneses, past the Neaves and turned left into a passage that led to a courtyard. On the right, the concierge's lodge wasn't a concierge's lodge any more but a small modern elevator made for two. I whispered up in this to the sixth floor, the lower of the penthouse duplex. The elevator opened directly on to a room and a tall slim man with a handsome face under auburn hair fluffed up to make the most of its last days. This would be Patrick O'Higgins, the ex-Irish Guards guard, secretary and *homme à tout faire* to Madame R.

He led me across a vast space entirely surrounded by Picassos and Africana into a small octagonal room with a chair in it that looked like a throne. He sat me opposite this.

'David sent us a cable about you,' he said and left it where it lay. He went out and came back with a serious-looking whisky. Good man, O'Higgins.

'Madame will be right with you,' he said, and went off somewhere a great way away.

A small black-haired woman with no visible neck came into the room with a kind of shy imperiousness. It could have been an Inca icon, if they had them, or Sam White's mother. She looked like a female Somerset Maugham, but then so did Somerset Maugham. She was wearing a floor-length tea-gown cut by Balenciaga from the original Mondrian. She looked very old but very well preserved, like a mummy.

'David says you are very good,' she said, in a soft English with a hard middle-European accent. She studied me as if, after all these years and with all this wealth, it still mattered. She was adding me up to see how much I was worth. I could have told her and saved her the trouble.

I pushed my book of samples across the low table between us and she turned the plastic pages slowly, making little mewing noises.

'These are beautiful,' she said, closing the book and staring at me again, adding a few decimal points to the total.

'You will go very far,' she said, a high-class fortune-teller now. 'I am never wrong about such things.'

There's always a first time, I thought, but this woman would always be more right than wrong, buying or selling.

'Have you seen my garden?' she said, more as an accolade for me, I thought, than as a proprietorial boast. She led me slowly, neatly up a staircase to the next floor and out through a wall that was all open window. We stepped into a *jardin suspendu* no longer than the Queen Elizabeth.

'My view,' she said with simple majesty, and raised an arm slowly, like a Pope, in benison. All of Paris lay below her, cut from the whole cloth.

'Where do you live?' Madam asked, as if that mattered too. I pointed down the *quai*.

'Just down there,' I said. 'Across from the cathedral.'

She spun round and stared up at me, the unloving eyes narrowed to slits you expected gun muzzles to come through.

'Is your view better than mine?' she asked.

I could have used the money. She was ready to buy it, sight unseen. Too bad it wasn't mine to sell.

'No,' I said kindly, and went back in to pick up my samples and ride down to the street and the real world.

The real world wasn't looking so good. Negotiations move at different speeds for corporations and individuals. Individuals can go broke. Lloyds Bank in the Rue Cambon, handy for the Ritz Bar, were getting edgy, the strain beginning to show. Marc Riboud and Elliott Erwitt came round with a cheque for a few hundred dollars – to buy a couple of shares in the new company, as they tactfully explained. Edward Behr offered to help. Everyone was kind.

Then David Ogilvy landed the Shell account, doubling his billings. *Les bonheurs des uns sont les malheurs des autres*, as the French say, almost. The trouble was that Bensons had BP, and shared it in Canada with Ogilvy. It was impossible for one agency

218

to service competitive clients. So Ogilvy was forced to break with Bensons, who were hardly ready to sacrifice BP. And with Ogilvy and Bensons unable to work together, my neat structure lay in ruins. Bensons could have gone it alone, but without the name of Ogilvy to serve as entrée to Europe what had I got to offer? I was once again what I had always been – no one.

So things didn't look good. No job. No empire. There was still Judy Douglas, though. She looked good, all right.

Chapter 28

Apart from the odd stint in residences in Phoenix, Arizona and Cannes, Alpes Maritimes (the bare minimum for social decency), the Douglases holed up in the converted lodge of a mansion in the Rue de Varenne, a party's throw from the Dillons, in the Faubourg St Germain.

They threw a party there one night that fall for the young set and the older crowd; qualifying for both, I was invited. In a courtyard like a parade ground stood James Douglas's black Cadillac and Judy Douglas's green Rover, the Rolls-Royce of the English middle class. Inside, the usual cosmopolitan crowd was in full shriek. Rented flunkies and the house man handed round champagne and whisky.

The word went round that everybody was going to bomb up to Montmartre and an amusing restaurant. I knew the joint. Not my favourite eating-place. Besides, I'd never been there. What's more, I hate crowds, especially when eating, which should be an almost solitary pleasure, like reading a good book. Apart from noise, mobs meant compromise, delay and sordid wrangling when they brought the bill. The problem was, how to get rid of this bunch without getting rid of Judy, whose perfect nose had now detected, as well it might, the damp odour of wet blanket.

Everyone was going around chirruping, finding out who was *motorisé*. I wasn't. Judy was. Gallantly, well, cunningly, I took the wheel of the stately, wood- and leather-scented Rover. As if by chance, our car became the sulky last in the junketing convoy. From our position of strength, we negotiated Concorde ('... the taxis missing each other superbly': Tessimond) and turned into the Rue Royale. Half-way down the Rue Royale I was struck by an idea I hadn't seen coming. With what I hoped was a squeal of rubber on tarmac, I swung the car into a U-turn (it is impossible to make a non-U turn in a Rover) and skidded to a halt in front of the burgundy-and-gold awning of Maxim's.

Beside me, Judy sat very still, her face saying nothing and everything, like Garbo on the poop, or whatever, in the long, last one-shot in *Queen Christina*. After a bit of that she said, in the quiet, level, unemphatic voice that women reserve for the great dramatic moments in life, 'We – can't – do – that – you – know.'

She turned her head just enough to fix me with an eye that was carefully neutral, judged to a fine shade. I gave her the calm beam of a man who has the lady over the saddle of a white charger, which is where, while denying it, she wants to be, rather like that girl in Byron's *Don Juan* who, 'saying no, consented'. We creative men understand these things.

She turned her head to the front again and studied Cleopatra's Needle on the *place*, as if she was working out the shipping cost from Egypt.

'You realise they'll all be waiting for us.'

I gave her the beam again, increasing the voltage slightly.

'We'll have to telephone them, then.'

There was a long pause, just the amount you'd need for an exit with dignity.

'All right?'

'But of course,' I said agreeably as the *chasseur* came over to hand her out, rapt as a bride, and take the Rover to wherever Maxim's park their customer's cars.

We started with the *Crêpes Maxim's*, which are those little *coups de genie* in which a *duxelle* of sea-food, with a hint of *sauce armoricaine*, is cradled in a lace-fine pancake, the whole no harder to digest than the first movement of Mozart's 21st piano concerto. There was the house champagne. And then I forget. Maxim's is the only place on earth that has music and good food. Any woman, seated on one of those old-rose banquettes, with the belle-epoque mirrors reflecting candle-light and a violin swooning in her ear, would be *en beauté*. And Judy was eighteen, and would have looked beautiful in a works canteen.

>And how did Lady Gaster's party go?
>Juliet was next to me, and I do not know.

She forgot about telephoning those people though. Nobody's perfect.

It had been, once, a plain stucco Provençal *mas* – the piney woods are full of them – up in the foothills above Cannes-la-Bocca. Mrs Douglas, the third, or current, Mrs Douglas, preferring the Normandy style, had added a couple of slated cone turrets, then had the whole thing faced in dazzling white stone. It was the Carlton, down the hill, without the icing. It looked rich enough not to need the icing.

They weren't holding the Olympics in the pool that summer, but it was there when they needed it. Leaning your wet elbows on the surrounding balustrade you looked down over lesser pools to a blue-grey haze that was the bay of Cannes. If that was too hot work you could pad over to the patio on your left, flop wetly on to the sun-bleached canvas of a bamboo chaise-longue, and if you flopped right, reach with your heel the bell that would bring them running with the gin-and-tonic. There were worse ways to ruin your health.

Inside the house someone descended from Adam – the eighteenth-century one – had fringed Wedgwood-blue walls with instant white carving. The cool, russet Provençal tiles had been carefully hidden by about an acre of white carpet that had spread everywhere, as if someone had thrown a pack of detergent in a fountain. The furniture was real enough though. What wasn't Chippendale was Hepplewhite, and vice versa. Outside it was Bel Air. Inside it was Mayfair. It didn't bother me at all.

I had arrived the evening before, winding up one of those last-night-I-went-to-Manderley drives that keep you wondering where the house is, or if there's one at all. When I got close enough to

222

see the whites of its shutters I saw the black of the Cadillac too and as I parked in a small piece of its shadow a man came through an archway that led to the pool and then to nowhere. James Douglas. Six feet tall and several millions rich.

The eyes were blue, kind and weak, the hair thinning and grey, brushed flat and straight back, like a thirties tennis pro (a kind of Fred Perruque). The liver-mottled skin had been seasoned by the sun of Cannes and Scottsdale, Arizona, some of the best sun there is. This was a man's man, but also a ladies' man, the kind of rare male who not only would dance well but would like to. And with the uncertain social judgement that goes with second generation money this man, you'd say, would be catnip to the tough, the ambitious and the vulgar woman.

Mr Douglas wasn't Judy's father. Judy's father was a minor civil servant in Washington, where everybody is a civil servant, and lived with his second wife and no children in a nice catalogue house on Chesapeake Bay, which some know for battles long ago and I for the chincateague oyster here and now. The first Mrs Kirkland was the third Mrs Douglas and when Jim Douglas pointed out that he could offer Judy a better life, whatever that meant, than her father, Judy went along too. She was thus transported from lower middle class, small-town America to international millionairedom and the strain may have told, for there were reports of emotional crisis when she was sixteen; she survived that, but she kept her appointment in Samarra anyway.

At the villa were two other guests, invited, with typical graciousness, by yours truly. I had been over to London for the wedding of my two protégés, Bill Binzen, art director at Ogilvy, Benson and Mather, and Gail Binzen, copywriter at ditto. I had brought them together, you will remember, and it had taken. Now they were heading down to Florence, the other place good Americans go when they die, for a sabbatical year. (They had their first child there, a girl called Claire. In New York, later, they told me that everyone had sent them letters and telegrams of congratulation. Everyone, that is, except the President of OBM. He had sent a cable addressed to 'Miss Claire Binzen' and it said,

'Welcome darling. David Ogilvy.' Be memorable.)

We swam in the pool and Bill took pictures as the butler brought drinks to the evening patio, and Jim Douglas, as he always waggishly did, cautioned us against too much ice because the ice-worms could make you feel bad next morning, ho, ho, and we had dinner off the Chippendale or else the Hepplewhite and drank Bordeaux because that is what the doctors of the rich prescribe for aging millionaires and that is how they stay doctors of the rich. It was a day like any other at the Château Garibondy, like any day, that is, spent *en famille*, for somewhere along the coast there would be the moveable party and one night that summer it was the Douglases' turn to throw it.

But first I made Judy over. Superb as she was in every way, she dressed in the manner that Americans in the international set dressed, and that was not good. Against the blare of the sun and the blaze of the bougainvillea the French, and also the Italians, wear solid navy and white, or all white, or navy and pale blue, faded strawberry and that's OK. But Americans take their colours from the surroundings and you get the sallow businessman in the Hawaiian shirt or his wife in hectic prints, coral necklaces (or the pastel-skinned Englishwoman in the pastel-flowered Royal Garden Party dress with, for the mad tropicality of it all, a cartwheel straw hat, the last straw). These things matter. If the trivial isn't important, what is?

So pausing only long enough for Judy to put the bite on adoring papa, or step-papa, for a bit of the ready, we climbed into the open red 1925 Renault that Mr Douglas had bought on his first trip to France and chundered down to Cannes. Stopping at here a dress shop, there a shoe shop, I snapped up, sparing no expense, little shorts and matching jackets in turquoise and in navy (Bardot had brought back gingham in St Tropez, and Cannes, waiting a cautious year, was on to it now), and plain white pants and navy shirts and a white broderie-anglaise dress with built-in petticoat (Bardot had brought back broderie-anglaise, etc.) and leather-coloured leather sandals that made the foot look not so much naked as nude.

That night, the night of the obligatory *soirée*, Judy put on the white dress, put on the sandals, and put up her hair. Then, it seeming the logical next step, she came out of the house and down the steps to the lawn and pool to greet her guests. You may recall the scene in *My Fair Lady* where the transformed Eliza descends the staircase to the wonder and amazement of all. Well, that was nothing on this. Women who had dandled her on their knees didn't recognise her. Pop, eyes glistening (ice worms perhaps), booked the first dance. Judy glowed, like a girl showing her engagement ring, which has changed everything, she knows, for ever. And I felt that warm sense of achievement that sometimes comes to us senior creative men.

There were tables set on the breathless lawn, between house and pool. Behind, the hills, that like the guests had seen it all before, had turned in early. Below, the coast glittered like costume jewellery. The sky lowered. Moisture hung in the air, biding its time. The chittering guests, greeted, introduced and primed with champagne, peered for their place cards, sat down, shook out their napkins and addressed their melon and prosciutto. The cream of the Villa, Boat and Hotel People fell on the food with little chirrups of joy, as if they'd never seen the like in all their puff.

The shop-worn caterers, who had served them the same meal last night, and the night before, and the whole season, and the season before, moved dully about, quietly clacking and wiping already clean plates and pouring wine with self-serving generosity. Inside, beyond the open French windows, the mandatory group of mop-headed young English rockers, in from Hamburg for the summer, tuned up, or plugged in, for the dancing, and leered at the upper-class potential groupies. Indoors and out, it was a night like any other night at that place, in that season, on that coast.

Then the rain came, all at the same time, in glops. The women, hair still hot-pressed from four hours at the Carlton *coiffeurs*, leaped to safety through the French windows. Men, mere accessories, followed at their skittering heels. Waiters, alive now, raced to the kitchens with salvers of gaping *loup au fenouil.*

I stayed, to finish a glass of Bordeaux before it got polluted with rain, idly watching whatever the opposite of an exodus is and reflecting how thin is the upper crust of our society, and how vulnerable to acts of God, or whoever. And James Douglas stayed, his tanned face in the gloomy light turning, one would have sworn, a shade of grey now. Then suddenly he began to scream.

'Help me!' he screamed, eyes staring, wild. 'Get those people back! Get this furniture inside!'

For the rain which, they tell us, falls on the just and on the unjust, now fell on the Chippendale and on the Hepplewhite. The guests were sheltered now, but who cared? Money talks, as Tessimond advised us, with a voice of fear.

I couldn't think of a bread and butter letter (which the French call *une lettre de château*) that would express my true feelings, so I went down to the right bank *quai* near Vilmorin where they sell pets to those who need pets and bought a Siamese kitten and a basket and put the former in the latter and both on the train with food and milk and instructions to the guard. The efficient SNCF delivered it at the Château Garibondy next morning and the maid woke Judy with breakfast and a kitten. She called the kitten Tiger, which is what, later, she was to call her son. More accurately, she called the boy Hogy, which is the Korean for tiger. And thereby hangs, so to speak, a tale.

We strolled in the gentle autumn sunshine from the Rue de Varenne up the Boulevard to St Germain des Près. On the terrace of the Deux Magots the returned *vacanciers* were topping up their tans under a sun past its prime. One face needed no help, the passively, impassively amused moon-face of Peter Hyun, riding high on his reputation as the only young Korean poet in town.

(With him I had met the Indian poet Dom Moraes, just down from Oxford, and that month's sensation. He was girlishly good looking and shy and throughout dinner kept the roll collar of his sweater unrolled almost up to his eyes, which, although perhaps giving him an advantage as an observer of life's passing show, made conversation difficult and eating distinctly messy.)

I introduced Judy to Peter. From my point of view this was a mistake. Peter had a fine eye for a pretty doxy, and Oriental poets were in that year. Although I began to see less of Judy after this encounter I failed to notice that anything was amiss, or alad either. Then one evening she arrived late for dinner and seeking to mollify me offered me what she had decided would be an appropriate gift – a small toy model of a Rolls-Royce. Dashed nice of her, of course. The trouble was that during dinner I remembered that Peter lodged in a room on the Boulevard St Germain, just about halfway between my flat and the Rue de Varennes. And directly underneath this room was a toy-shop that sold, as most toy-shops do, small model cars.

Hurt of course in my pride by this atrocious act of duplicity, but ever the philosopher in such matters, and possibly somewhat relieved by the lifting, once more, of a threat of marriage, I said and did nothing – a stance I have often been known to adopt in times of crisis. And what we had here, in fact, was a crisis of the most critical sort, though not, as it happened, for me.

The telephone rang one evening in my flat and I heard the voice of Jim Douglas, a voice that had in it now all the hopeless sadness of a man whose world lay shattered about his erstwhile dancing feet. What he wanted to know was if I knew. Well, as it happened, I did, having started the whole thing on its way. But, it seemed, if more or less *au fait*, I was not absolutely *au courant*. In a stricken, mournful tone he announced that Judy had gone mad. Could I come over and see him? Well, I hate to see a millionaire down on his luck, so over I went.

Over a large scotch in the small but plush living-room in the Rue de Varenne I watched a battle rage over the handsome spoiled face of a wealthy WASP whose adored, if adopted, daughter had betrayed his trust, and what's more with a penniless poet, and worse, with a penniless Oriental poet, that year's model. He truly had my sympathy, especially after a second thoughtful scotch.

227

He told me brokenly that he had tried to persuade Judy to do the sensible, indeed only possible thing, i.e. and to wit, get rid of this Chinese-type poet guy who was obviously only after Judy's, that is, his, money. Faced with her baffling and shortsighted refusal to comply with this perfectly reasonable suggestion, he had made the only deduction possible – that she had gone right off her rocker – and, with great patience and forbearance, had tried to persuade her to see a psychiatrist. She told him he was out of his mind.

So he had reluctantly decided to take the only course open to him and cut her off with a penny (or without a penny – I forget the details). And that included the Rover, which was mine for a nominal sum. Having been obliged to exchange my Renault with Jacques Sorbac of JWT for a bit of the ready I gratefully accepted his kind offer.

It was thus with the bottle-green Rover that I moved its one previous owner, careful driver, and her lover from the room on the Boulevard St Germain to a basement flat in the 16th *arrondissement*, and after a bit of that, out to the airport for a flight to London. There they stayed with friends, and married, and then moved on to New York, where Peter had relatives and where he thought he might more easily find a job than on the Left Bank of Paris.

It's a long way, in every sense that matters, from the Deux Magots to Manhattan, and I did not expect to see the two of them soon again. And yet, such is the way the world wags, I did.

Chapter 29

All very well, these social shenanigans and carryings on, but life is real, life is earnest, life is for the very sternest, as we had written to sell more Guinness. And here was I with one more high-flying fantasy − the instant big deal − shot down in flames. I was broke and jobless. Now though I am often broke I am only infrequently jobless − about once a country, on average, rather like George Orwell. Perhaps it was another country's turn to face up to its responsibilities and shoulder the burden for a while? I was, after all, a British citizen. That still meant something, I hoped. Leaving Paris, as usual reluctantly, and I hoped temporarily, I flew to London to circle, like a homing albatross, about the neck of my younger brother Tom in Lexham Gardens.

As I said, I didn't want to leave Paris, to understate the thing somewhat, and if I did, I didn't want to leave it for London. New York, OK, but not London. Still, needs must when the devil drives, whatever that means. These were desperate times, calling for desperate measures. So, sponging like someone born on an ocean bed, I hung around the gloomy city, prowled the squares where, as the poet Tessimond observed, it is always Sunday afternoon, and breathed the sooty air that smells like an old railway carriage of the non-no-smoking kind. Other times I lurked in the empty flat, looking at the telephone, in Hot Line red, that slept curled up like a cat in the kitchen. Nobody called. Nobody offered me a job. The time was full of nothing happening.

Then, one morning, as I was brooding alone in the flat, the employed members of the family being out winning my evening bread, the telephone rang meaningfully. Down the hot line and into my shell-like ear came the always welcome voice of Lorraine Davidovici. *'Eh ben,'* she said, as the French tend to, *'eh ben,* once more, it seems, you fall, how do you say, on your feet.' She had, with typical kindness of the sort that I tend to take entirely for granted, been along to the Rue le Regrattier to see if there might be any vital mail for me. Among the bills was a telegram which she now proposed to read to me. 'Right-ho,' I said. 'Shoot the *sorbet* to me, Herbert,' although that was not her name of course. Then she read, in capitals, the following communication:

HEREBY OFFER YOU JOB IN NEWYORK AT SALARY OF TWENTY-FIVE THOUSAND DOLLARS STOP YOUR FIRST ASSIGNMENT WOULD BE THE UNITEDSTATES TRAVEL SERVICE ACCOUNT WHICH WE HAVE JUST BEEN AWARDED FOR ENGLAND AND FRANCE STOP IF YOU ACCEPT WE WILL PAY YOUR FARE TO NEWYORK AND WILL CABLE THE MONEY IF NECESSARY STOP WHAT IS EARLIEST DATE YOU COULD START
DAVID OGILVY 521 EAST 84 STREET
NEWYORK

Then she announced that there was another cable, referring to a letter that she held even then in her hot little hand. This one went:

SEE FIRST PARAGRAPH OF MY LETTER OF JUNE 29 ARE YOU COMING? WE HOPE SO OGILVY

Funny thing, life. I mean, one minute you're down and out in London and Paris and the next – Orwell again! Cutting through this miasma of cables snapping at each other's heels and mysterious letters not yet arrived, and acting with that decisiveness of which I am capable whenever someone makes me an offer of twenty-five grand, plus some more up front, as they say, plus carfare, I grabbed the phone again, with the same sort of grip, and for the same sort of reasons, as a drowning man clutching at a straw.

I asked for Murray Hill 8-6100. I got the switchboard girl at OBM. Then I got the President's bi-sexual outer office (Harry the male secretary, June the female). Then I got the corner office and the throne.

'Oh, hello,' I said.

'You there?' I asked.

Just as well to get the characters lined up for the big scene.

'Charles here,' I said, making sure he was in the picture. 'Got your cable. I mean, I didn't exactly get it. As a matter of fact it's in Paris and I'm in London, but someone read it to me. Both of them, actually. I mean, there were two cables, weren't there? And a letter. Haven't got the letter though. She'll send it on I expect....'

Cutting through this idiotic waffle like a knife through stutter came the voice of David Ogilvy, with its measured, vaguely theatrical, almost Churchillian cadence.

'Is − it − a − deal?' he asked.

Getting a grip on my emotions and taking a deep breath I said out loud, 'Yes,' but within me another voice, like the inner voice of Molly Bloom, went on saying 'Yes, and yes, oh yes....'

Then I went back to Paris, left the Rover with a friend in Digby's office and clanked the steel shutters closed on the Tour d'Argent, the Pantheon and Notre Dame; and on the barge-heavy Seine, which took no notice and, like life, like time, flowed imperturbably on.

Amble IV

Chapter 30

The Gladstone, though smaller than Mies van der Rohe's Seagram building across the street ('Less is more,' I cracked to Mies one day, and the thing caught on), had the attraction of those quiet, family-sized hotels that exist still in Paris but no longer in mid-town Manhattan. I had moved in here because it was a block or two from the offices of Ogilvy, Benson and Mather, and because I had not had time for that demanding sport, apartment-hunting.

As soon as I moved in I took to my bed, felled by one of those psychosomatic short jabs to the stomach – always, as I may already have said, my Achilles heel. The head-swelling thought that I alone had been selected by the Master for this vital post was now replaced by the head-shrinking thought that I was faced with new and terrible responsibilities. Here was I, a kind of lightweight European bohemian who, by the more or less adroit juggling of wits and words, had managed just to keep his balance on the slippery surface of life, suddenly translated into a heavyweight trans-Atlantic executive with a client in Washington (the US Government, no less), a key job in New York and advertising agencies in Paris, London and Frankfurt waiting on my word. It was enough to make a fellow sick, and it did.

For a couple of days I skulked there, calling in to report on my state of health. Then, suddenly recalling that my self-indulgent cowardice might put in jeopardy the twenty-five thousand on which I was even now living, or dying, I hauled myself up and dragged myself over to 589 Fifth Avenue and took the elevator to the ninth floor.

The President was out to lunch and I sat in the austerely plush reception room to await his return. After too short a while (I would have been really braced in about five minutes more) the elevator doors glided open and Ogilvy, followed by Cliff Field and Joel Raphaelson, strode in his spring-heeled way towards me, held out his hand, threw back his head like a dentist, the better to focus through his horn-rimmed glasses, bared his teeth in a sardonic grin and said, 'Doctor Livingstone, I presume.'

My office now was next but one to his. Between us was the office of the Copy Chief, Dave McCall, the crew-cut, buttoned-down, J. Pressed, steel-rimmed Princetonian Dick Stover redux who had been the cub copywriter when we first, and last met. Reva Fine, now Mrs Korda, was a Copy Group Head (like Cliff and Joel) and would supervise the copy on the account. Bill Binzen, back from Florence and freedom, would be my art director. Borgie Baton, but who else, would do the typography, for which her fluent French and German would by handy. The old crowd. You *can* go home again.

Working for me, under Reva, were two copywriters, in shades of black and white. Don deLillo was a slight, watchful, quiet man with some of the looks and a lot of the almost fearful, *à fleur de* pock-marked *peau* sensitivity of Montgomery Clift. He wrote well, but then Ogilvy writers were supposed to. They were also supposed to be nice and he was that too. He left Ogilvy after a while, as copywriters often do, to write a novel, and unlike most, he wrote one, and got it published, and then a couple more.

Reversing this more normal procedure, the black chap, Junius Edwards, had published a novel, and several prize-winning short stories, before he joined Ogilvy as a trainee copywriter. (The novel was called *If We Must Die* – published by Laffont in France as *S'il faut mourir* – and was the story of a young Chicago black's struggle to get the vote; when Ogilvy wrote his first book Junius kindly introduced him to his agent, who found himself with 10 per cent of a best-seller.)

If Central Casting had been looking for blacks, with special emphasis on the kingly, Zulu-chieftain type, and you'd rolled up with Junius Edwards, they'd have been tickled pink. He was about six foot three without trying, upright, grave, majestic, with the kind of refinement to the head which suggested that they had brought his batch from Senegal rather than the Ivory Coast. He looked down through gold-rimmed tinted glasses and his teeth protruded slightly: when he laughed, which was often, it was as if a coconut had been suddenly split.

Thanks to Senator Fulbright's bill, Junius had pursued, and caught, his higher education at the University of Oslo, and there had met and married a blonde, pretty and gentle Norwegian called Inge. There are four children, two boys and two girls, who, apart from sharing a rare beauty, have the unusual distinction, for people of their complexion in Manhattan, of speaking fluent Norwegian.

Before, however, these assembled talents, under my nervous command, got started on the relatively pleasant task of turning out headlines and matching them to photos for the United States Travel Service campaign (the first tourist advertising ever conducted by the American government, and hence a bit of a catch for the Scottish-Irish Ogilvy) there was, as usual, research to be done.

Consumer research demonstrated that what the European consumers wanted to see in America was – surprise – what they didn't have at home: the great American stereotypes of skyscrapers, the Grand Canyon, Mississippi river-boats, cowboys, Indians and rodeos. Again, to the surprise of hardly anybody, what they feared most was the cost of living in America, a fear no doubt engendered in part by the gaudy big spenders encountered on their own shores.

Burrowing away, the media researchers established that the best buy for the money (which was strictly limited, for tourist advertising budgets, being government controlled, are rarely lavish) was the newspaper, and since the American image of big-ness required, as it were, wide open spaces in which to express itself, whole pages were recommended – 'blockbusters', as Ogilvy calls them – in a few selected papers reaching an audience disposing of enough of the ready to be able to contemplate a week or two in America. The papers chosen were *The Times*, *Guardian* and *Telegraph* in England, *Figaro* and *Le Monde* in France, and the *Frankfurter Allgemeine Zeitung* and *Die Welt am Sontag* in Germany. It was to be a black and white keyboard on which I would play my New World Symphony.

These cogently argued propositions were totally ignored, at least at the beginning. Ogilvy had won the account with 'Ogilvy' layouts. And for Ogilvy, who had become a specialist in the field, tourist advertising demanded colour and superb photography – and hence magazines. For the Puerto Rico campaign Ogilvy had used photographers of the calibre of Tom Hollyman, Elliott Erwitt and Burt Glinn (these last two members of Magnum). The employment of such 'editorial' photographers had its origins in a curious phenomenon cursed with the unlovely name of 'scrap art'.

Scrap art consisted of compelling photographs on any subject under the sun torn out of magazines and books specially purchased for the purpose. Ogilvy, who was no doubt drawn to this procedure by some private passion, had given it a sophisticated structure within the agency and liked to boast that OBM 's scrap art collection was the most complete in the world, not excluding the basements of the Prada and the Louvre. Scrap art now occupied a whole department of the agency, under the supervision of Billie Sutter, a woman of charm, intelligence and Grecian beauty.

When an art director had a campaign to prepare he came to see Billie and explained the kind of mood or climate he wished to convey with his illustration. She then prepared a portfolio of appropriate scrap art and the chosen picture, blown up or reduced if necessary, would be pasted down on cardboard with a space left for the headline and copy. This photo was not meant to be definitive. Its function was to demonstrate to the client, in a way that an art director's rough sketch could not, the genre and quality desired for the final photo.

In the case of our tourist campaign, Ogilvy claimed that all the great photos of America had already been taken and that reproduction rights, for such a noble cause, could be easily obtained, and at less cost than employing a leading photographer to wander around the nation. So Bill Binzen, pillaging Billie Sutter's hoard and his own memory, chose the pictures and stuck them down, David Ogilvy, Junius Edwards, Don deLillo, a girl called Doris Lockhart who is now Mrs Charles Saatchi, and I wrote headlines and subheads which Borgie set in type; and the boys in the bull-pen assembled 125 cardboard-mounted, cellophane-wrapped, double-page colour magazine layouts.

The effect was dazzling. Ogilvy, ever, as we have noted, the showman, commandeered the boardroom and mounted a two-week exhibition. I was invited to address the Senior Vice-Presidents on the preparation of the Great Works and by the skin of my teeth managed not to. Every employee was adjured to go and bask in the glow emanating from the massed layouts. Clients were invited for lunch and a post-prandial tour.

I flew with the huge pile of advertisements to London, Paris and Frankfurt and presented them to the awed staffs of our three collaborating agencies. The praise elicited by this flying exhibition was merited. The advertisments were enticing, lavish, mouth-watering. They attracted by the force of the photography. They compelled readership of the crisply written copy.

There was only one snag. Not one of them was usable and not one of them was ever used. For not one of them could be justified by the research the agency was obliged to present to the client. They had, however, served a purpose: they had enabled us to win the account for Germany, a valuable part of the budget which had not yet been assigned. They had also served to let our European collaborators know just what sort of chaps they would be dealing with. Yes sir.

So we started all over again, and produced just four black-and-white advertisements to run as full-pages in the selected newspapers. At the top of each was a narrow horizontal photo: the skyscrapers of Manhattan at night, a cowboy on a ridge with a mesa backdrop, a steamboat, last of the line, on the Mississippi.

The copy was long, factual, informative – about 1500 words of it. Under headlines like, WHAT TO SEE IN THE USA – IF YOU'VE ONLY GOT THREE WEEKS, ran subheads like:

For £35 a week you can see New York, Washington, San Francisco. You can visit Niagara Falls, see the Rockies from the glass domed car of a luxurious train, spend a week on a ranch, have more fun than a barrel of monkeys – and dine out on the experience for the rest of your life.

As prose, it wasn't Gibbon or Sir Thomas Browne, but it did the trick.

The famous Fairfax Cone, golden oldie and head of Foote, Cone and Belding, wrote a letter to Ogilvy:

> I would like to congratulate you all on the U.S. Travel Service advertisements.
>
> What you have done is down to earth and tells people what I am sure they want to know about travelling in the U.S., and what they should see and what it should cost.
>
> I used to write travel advertising and I think I have some knowledge of it. This is the kind I used to try to make.

We took the stuff down to Washington, Ogilvy's old home in his Intelligence and polling days, to present it to Luther Hodges, Secretary of Commerce. After the meeting we had a beer at the station, a concession from Ogilvy, who loathes bars. Then he took the night train to Chicago ('One pill and I sleep like a log') and I went down to Chesapeake Bay to see how things were with Judy Hyun, *née* Kirkland, adopted Douglas, and late of Paris and Cannes.

Brides are supposed to be radiant, and so are new mothers. Judy cashed in on both traditions. Her father's house was a nice house, but it wasn't the Château Garibondy. Budweiser took the place of Bordeaux with dinner. It must have been the servants' day off. Peter was away too, back in New York, or more accurately, at Idlewild where, in the metallic grey uniform of TWA, the Parisian poet shepherded passengers from the Orient. Mia, their daughter, in whom the twain triumphantly met, played at my feet in sweet oblivion of time or place and the changes they can bring, for rich or for poor, for better or for worse.

I flew the drinkless, foodless, sexless shuttle back to La Guardia with the other brief-cased automatons, thinking in the turbulence turbulent thoughts, striking the occasional glancing blow at truth, catching the odd snatch of wisdom on the wing.

I was flying again soon, on a second Grand Tour of Europe, to show our black and white campaign. As I packed my bag for my return flight in the Crillon in Paris, a letter arrived from David Ogilvy:

> Dear Charles,
> I congratulate you on sustaining the pace and pressure of the USTS account for the last five months.
> Baptism by fire.
> I hope that your spirits and your nerves are being restored in Europe.
> When you get back we will work out ways and means to get the account organised on a more *liveable* basis.
> Yours ever,
David

Nice to know that someone cares.

Chapter 31

There was a Frenchman, an Englishman, a Hungarian and a Swiss, and they had one thing in common. They were all practitioners of a medium – photography – which had recently been liberated by the invention by Leica of the 35-mm camera. When the four men founded a co-operative of photojournalists in Paris after the war it seemed natural to them to toast the new venture in champagne. After a glass or two of the stuff, it seemed perfectly logical to name the new venture Magnum Photos.

In those pre-television days when, for the non-picturegoer, magazines were the only source of news in pictures, the agency thrived. The four founder-owners, Henri Cartier-Bresson, George Rodgers, Robert Capa and Werner Bischof, soon opened offices in Paris and New York whose function was to seek out assignments for the photographers and to take care of distribution, finance and the invaluable archives. They also recruited like-minded younger photographers who, as the four founders did, agreed to pay back almost half their earnings to maintain the offices and pay their employees. They elected their own officers at annual general meetings held alternately in Paris and New York.

There was no credo, no written philosophy, to guide the new members of Magnum. But each new recruit was proposed by an existing member and his work, views, personality and general suitability to this curious group of independents assessed by all the members before he was voted into the group. To be invited to become a member of Magnum was, and is, regarded as the highest honour that can be conferred on a reporting photographer.

241

The man through whom I became a familiar of this privileged élite was himself a protégé of the acknowledged master, Cartier-Bresson. I met Elliott Erwitt in Bill Binzen's office during my first sojourn at Ogilvy, Benson and Mather. He had recently taken a photograph for the Puerto Rican tourist campaign which has become an advertising classic. It is a colour photo, lit by Vermeer, of Pablo Casals' cello leaning against an upright chair in an otherwise empty room.

Ogilvy maintains that the undeniable power of this calm picture is the result of a stroke of genius: by leaving Casals out of the shot a tension is created and the viewer, perhaps unconsciously, wonders if the great man has just left the room, or is perhaps about to enter it. While I yield to none in my admiration for Erwitt's genius, the facts behind the taking of the picture suggest quite otherwise (unless of course genius – as it may well be – is an infinite capacity for taking advantage of accidents.).

Erwitt and the copywriter on the account – Cliff Field, the brilliant English burbler – had been sent to Puerto Rico to explore various agreed themes chosen to trade up, as they say, the lowly image of that exploited island: a debutante ball, a ballet performance, and the country's chief claim to culture on an international scale, the Spanish refugee Casals.

An appointment was made with the Master, but when the time came for shooting he was, unfortunately, indisposed. Faced with the prospect of flying back to New York without a picture, Erwitt, turning, as the poet so neatly puts it, his necessity to glorious gain, suggested that he should take, *faute de mieux*, a Casals picture without Casals but with his cello. This inspiration, however, met another snag. Casals, it seemed, was not too keen to let a bunch of advertising people fool around in his absence with the precious instrument. A cello was, therefore, rented. Thus the final picture, so evocative of the great artist in his exile, is totally false – and yet totally true, for, as we know, the poet lies in order to tell the truth.

The poet in question, Elliott Erwitt, was a man of about my own age and about my height – just about right, in sum. He was slim, quiet, handsome with black hair brushed straight back, like a wavy-haired Kafka. He had the fine eyes, faintly startled and at the same time concerned and not a little wary, of Gerard Philippe – eyes that conveyed, in about equal proportions, kindness and irony. He was *malicieux*, in the unpejorative French sense. The nose was straight and fine and the teeth were Californian surfer white. His mouth had that gently fixed faint smile you see on the faces of the more sensitive among us: Tessimond had it, Ewart has it. His jaw was firm and lean. He looked like a rich man's Eddie Fisher. He dressed, as Magnum photographers tend to, in good but unplaceable everyman clothes: greyish tweed jacket, shirt, tie unremarkable, grey trousers, correct in any country, belonging, somehow, to none. Sartorially at least, Magnum has no homeland.

There may well be other Jewish Buddhist priests, but Elliott's father, Boris, is the only one I know. He had eloped from Odessa, to the chagrin of both families, with the White Russian daughter of a wealthy manufacturer and had arrived, by way of Rome, in Paris where Elliott, their only child, was born in the American Hospital. Returning to Rome, his father became a professor of science at the University but, with fascism becoming fashionable, the family moved to America, where the professor took to the road with a snappy line in wrist watches. Elliott attended high school and art school in Los Angeles and went to work in the dark room of a Hollywood still studio, developing and printing glossy pictures of stars for promotional purposes.

Elliott was separated from his first wife (who appears in some of Elliott's most famous pictures, reproduced in *The Family of Man*) and lived now with a Rio-based blonde Austrian model called Okky Offerhaus.

One evening I invited Elliott, who was temporarily Okky-less, to join Borgie Baton and Bill and Gail Binzen, my protégé couple, for drinks and dinner. Elliott, a man who knows me as well as anybody, telephoned before the party to say that a girl had arrived in his care, sent from Rio by the absent Okky. Could he bring her along? He added, thoughtfully, 'I can't be sure, but I think she might just be right for you.' She was.

She came into my life and my apartment shyly, always a good sign. She was young and fresh and slim, poised in the unsophisticated way of children and − foretaste of her unfailing tact − just the right height for me. Her hair was light chestnut and straight not in the way straight hair is but with the body of hair that would be wavy if it hadn't been dried straight. Her eyebrows and her eyes were finely drawn and her look was warmly brown and candid. Her nose was straight and a breath too long and her lips not plump but well-formed.

She had what are usually referred to as good bones, the so-called secret of photogeneity. She would weather well, the youth shining through the old. She was willowy, the legs beautiful in an under-stated way, the shoulders held forward and slightly hunched, as if from suppressed eagerness. In a trenchcoat she would be Garbo's Ninotchka, contained and dignified, with, behind the eyes, a warmth that had the scope for laughter and also tenderness and care. Her name, according to Elliott, who had been briefed, was Patricia and, *plus loin*, Hermes. The gods had been kind, to her and to me.

Although I am by nature, or adaptation, almost actively passive, it was I who made the early running, or walking, in our relationship. She allowed me to do so, not from attraction but for diversion, for her mind, if not her heart, was still in Rio de Janeiro where her first and only boy-friend (every girl I ever met has had only one boy-friend, but in this case it happened to be true) had failed her. He was, I gathered, a mother-dominated architect and film designer who could not be brought to the point of marrying her. Well, I can see how that might be....

So, in order to distract the distracted maiden, if you follow me, and perhaps also to make something interesting out of a suitor without much inherent interest, I pitched into my Svengali, or is it Pygmalion, act again. Just as it is very hard to eat badly in France, so, if you are a woman, it is difficult to dress badly. The same cannot be said for America. However, through diligent research and close observation, I discovered, for example, that Messrs B. Altman, of Fifth Avenue, were the sole, as it were, importers of the footwork of a new young French designer called Charles Jourdan, and I rushed Patricia over there hot-foot. Then there was a small shop on Madison in the Fifties that sold French sweaters and swimsuits and underwear from Dior and Lejaby and so on. And the French newsagent on Rockefeller Plaza helped one to keep up to date with what the girls were wearing in *Elle* and *Marie Claire*.

And since I was working my way at the time through that indispensable classic, *L'Art Culinaire Français*, we were obliged to spend a good deal of time and not a little money in havens like Bloomingdale's delicatessen and a small cheese shop, run by a French family, which I had discovered around the corner from Alexander's department store on Lexington. So Patricia, who had known only America and Brazil, which is admittedly quite a bit of desirable freehold, now discovered France in mid-town Manhattan.

That first winter, as a kind of acclimatisation for Patricia, we flew down the Caribbean to France, to the island of Guadeloupe and her first sight of uniformed French *douaniers* (in a Rousseau jungle) and *flics*. We stayed at the Fort Royal – now, like most places, a Club Mediterranée – and swam in the blood-warm, glass-clear sea. And, flashing my French driving licence, we rented a Renault and explored the interior and found a snack bar run by a nostalgic Parisienne who had decorated the place with a map of the Metro. Here in the jungle the familiar names brought back the too warm air, the tiled corridors and the smell of hot metal: Montparnasse-Bienvenue! Kremlin-Bicêtre! Chaussé-D'Antin! Menilmontant!

Back in New York, Patricia enrolled for a course in French. For once, I was making plans.

Chapter 32

As the glamour of my trans-Atlantic translation wore off, and I became more and more enmeshed in the routine mechanics of the agency, that morning sickness that I share with pregnant women returned once more. Eased out from under the warm wing of David Ogilvy, my mentor who, having delegated this piece of business, had other things to attend to, I found myself responsible to others for whom I had less regard, or less respect. Humanly as well as professionally concerned at my increasingly late arrival at the office (vomiting, you will appreciate, adding to the time needed for one's morning ablutions), Ogilvy felt obliged to send, to my home, a four-page, handwritten letter. The envelope, forebodingly, was marked 'Private and Confidential' and the letter bore the inscription, in blaring red, 'BURN!' I later decided that this, which I had at first taken to be an imprecation, was a hangover from Ogilvy's days in Intelligence.

The letter was full of kind concern. He pointed out, with great tact, that he could not be expected to devote a disproportionate amount of his time to an account that, prestigious though it undoubtedly was, represented a tiny percentage of the agency's total billing; and that if I had problems, professional or otherwise, I could always discuss them with one of my superiors – the estimable Jock Elliott, for example (today head of the agency). He noted gently in passing that the need for a 9 o'clock start was 'a fact of corporate life' (a phrase in itself guaranteed to induce a spasm or two in my gastric regions) and that he himself had found, early in his career, that late arrival was 'self-destructive' (whereas I found that going to the office at all was killing me).

Still and all, it was a nice, thoughtful letter. Few, it occured to me, were the presidents in this harsh world of advertising who would spend the time and take the trouble to communicate in such a human and apparently caring way with just one, and by no means the most important, among hundred of employees.

Feeling that some sort of response was required, I went to see Ogilvy in his corner office. On the Fifth Avenue side, crisp New York light was cleanly filtered by filmy nylon. On the opposite wall, work in progress in the form of flimsy roughs was pinned to a cork board that covered the whole surface down to a waist-level ledge on which a mounted layout or two stood. Seated beside me on the couch in front of the low table, he served me tea and biscuits brought by Bridie, the Irish maid.

Seeking to explain my side of things, just as if I understood them, I burbled on a bit about the workings of the unconscious, the conflict between the desire for liberty and the need to earn a living, and such bromides, to use a favourite word of Ogilvy's. Suddenly I became aware that this last-named had vanished from my side. Lifting my gaze in mid-monologue from what had been a singularly unresponsive carpet, I saw that Ogilvy had covered the space from sofa to coffee table in one bound and now stood, feet on marble table-top, looming above me with his arms stretched up towards the ceiling.

As I gazed, speechless – as who would not be, confronted with such a *tableau vivant* – Ogilvy lowered his arms to a position that might be assumed by a child at a pool's edge learning to dive. His knees began to tremble in a sort of strip-cartoon symbolism of fear.

'Your trouble is,' he said, in his quietly urgent voice, 'that you are standing here, at a level below your true abilities, looking at the gulf before you and saying, "Ooh dear, if I jump I might fall in!" '

Then he straightened, turned half-right, and vaulted upwards and outwards, in a leap only slightly below the standard required for Olympic qualification, to land on the waist-high shelf, more accustomed to supporting layouts than agency presidents.

'You are down there,' he declaimed, pointing dramatically towards the innocent coffee table, 'and you should be up here!'

Brooding on Ogilvy's diagnosis, and with my dawn nausea still going strong, I decided to see a doctor. Dave McCall gave me the name of his, a Dr Peters, of Park Avenue. Nothing but the best, I always say. I trotted along to his office and gave the kindly fellow a quick run-down on my vomiting, up-tightness, indigestion and other exciting items from my medical check-list (items that I now might recognise as the banal symptoms of clinical depression; but you live and learn, that is, if you live).

Sizing me up with a glance – the kind of glance that sets you back twenty-five bucks – this medico said that what I needed was to go and see a colleague of his, name of Dr McKinney, who practised psychiatry just up the block. 'Go see him,' he said, intriguingly. 'You'll find he's quite a character. If, uh, you don't get along with him, and some don't, let me know and we'll try something else.'

Well, St George's Psychiatric Unit had tried, and persumably failed. At least I wasn't in as bad shape as the poet Tessimond, having his noddle zapped with a few thousand volts by the ECT freaks at St Thomas's. I'd give it a whirl. I was born free, and had nothing to lose but my brains.

At the startling hour of 8.30, showered, breakfasted and vomited (and amazed at the number of people who had also decided to rise early that morning), I took my psyche along to meet Dr John McKinney, Park Avenue analyst and, like Freud, former neurosurgeon. The doctor's office, or consulting rooms, adjoined his apartment, six floors up in one of those metal-window-framed, faceless brick blocks you get in the East Seventies between Park and Lex. I was in sunny mood as I rode the elevator. After all, this beat going to the office. Almost anything did.

A pleasant nurse led me through a small reception lobby into a room which was shut off from the sky, or the neighbours, by a

248

lowered venetian blind. A heavy, senatorial desk stood under the window. Along one wall was a couch on which I sat, presenting my left profile to the empty, high-backed, cloth-covered armchair that stood at an angle between couch and desk. On the wall across from me hung a Steinberg diploma that reassured me that Dr John C. McKinney was a paid-up member of the American Psychoanalytical Society. Moored alongside was a large photograph of a ship's officers, in Pacific whites, aboard some dreadnought. So this was going to be a naval encounter.

As I was contemplating this marine view, the door to my right, which led to the small lobby and, beyond, the wardroom, opened and a tall, bald, pink-faced man of about seventy, looking like an extravert P. G. Wodehouse, shuffled eagerly into the room, large hand extended. His progress recalled that of Boris Karloff, or perhaps I mean Lon Chaney Jr, in *Frankenstein* – the result, I concluded, of his glasses, whose lenses, thick as bottle-bottoms, tripled the size of his sea-going blue eyes. The lenses acted like blinkers, so that he saw only what was in front of him and was constrained to walk by pushing one foot in front of the other in the way one might if one were negotiating a tricky mountain path at night.

He aimed accurately enough for me, shook my hand, gave me a warm smile as if he had plenty more at home and said, 'Hi there. John McKinney.'Assuming that he had a pretty shrewd idea of who I might be I remained silent and, finding little of moment to say, contrived to remain so for the next fifty minutes – making my silence, at a dollar a minute, almost golden.

Dr McKinney lowered his large but stylish frame (like one of Saxon's characters in the *New Yorker*) into the armchair, unbuttoned the two buttons of his navy (of course) blue, lightweight Brooks Brothers suit, placed his large pink hands on his knees as if he were sitting for Graham Sutherland, and beamed his lenses like a cruiser's searchlights on my left profile.

'Well, what can I do for you, young fella?' Dr McKinney asked in a voice that was a sort of kindly bark, of the style favoured by the white-haired judge in western movies.

I sketched in briefly the symptoms I had laid out for Dr Peter's scrutiny.

'Well, why d'ya think you can't sleep an' all?'

The content may have been according to the book but the form was a long way from Vienna, Europe.

I mumbled. Our dialogue, descending from its peak of desultoriness, fell into a black hole of silence, a place that felt like home to me.

'Thing is,' said Dr McKinney, after a long, expensive pause, 'what we like to do is get people talking, y'see. Matter of fact, we can't get you talking, don't see how we can help you much!'

The silence I was doling out so generously was interrupted by the telephone on the noble desk.

'Oh hi,' said Dr McKinney into the receiver, which accepted the message and passed it on. 'Yeah, wanted to talk to you about my portfolio. Ain't looked at it in a while. Yeah. Right. Oh, you do....'

The chat went on for a good five dollars, the warm bark occasionally interrupted by a duck on the other end of the line. After a while the doctor hung up, beamed in again on my left profile and said, 'Sorry about that, Charles. My broker. Those scallywags are hard to get hold of. Got to catch them when you can.'

I doled out some more expensive silence, like a shuffle-footed boy before a stern but understanding headmaster who wants him for his own sake to confess to some sin he hasn't committed, or doesn't know he has.

'Now we got ways we can help people to talk,' said the patient Dr McKinney to his patient. 'So if you agree, next time you come and see me, we'll just give you a little shot and that'll loosen you up a bit and then maybe we can get along a little faster.'

I nodded and got up to leave. Dr McKinney rose, back of the head, shoulders and heels in a straight line, as if he was about to have his height measured, and did his hearty shuffle to the desk. Fishing in a drawer, he peered to make sure he had found what he wanted.

'Here,' he said, 'Want you to take this and have a good look at it from time to time. 'Cause that's what it's all about.'

I glanced at the object. It was a black and white picture postcard of a polar bear hugging its cub.

'Come'n see me now,' barked Dr McKinney warmly, shuffling and beaming me out of the door.

Out in the lobby an elegant and beautiful woman sat, looking at a magazine and looking about two million dollars. The upright doctor leaned back a little farther and spread his practiced hands in welcome.

'Why Gloria! Mighty snappy boots you got there. C'mon in, won't ya!'

Downstairs in the street a grey-green Bentley waited, grey-green uniformed chauffeur at the wheel. It became a familiar sight over the next year or so as, in a methedrine glow, I handed over Dr McKinney for the next fifty minute slot to Gloria Vanderbilt, who could better afford it than I.

Chapter 33

Advertising, like other trades, boasted its Great Men. The golden oldies were represented by Stanley Resor. In the next age group came Fairfax Cone, a founder of Foote, Cone and Belding and a champion of literacy in advertising, and Leo Burnett, the Chicago agency that opened up Marlboro Country to what had been a woman's cigarette.

Younger than these men was Bill Bernbach, of the hot shop Doyle Dane Bernbach, creator of the hand-rubbing, self-pitying school of advertising exemplified by such headlines and slogans as 'Think small' and 'Lemon' for Volkswagen, 'We must be doing something right' for Reingold beer and 'You don't have to be Jewish to enjoy Levy's rye bread'.

In the Bernbach generation there was, of course, David Ogilvy. There was also his brother-in-law, a fellow by the name of Rosser Reeves, who became chairman of Ted Bates, an agency with a reputation for rough and tough 'hard sell' – a quaint coinage of the time. Reeves had published a book which revealed to an astonished world that the secret of successful advertising was the isolation of what he called the USP, or Unique Selling Proposition. Every product, it seemed, had one of these. All you had to do was winkle it out and ram it down the throat of the public by dint of repetition. It is quite possible that it was his relentless advertising of Anadin that gave people the headache that the product purported to cure.

The USP, you will have deduced, was nothing more than Ogilvy's Brand Image wearing a cloth cap and speaking out of the corner of its mouth. It would hardly be surprising if the two men had not hit upon the same fruitful theme, for as beginners in the business they shared an apartment. Though rivals in philosophic conception and, later, in fame, the two men remained friends, a fact which was to cause me no little embarrassment, for when eventually I left David Ogilvy it was at the behest, nay, insistence, of his old room-mate.

A kindly Frenchman called Pierre Garai who was a fellow-copywriter at OBM invited me one evening to share a Ricard at the bar of the Marmiton, across from the office. Ted Bates, he told me, had recently acquired an agency in Paris – AFP, or Agence Française de Propagande. Earlier, Bates had established a London base by purchasing the highly successful agency founded by John Hobson, an account executive, and John Metcalf, a copywriter who also reviewed books for the heavier Sunday papers. Impressed by the work in tandem of these two, Rosser Reeves was now looking for a creative partner for the Frenchman, Armand de Malherbe, who was now head of the new agency.

Garai had been offered the job and had turned it down: he had an American wife, and his roots were now here. Would I be interested? Well, yes. After all, it would hardly be a step down, or anyway, one small step, as the NASA scriptwriter put it. Bates was a solid agency. Reeves was a celebrity, like Ogilvy. I would be joint head of a new joint. I would be back in Paris, this time with American prestige and dollars behind me. And I would maintain my ties with New York – for I had discovered that although in New York I was nostalgic for Paris, in Paris I missed New York. Slice it where you will, the thing looked good.

The next week I was seated at 'the Ted Bates table' in one of those false-French, expense account restaurants that abound in mid-town Manhattan. Opposite me at the dais-mounted table, looking down at the other expense account junketers and with a good sight-line to the door, was Rosser Reeves, Chairman of the Ted Bates Company. If you compared this to lunching with David Ogilvy it was rather like swapping a star performance of the Royal Shakespeare Company for a top-of-the-bill show at Caesar's Palace.

253

Rosser Reeves's face, which in a kidnapping crisis could be used as a double for that of President Andreotti of Italy, wore that look of patently false surprise, of innocent bafflement, that might be adopted by a polished stand-up comedian attempting unconvincingly to convince an audience laughing at a *double entendre* that it was the other, purer, meaning that he had intended. Below thick black hair brushed flatly back, the eyes, behind double-glazed glasses, were twinkling, watchful but not unkind, and the thinnish mouth below the fine straight nose seemed poised to laugh. When he spoke, this mouth, pulling down at one corner, resembled that of an old lag or ventriloquist, so that Reeves talking to you across a table seemed to be projecting his voice to someone seated beside him. It was a face that never seemed to have suffered or even doubted; a sensitive, intelligent face that shone with that assurance that success brings. Alert as a beacon on top of the tall, well-built, city-suited body, it was the face of a hard American businessman with a soft American heart.

There lurked behind the polish of Reeves a capacity for aggressiveness you do not find in Ogilvy; and there was an aggressiveness, I discovered, about Ted Bates that I had not found at OBM. For this super-salesman, whose greatest satisfaction, one might guess, would come from selling anything to anybody, had little trouble in persuading me that my best interest lay in leaving Ogilvy to join him for a few months' indoctrination in New York before returning to Paris as one of the two heads of AFP/Ted Bates. I would start at 30,000 dollars a year. Hell, it would have to do.

I composed a soapy letter to David Ogilvy, well-tailored for the consumer, I presume, for readers anxious not to miss a second of this thrilling drama will find it reproduced in his memoirs (page 27, English edition), where he uses it as a slippery platform from which to sermonize about those 'poor fellows' who, misguided enough to leave his *atelier*, 'find that their paradise is lost'. There's something in that.

His reply was reassuring:

Dear Charles,

Thank you for your letter. It has given me great comfort. I hope
things go swimmingly for you at Bates. A splendid opportunity.

Yours ever,
David

All, it seemed, was at peace between us. That's the way
everybody felt after Munich, too, in 1939.

666 Fifth Avenue was variously known to New Yorkers as the
sick, sick, sick building, the package the Seagram building came
in, and the world's largest urinal. This last image owed its
dubious inspiration to the presence, in the heavily pillared arcade
entrance, of a non-stop fountain of quite riveting ugliness. I felt as
miserable going to work in this place as I would wearing a cast-
off suit bought from the YMCA.

To the amazement of many, the agency had recently acquired
the Cunard account, though some would have maintained that
the victory went well with the agency's somewhat piratic
reputation. It was concluded by the management that, the two
Queens being, as it were, noble subjects, and the target audience,
as they say, being the upper-crust executive, the ideal creative
man to put on the job would be a British copywriter, preferably
with some grounding in the Ogilvy style. It could have been
worse. It could have been Wonderloaf, which builds healthy
bodies seven ways.

Apart from a 'Hi Chuck!' here, or a 'Nice to have you with us,
Charlie' there, I was left alone to mull over the approved 'copy
strategy'. The advertisements, if I could think of any, were to run
as whole pages (Ogilvy blockbusters) in the *New York Times*, the
Herald Tribune (still a New York paper) and the *Wall Street
Journal* and in double pages in colour in the *New Yorker*, these
being required reading for top executives – the target audience for
the ads. The fact that this select group included, by definition, the
leading men in the New York advertising industry did not
impinge upon my conscious as having any great significance, so
that I was quite unprepared for the rather unfortunate
consequences of the campaign. This brou-ha-ha was hurried

255

along by the arrival of Junius Edwards, my friend at Ogilvy, to join me as my assistant.

This move, however, was not so easily accomplished, for not only did Bates already possess its token black but the fellow was a copywriter too. But because of the way things were developing on the Cunard account, my wish at the time was Rosser Reeves' command, and my wish was that Junius should be my assistant. To envious mutterings about Hennessy and his shadow, Junius joined me at Ted Bates, and one more foolish fellow had quit the paradise of Ogilvy's *atelier*.

The art director assigned to the Cunard account was called Joe Gauss. Like most art directors anywhere he was a pleasant, calm, quiet-spoken and courteous man. He was of German origin and his thick, almost blond wavy hair and handsome profile reminded one of Werner von Braun, who was also constantly reminding one of Werner von Braun.

Joe had spent most of his career at Ted Bates, a fact which caused a certain amount of friction between us when he began to lay out my copy in traditional Bates style, i.e. and viz., with punchy, sock 'em typefaces, addy tricks, explosions and such doodahs. Since the stuff I had written was long, factual, almost journalistic in style, I had to persuade the good and patient Joe that what we needed was a sober, 'editorial' kind of layout, full of authority and free from gimmicks.

The friction gradually changed to non-friction. After prolonged and severe internal struggle, Joe saw the light and began bursting into my office with an enthusiasm that almost had me removing my feet from my desk, brandishing roughs that he presented with the curious but compelling expression, 'It's a bitch, Charles! It's a bitch on wheels!' What we now had, as was apparent to the informed eye — and there were a lot of them about on Madison Avenue — was a piece of typically Ogilvy copy in a typically Ogilvy layout. And that's where the trouble started.

Reeves, though, gave no sign that things were anything but dandy. *Au contraire*. Little *billets doux* began to flutter into my office. The first note, however, struck an ominous note.

From: R O S S E R R E E V E S   19 Feb. 1963
To: Mr Charles Hennessy
Charles,
I think one of the best things that ever happened to the Bates
agency was you.

    I hear the Paris agency is getting into more and more trouble and
we may lose you to our Gallic friends ... but I hope not.

                                                  R.

Next came this:

From: R O S S E R R E E V E S   7 March 1963
Route: Mr Bates, Mr Reeves
Ted,
Read the last four paragraphs of Charles Hennessy's copy.
    We have a poet in our ranks.

On this simple paean the busy Ted Bates had scrawled 'Great!'
which, as we have noted, is merely the American for 'Good!'

Finding his stride now, Reeves swiftly followed that with this:

Charles,
I think you are a vast addition to our creative staff. I want to talk to
you about whither!

                                                  R.

A theme was beginning to emerge. What our author needed
now was a good strong climax. Trust old Rosser. Returning
thankfully to my office from a meeting one Friday afternoon I
found scrawled on the top sheet of my writing pad these words:

Charles –
Remind me next week to make you a Vice-President.

                                        Rosser

As I sat riveted before this gem the phone rang. It was Rosser
Reeves' secretary, telling me that Rosser had called up from
downstairs to say that if I was still there he'd like me to join him.
The really interesting thing about this message was that
'downstairs' meant the local, which was the bar of '21', around
the corner from 666 Fifth Avenue. I could use a drink.

I found Rosser at the bar, raising elbows with Jerry Gury, a nattily dressed man with cuff-links like die-stamps, who was the creative director of the agency and thus ostensibly my superior (with my kind of effortless inferiority, most people are). I stood awkwardly between them, for they were a drink or so ahead of me and hanging loose, while the barman worked at one of those fearsome, 'Hit me, Mario' American drinks.

I took a fast gulp of the brew, which was a good move, for Rosser had adopted the stance of a king about to confer an accolade upon some humble courtier. The fellow he had in mind, it turned out, was me. In his rich, deep, room-filling voice, trembling with controlled emotion, he declared that not only was I henceforth a Vice-President of the Ted Bates agency but that, as a mark of that elevation, my salary would be doubled, effective now. I would, unfortunately, have to wait until Monday to receive the emblem of my new status: the key to the executive washroom.

I felt, not for the first time in my life, like a character in a rather bad book. Suddenly I longed for the flat that happened to be home this year, and for the sweet sane decency of Patricia. The brief ceremony over, my two fellow-officers decided to rent a Carey Cadillac to cruise them to dinner and then home. I made, as they say, my excuses and walked, in more of a daze than they, back towards 64th Street, twice as rich as I had been when I left it that morning, newly ennobled, and feeling just faintly sick, sick, sick.

The Cunard blockbusters dominated, which was the whole idea, the city's newspapers, and since these were the morning and evening pabulum of the commuters on the New York and New Haven Railroad they were read, all three thousand words of them, by my fellow-practitioners. We had put it on the train, and it had got off at Westport.

Advertising Age, the paper of our trade, reproduced the first advertisement under the headline, 'When is an Ogilvy ad not an Ogilvy ad?' My copy was subjected to a textual analysis that would not have shamed F. R. Leavis; my prose was given a thorough Barthes. And from the heart of Paradise Lost into the shaded corner office of Rosser Reeves came the first angry letter from David Ogilvy. Unforgivable things were said about rapscallions who perpetrated plagiarism. Alas for Ogilvy, there is no copyright in copywriting.

The battle, once joined, raged for weeks. A Reeves reply, even with his memorable prose style, failed to mollify the angry Ogilvy, who saw himself as a man betrayed. Further protests from him were passed on to me, accompanied by the Reeves scrawl. 'Charles – ,' he wrote, 'David is still doing a slow burn. Please draft a reply.' At OBM I had drafted letters for Ogilvy. Now I wrote to him as Reeves' hired scribe, which of course, although a Vice-President, is what I was.

This houha bothered me, but what bothered me more, as the flattering notes continued to arrive from Rosser, was that he had a plan and that plan was for me to stay in New York. I, on the other hand, had no plan, but if I had had a plan that would not have been it. Confirming this suspicion, in a roundabout way, Reeves called me into his office one day and said, 'Charles, Armand's acting difficult. I want you to go have lunch with him Sunday.'

I took the overnight Air France flight to break *baguette* with Monsieur de Malherbe but even through the haze of time-zone fatigue it became clear to me that if ever there was a Frenchman who felt absolutely no pressing desire to share his newly won power with some interloping Anglo-Saxon imposed on him by head office, this Frenchman was that Frenchman. The lunch though, at Prunier Traktir on the Avenue Victor Hugo, was, in Ogilvy's phrase, a great comfort to me as I took the afternoon plane back and returned once more to the social round, the common task in New York. But the glazed stare of the Prunier oysters was doing its devil's work in my unconscious. *L'appétit vient en mangeant* – and I wanted more of the same.

Chapter 34

Twice a week now, at what was dawn to me, I took the above-mentioned unconscious for a work-out at the hands of Dr John McKinney, the bluff old sea-dog of the psychoanalytic world, voyaging bravely into the uncharted deep, delving daily in Ernest Jones' locker. Twice a week I sat on his couch, took off my jacket and rolled up my sleeve for my morning fix.

The ritual was unchanging. Dr McKinney did his looming shuffle towards me from the desk, first with the red rubber tube that he tied around my upper arm, peering with jumbo eyes behind his stamp-collector's lenses, then with the alcohol-soaked wad of cotton that chilled the instep of my elbow. Next came the smart tap with two old dry fingers to raise the vein. Then he examined the syringe against the lamp beside his chair, pressing the plunger slightly to expel the air. Pop goes the needle into the turgid vein, ping goes the rubber tube as he flips the knot and it falls aside, and squish goes the plunger as the blue methedrine joins my red and white corpuscles for the round trip. 'There y'go,' said Dr McKinney, replacing the needle with a dry wad of cotton and bending my arm over it; and there I went.

Within three seconds, par for the course, my heart began to race, warmth flushed my throat, my head cleared of morning mists, a brief feeling of nausea swayed me and then went away, leaving me for too short a while in that state of benign, almost loving calm, of poised serenity, of warm detachment, of freedom from conflict, hate or envy for which someone invented the word euphoria but which may be, for all I know, the happy state of most people most of the time.

260

The flush in my throat moved out to uncrank my tongue and for fifty minutes, which is all you got of the hour you bought, I chatted happily and easily while the good doctor listened with great care, upright in his upright chair, moving only occasionally to lean forward and touch my forearm in a gesture of approval or support.

Topics were interestingly varied. There was Marilyn Monroe's mysterious death, for instance.

'Yeah!' Dr McKinney said. 'You see about that in the paper? You know, she used to remind me a lot of you, young fella.' He didn't explain that. They don't have to, even at a dollar a minute.

Civil rights was in the papers too. 'See them nigras are getting uppity again,' said the doctor, thoughtfully.

Once he brought me a speech that Ogilvy had made to the New York Hibernian Society, or some such crowd. He seemed tickled to have made the acquaintance of this subject of some of our chats. He seemed impressed by the fella, though it was his considered opinion that most advertising men were scallywags. He asked me what I thought about my colleagues and I said that sometimes I felt superior to them, and sometimes inferior. Dr McKinney leaned forward and put his hand on my arm, eyes big and milky blue.

'Ask me,' he said, 'you're way superior! Scallywags,' he added, mildly.

Encouraged by Dr McKinney's warm, spontaneous and constant approval of almost everything about me, I mentioned one morning that I kept an occasional notebook of Great Thoughts. This news excited him and he said, suppose I wrote some stuff down and then brought it in and read it to him. Might make a lot of progress that way. These readings, and his occasional exegeses, rather in the manner of an Oxford tutorial, took up the greater part of my sessions with him over the next year or so.

'What ya got for me today?' he would ask eagerly.

And one day, during a pause in my reading, he said, looking at me in wonder, 'Y'know, that stuff you write reminds me of a fella

261

we used to have to read in college. Carlyle. Hearda him?'

He asked me why I didn't think of getting something published. I pointed out that my Great Thoughts, which were by way of being rather self-indulgent soul-searching, were not intended for the eyes of others, except his of course, and anyway were hardly the kind of thing that publishers were beating the bushes for.

'What I mean is,' he said, 'you write this for you, and me of course, and then in the afternoons, or whenever, you write something else for them. Get it published, see!' He leaned forward, the pink-white dry hand fell on my sleeve and the cataracted eyes zoomed in behind the prisms. 'Cause I feel sure that that's where your salvation lies,' he said.

The vocabulary may have been a touch un-Freudian, but then Dr McKinney was very much his own man. When I told him that I had been surprised to find myself sitting down to write in a notebook and had often wondered what had started me off, he barked, triumphantly, 'Desperation!'

I had begun the Work when I returned to London after my first stay in New York, and I had felt curiously euphoric and serene. I had somehow cut my ties with a previous existence, and knew that I would not stay for long in my former job with Bensons. He seemed to understand that too, even to relish it. 'Freedom!' he shouted.

I told him that at the time my friend Anthony Blond had said that all my troubles would be cured if I only repeated to myself, ten times a day, 'I am a perfectly ordinary chap.'

'Heh, heh, heh,' went Dr McKinney. 'Guess he was trying to give ya some kind of an insight.'

My stumbling efforts to put into words the things I felt were quickly interpreted by the doctor.

'Yeah, well, what we call that, see,' he said with a reassuring wave of the hand, like one greeting old and trusted friends, 'that's what we call the blessed trinity – fear, guilt 'n' shame, see! Yeah, fear, guilt 'n' shame.'

He could be grave when no change seemed to be forthcoming,

262

taking me by the arm and saying, with a look almost of wonder in the enlarged eyes, 'Y'see, these are heroic things we're talking about.'

Sometimes he stared at me in accusation, saying, 'You *know*, dontcha, you *know*.'

But I didn't, or didn't dare to know I knew. Hoping to be helpful and give him a rich lode of material to work on, I suggested one day that perhaps my problems stemmed from my being a repressed homosexual. The good shrink had a short way with this.

'Well are ya?'

I gave him a blank look.

'I mean, some guy sticks his dong in your mouth, you gonna suck it?'

When I left my twice-weekly main-lining sessions I stayed in my state of relaxed, benign volubility through lunch (and if I had a drink with my lunch the alcohol gave the puttering rocket of the drug a boost into a higher apogee). I found that I could chat without strain to the cab driver who took me to the office and although I was incapable of writing copy under the influence, I was an unwonted whiz at meetings, which normally reduced me (though not, apparently, apparently) to a state of squawky terror, the state you may recall from nightmares when all you can produce at a time of great need is a kind of Munchian silent scream.

I wondered if this pleasant state was that of those 'normal' people who chatted easily with strangers, expressed their views unhesitatingly at meetings, addressed conferences and gave interviews on television. But this, to me, heavenly state had to be paid for by a bit of hell. For in the late afternoons and evenings of these morning highs the curve on my euphoria graph plummeted in compensation, and a speechless despair descended on me which nothing, not company, not food, not drink, not sex, could dispel. For this easy riding excursion into the what-might-be, the mind and body paid a black and bitter toll.

Dr McKinney (no Doctor Feelgood he) worried that I was not

263

making fast enough progress towards whatever goal he had set for me.

'You can get too old for this sort of thing, y'know,' he said with truculent concern. Now he suggested a new tack.

'Coupla young fellas up at Harvard got this new stuff,' he announced. 'Sent me a sample. Thought we'd try it out on you. If you go along with the idea, that is,' he said, with a kind of eager supplication.

There had been reports in the papers about these Harvard researchers, Leary and Alpert, who were experimenting, not altogether judiciously, it seemed, with a new mind-altering drug called LSD. They had made some of the product available to a few selected psychiatrists to see if it might do their patients a bit of good. Dr McKinney, I was not surprised to learn, was among these front-runners.

He proposed a deal. The experiment would take the best part, whatever that part is, of a day and he would have to cancel his appointments for the period, at some considerable financial loss. If I would pitch in with a couple of hundred bucks he would make himself and his nurse available. I'd be one of the first in the world to go on an LSD trip. It was an offer I couldn't refuse, which may tell you something about the state of my mind at the time.

The caper would happen *chez* Hennessy. Having prepared me by the loan of a couple of books – including Aldous Huxley's account of his experiences with mescalin, *The Doors of Perception* – Dr McKinney instructed me not to eat breakfast on the day that my mind was to be blown. Ever ready to make a sacrifice in the cause of scientific progress, I agreed. We would start at 8.30 and I would stay in bed – always an agreeable prospect.

At 8.15 I opened the door of my apartment to Dr McKinney and his nurse. The doctor beamed his eyes around the place.

'Swell joint you got here, young fella,' he barked, bright as a button, at dawn.

We fetched an armchair from the living-room and put it beside the bed. I got into the latter and Dr McKinney into the former.

The nurse handed him a glass dropper with a rubber bulb at one end. He asked me my weight, to get the dosage right, and squeezed three pale blue drops on to my tongue. (The same colour as the methedrine: pale blue was the fashionable colour in drugs that year.)

Nothing happened. Dr. McKinney sat in the armchair, with what is called for some reason a yellow legal pad on his knees, and waited. The nurse went into the living-room to catch up on *Elle* or the *New Yorker*. Nothing still happened. Dr McKinney looked at his watch, eager for action, and grunted.

'You feel anything? Oughta feel something by now. Five minutes, they reckon,' he said, almost querulously.

Five minutes gone. Ten minutes. Nothing kept on happening. Maybe pale blue just wasn't me. Horse of another colour. Clear as a bell still. Bell for the last round. Fight the good fight. Half an hour. Beat the bastards.

Then something happened, and then unhappened. I was like a jet in the cloud-layer, sometimes in, sometimes out, now under, now over. When I was under I felt terror in its pure, unsullied state, for I was changed, changed utterly, and a terrible ugliness was born. I was born.

I did not see myself as something else: I became that something else, and that something else was me, good old Chuck, at other ages than the present, getting younger every year. And then I was a baby, I had given birth to this baby in me, the one that never grows up. I looked to right and left in the bed and saw, at the ends of tiny arms, a baby's hands. I felt stunted. I put these tiny hands to my head and was amazed to discover thick locks of hair. Babies weren't wearing long hair in 1925.

I grew older and priests and nuns came in long black sinister queues, remonstrating, chastising me. Getting back at me for chucking the awful catechism and all the other superstitious junk food for the mind, back when I was eleven, and God save us, an altar boy. But now I was an altered boy and the catch was, these were *my* priests. Superego, or whatever. I fought the priests back, I made them vanish.

The struggle showed. All this immeasurable time I was fighting for my life, bathed in sweat, pyjamas clinging, sheets damp, hair tangled. I was kicking and punching to keep control, not to go under the cloud for ever, not to let the painfully built defences be breached and some unknowable truth be revealed, not to go back to the womb and its dark unutterable secrets.

But all the time too, through the morning and past noon, I responded coolly, clearly, to the questions put by Dr McKinney. Fighting to dominate the inner chaos that threatened to wreck me I became, as one sometimes does in moments of great danger, superhumanly calm.

'In case you're hungry,' I said, 'there are sandwiches in the icebox.'

I came out of the drugged state, as programmed, around 3.30. I could stand, with help, and I was weak as a man recovering from a long, near-fatal illness (which may be what life is). My hair, unwontedly, was matted. I smelled rank. But these were the arms and hands and legs I knew. I felt as if I had returned from that bourne from which no traveller returns. I shuffled on that mortal coil again. It felt good, made-to-measure for me. It was nice to be alive. And thanks a lot, Timothy Leary.

Dr McKinney put away the antidote that, he said, had been ready in case I had a bad trip. Now he tells me. He asked if there was a friend who could come and stay with me. I shouldn't be left alone, it said on the instructions. Marianne Spottiswoode lived in New York now. The nurse called her and she said she'd come, to make supper and to stay over.

'Come and see me in the morning!' barked Dr McKinney, and left, in search of food I hoped, for he had not eaten all day. His nurse stayed, to keep an eye on me until Marianne arrived. (You just try and throw yourself out of a window in Manhattan – the damn things are all sealed.) She spoke of her admiration for the doctor, of his generosity of heart, of his dedication, of his courage in the face of approaching blindness and in the aftermath of two coronaries. I thought he was pretty cool myself.

Next morning I reported as instructed, for a de-briefing after my trip. The indomitable doctor opened the door to his consulting room himself, and stood there pink and beaming and bolt upright, leaning, as usual, slightly backwards, eyes looking down, large and in soft focus behind the thick lenses. He threw wide his arms and cried out to his nurse, 'Why, whaddya know, Nancy, he's alive!'

We went together through his notes. They were disappointing, he said. Trouble was, I'd held out. That bit with the sandwiches.

'Yeah, we thought that was just a bit much, young fella!'

The dose, it seemed, hadn't been strong enough to break down my resistance, which had been even stronger than he'd suspected. Next time we'd increase it. Then we'd see, young fella.

There was no next time. A card came to say that Dr McKinney had suffered one more heart attack, leaving me, and Gloria Vanderbilt, and the rest of the bunch, once more alone, as we always really are, with our troubles.

Chapter 35

The front page of the *Daily Express*, bought on my way home at the foreign newsstand on the corner of 59th and Madison, announced that the Danish wife of an Englishman, a Mr Digby Neave, had been killed by an avalanche while skiing in the Swiss Alps. There were two daughters, it said. You have to believe some of the things you read in the papers.

Hilary Rubinstein, Merton friend, then at Gollancz, came and we took him to an unspeakable Greek place, a favourite of Elliott Erwitt. Available Magnum photographers joined us. A civilised evening, in spite of the food.

The *Express* does it again. James Cameron, Merton friend and wit, whom I had introduced to Bensons, where astonishingly he became Director of Research, had been found shot to death, tied to an armchair in his flat. Later a Scottish labourer, what James would have called rough trade or a butch piece, was tried and found guilty. Dear James. That's what people who knew him always said if you mentioned his name.

Edward Behr, who had been at St Paul's with Alan Cooke and was about to become *Newsweek*'s man in Paris, came, went shopping, cooked us curry and gave us the hot news.

Europe was impinging and could not much longer be ignored.

Unaccustomed as I am to sudden decisions, or to decisions at all, come to that, I nevertheless sprang one day into action. It was 13 July.

I went and told Rosser Reeves that I needed a vacation and since I was Hero of the Month he readily agreed. Junius took over my work and when I walked home that evening I stopped in at a travel agent's.

'Tomorrow,' I announced to Patricia, 'We are going to dance in the streets.'

'What fun,' she said, ever ready, like most girls, to trip the light fantastic. 'Something on in the Village? They had the Italian Festival. Remember?'

'Village pah!' I replied, savouring the moment. 'Italian Festival pooh!' I added, to underline the point.

I played the thing for suspense for a while, walking about her with a mad gleam in the eye. If Hitchcock had been there he would have been taking notes.

Nicely judging the moment when the audience couldn't stand the tension any more, I halted in front of her and said, with a manly authority picked up from Cary Grant, 'Paris, that's where.'

She stood absolutely still. Actually, that's what she had been doing all along, saving her strength. I was the one who was jumping about.

'Dancing in the streets of Paris,' I added, elaborating on the earlier proposition.

She didn't move. Inaction speaks louder than words. Then, 'Oh,' she said, and then, more softly, 'Oh' again. She liked the idea. You can tell.

I explained that I had, that very evening, and not a block away, booked a hotel room in Paris and purchased two airline tickets to that city. I waved these last-named under her astonished nose.

'Les voilà!' I said, perhaps superfluously.

And I explained, for she still looked a bit baffled, that in France, on 14 July, for local and historical reasons, it had been for some years now the custom of the citizenry to dance in the streets. This year, for local and hysterical reasons, it was my intention to join them, and I was inviting her along.

Impressed by my learning and swayed by the cogency of my reasoning, and after a brief pause – roughly, I'd say, a second – to verify that in fact she had no conflicting engagements for the morrow, she threw herself into my arms. Luckily I was there to catch her.

269

At about 6.30 on the evening of the 14th the Air France 707 began its descent over Paris. My timing was just about right. As the jet bellied flatly down and circled, slowly turning the sunset-gilded city on its axis of the Eiffel Tower, up towards us from the different *quartiers*, pretty but pathetic as they challenged sun and sky, fireworks rose, expanding like paper flowers in water. I waved a languid arm over the scene below us and said, 'Paris is vulgarly known as the City of Light. There are fireworks all the time.'

Our pale grey-green and gold Louis XV room at the Plaza Athénée looked out on to a pink-white balcony that curved like a breast over the Avenue Montaigne. Above it were poised, still in the sultry air, two crossed *tricolores*. Slipping rapidly into our dancing-in-the-streets outfits, we shimmered forth to mingle with the cake-eaters.

There were millions of them out there, half on foot, half in slow-moving cars that klaxonned from habit, with a French accent. No cab to be had out there though. We surged therefore with the *sans-culottes* down to the Place d'Alma, up the Avenue George V under the spreading chestnut trees, and down the Champs-Elysées and its wall-to-wall *festivants*.

There, on one of the ranks in the middle of the avenue, like an oasis in the desert, was the only free cab in Paris that night. Handing the companion thoughtfully into the interior, I commanded the driver to take us to the Ile St Louis. My choice of destination was dictated by two considerations: first, I wished to do my stamping on my old stamping ground; second, the dance there, on the point of the island, was universally reckoned to be *le bal le plus sympathique de Paris*, featuring as it did a small bandstand, surrounded conveniently by wine and beer refuelling stops, on which, beneath the aristocratic windows of the *hôtel particulier* of the Princess Bibesco, played the band of the Communist Party of the 4th *arrondissement* – an area which includes, to add piquancy to the occasion, the Bastille.

The cab driver responded with one of those gallic shrugs which, as somebody has said, so nicely combine arrogance with ignorance, pointing out, with irreproachable logic, that the island was halfway across Paris, but that *tant pis*, and *pourquoi pas, allons-y, on va essayer quand même*.

We nudged slowly forward through the determined gaiety of the throng. About one kilometre and half an hour later our driver, solicitous no doubt of our welfare, and conscious that this was, *tout de même*, a night of celebration, asked if we would like to hear some music, to pass the time. I assured the man that we would have no objection at all if he wished to turn on the radio.

Heedless, apparently, of the damage that his gesture might inflict on the massed *pietons* milling about our float, the driver turned his head and fixed me with a Latin eye, at once fiery and sombre.

'*Je ne parle pas de la radio, Monsieur. J'ai la mange-disque, moi!*'

We had found, it seemed, not only the only free taxi in Paris but the only one equipped with that innovation, a record player, or disc-eater, a kind of horizontal maw below the dashboard into which, in the days before Philips invented the cassette, records were fed.

'*Qu'est-ce que vous aimeriez entendre, alors?*' asked the proud owner of Deep Throat, winging a pedestrian or two the while to keep his hand in. '*Vous avez un chanteur preféré?*'

As a visitor to his city, and aware of the importance to a stable Europe and world peace of the *entente cordiale*, I suggested that perhaps we might give a little air-time to one of his compatriots. Piaf, perhaps? Trenet? Montand? Aznavour? (An Armenian of course, but still, their Armenian.)

The eye turned on me again and darkened a shade. In a tone which managed to combine disappointment with discouragement he said, '*Vous aimez ça, vous? Moi, je n'aime pas du tout les chanteurs français. Mais pas du tout.*' Emotion caused ash to shake from the Gauloise on to his lapel.

One of those *pieds noirs*, was he, perhaps? Or worse, a Corsican?

'*Et Sinatra, vous n'aimez pas? Ou Bing Crosby? Le croonair.*'

271

I quickly reassured him. Nobody rated higher as a singer, in my estimation, than Frank Sinatra, unless possibly it was Bing Crosby.

'Ha!' said the *chauffeur*, and thrust a 33" into the mouth of the plastic apparatus.

And thus it was that we progressed, my true love and I, through the streets on a warm *Quatorze Juillet*, to the familiar, if anachronistic, sound of Berlin in Paris, the voice of the Old Groaner singing 'I'm Dreaming of a White Christmas'.

At last, on the prow of the island, under the yellow-white blobs of the *lampions* strung between the screening chestnuts I stood on the cobblestones beside Patricia, like one who has brought his bride home, looking at the known faces of the self-absorbed dancers who footed it featly to the Commie beat as Tessimond's accordeon 'gaily grieved'. These were the faces that had been my familiars, encountered daily in the narrow streets of the island: the thin, weak bistro owner, an alcoholic like so many of them, and his solid, coping wife; the fresh-faced country girls from the *fromagerie*; the ruddy Alsace family and their athletic waiters, lithe as Tour de France cyclists, from the Brasserie round the corner by the *passerelle*. I took her to dance among them. I felt at home, with them, and certainly with her, and almost with myself.

Dawn brought a working day for the French, but not for us. Far from the Madison crowd, from the sick, sick, sick building, from soft sell and hard sell, from impact and aided recall, replete, we rested. Then back at noon for a *choucroûte* and Mutzig beer at the *brasserie* and a lovers' stroll along the *quai* and past my old apartment. Further on, at the corner of the Rue Budé, Gloria Jones, holding a new baby, looked out of the curved corner window at the view, which now included us as we ambled into the frame in fetching two-shot.

'Hi!' she called, as Americans do. 'What are you doing here?' I shouted back a brief explanation, introducing Patricia. In return she introduced the baby, her first, a girl.

'Hey,' she continued, jiggling the baby, the mother on automatic pilot now, the hostess swinging into action. 'We're

272

having a party tonight for Jim's agent. Why don't you come?'

There weren't any other plans. There never had been any plans. So we went that night, to find James Jones serving drinks from behind the mediaeval pulpit that was his bar. Gloria was wearing a see-through dress in what she described as sharkskin, bounty from a winter spent sharkskin-diving in the Caribbean.

'I'm not wearing anything underneath,' she said, a trifle redundantly. 'Does it look all right?'

'Sure,' I said, looking her straight in the thigh.

I slipped out and round the corner, down the Rue St Louis en l'Ile that divides the island, almost to the church with its spire holed like gruyère and up the stairs for a quick house-warming with Lorraine Davidovici who, realising an ambition, had bought an apartment on the island.

When I got back, Gloria, who had straight away become protective of Patricia (when women become the mother of one they become mother of us all), reproved me for leaving Patricia alone.

'That's a great girl you've got there,' she said, adding with that frankness that some say is part of her charm. 'Too good for you.'

The next day I called Digby Neave. He was giving a party. Everybody was giving a party. Who needed plans? He lived now, a widower, in the suburb of Marly-le-roi.

It was the kind of place made for this sort of caper. You entered the sober, L-shaped eighteenth-century house by the second floor and descended to the dining- and living-rooms by a modestly grand staircase enlivened by a portrait of a red-tuniced, pink-faced, white moustached British general, an ancestor of Digby's who had the dubious distinction of being the booby who signed the order for the unfortunate charge at Balaclava. Faces of a swarthier hue adjoined the Crimean bungler. These, represented in oil, etching and sculpture, were the likenesses of Alexandre Dumas, *père et fils*, in chronological order and going from the darker to the lighter skin tones. The reason for the presence of these two literary chaps is that this was the home of Dumas *fils*, a thoughtful present from dad.

273

Digby had been alone in this large house – alone as you can be with two daughters and a nanny, which is as alone as any other way – since Ulla's death, and the party seemed to herald a return to the living. (He had come to New York after the tragedy and we had walked in Central Park, but the sight of couples strolling had been unbearable and he had left alone.) Now he took my arm and led me out through the Anglo-French windows to the garden, between house and hot-house, where visitors may see, free of charge, mounted on an easel among the potted plants, the view from my Ile St Louis apartment, painted by Ulla.

'Old boy,' said the man who had been instrumental in getting me that apartment, 'if I were you, I'd marry that girl. Because if you don't, I will.' I told him I thought I'd take Patricia down to the South of France for a bit, and he suggested we go by way of Maillebois and stay in his *moulin*. With that graciousness which has so often impressed my friends, I accepted his kind offer.

The hidden Hansel-and-Gretel mill-house was haven after the glamour and clamour of the city. We were alone, except for the visits of Monsieur Reynou, Digby's ancient and gnarled gardener, who brought us fresh, warm, bubble-topped milk each morning for our *café-crème*.

We hopped over to the next village of Blevy and swam with Bill Murray in a mill-pond calm as the sea while his wife Ariane read in a deck chair.

'You know,' said Bill, 'People think I never read anything. That's not true. Why, I've read *Gone With the Wind*, and some other book.'

We burbled down the shimmering asphalt of the Nationale Sept to Ramatuelle. Edward Behr, *Newsweek*'s bureau chief in Paris, had offered us the use of a house he had rented from the painter Michael Wishart. Above the beaches in the untacky air of Ramatuelle we dined on the terrace of L'Ormeau, looking at the villagers sitting around the ancient tree not looking at us, and wondering if Gerard Philippe, the village Keats of the screen, would trundle by in his old open Renault.

We meandered back to Paris and from Orly Caravelled to

274

London and the Ritz, that displaced piece of Paris. We took the train to Oxford and on the regency-striped lawn of Trinity listened to the band of the Oxfordshire and Buckinghamshire Light Infantry play brassily for a garden party. 'My regiment, actually,' I murmured. At Merton lodge the porter, Arthur, looked out from his cubby-hole and said, 'Why, Mr Hennessy, C.P., isn't it? And how is Mr T.M.?' It was terribly BTA.

From our room at the Mitre on the High I called my mother in Aylesbury – a forty-minute bus-ride away – to say that we would like to come and visit her. She declined the kind offer.

She noted that she had been without news of me for some four years, adding not unreasonably that, the time having passed agreeably enough, she thought she had sufficient fortitude to bear another four years of the same.

It was a bad omen. We were running rather late on our trip. In fact, it would be impossible for me to be back in the dark satanic mills of Madison Avenue on the due date. I sent a cable to Junius to explain matters. This was a bad move, for two reasons. First, Jerry Gury was my immediate superior and it was to him that I should have made my feeble excuses. Second, Junius had decided to take a few days off himself and therefore never got my cable.

Gury, already offended because I had been appointed by Reeves and had never reported to him on copy matters, was now understandably affronted by my failure to communicate with him directly or, as it happened, at all. In a brief but cordial exchange, as they say in communiqués about matters of far less moment than this, Reeves informed me that Gury, not feeling perhaps that the situation demanded a lot of nuance, had told him that either he went or I went.

Reeves, a warm-hearted but cool-headed man, took the more prudent and more economical course. In the great corporate tradition, I cleared my desk and in a brief ceremony which lacked only the slow beat of a solitary drum I handed in my key to the executive washroom. Then I floated down and out into the street with all the gloom and bitterness of a man whose doctor has just given him seventy years to live.

Chapter 36

New York City, richer then, allowed me fifty dollars a week from its coffers as unemployment benefit. So I signed on every Tuesday morning with the desperate immigrants and the shamefaced ex-executives, their heads buried in their newspapers as they stood in long lines for their turn at the purple indelible pencil.

I moved out of my swell joint on 64th Street, bequeathing my fine and stoic cleaning woman, Tilla Bonsell, to Elliott Erwitt (she is with him still). I moved into a one-room apartment a block away with Patricia. It was not the first, nor the last, time that my friends have been obliged to help me out by taking me in.

Merely not going to an office, simply not being part of a corporate body, was in itself enough to waken again faint, ephemeral feelings of *joie de vivre*. Live, I say, or go to the office. You can't do both. Each morning, I made breakfast and saw Patricia off to work at Magnum Photos. Totally absorbed, all morning I wrote Great Thoughts in my notebook. For lunch I ate two poached eggs and an apple. It seemed the right thing to do.

Then, the conscience relatively clear, I went out, down the steps of the brownstone and left towards Central Park, pausing to pick up the *New York Times* on my way. Through the Zoo, the seals (we had named them Codicil, *Domicile*, and *S'il vous plait*) on my right, then the cafeteria, then under the tunnel, a slight left, as winter came on, to watch the skaters at the Wollman Memorial Rink. After the kibbitzing, like any other bum I found an unoccupied bench and scanned the narrow columns of the *Times* to see how the world wagged, carefully avoiding the jobs vacant pages in case my idyll ended.

I was thus employed, so to speak, one pleasant afternoon when the top-hatted coachman of one of those *fiacres* you can rent in front of the Plaza halted his vehicle in front of me.

His woman passenger, seated beside a child in the open carriage, shouted 'Hi'. I recognised the voice, and the pearly teeth, as being those of Gloria Jones, my neighbour on the Ile St Louis.

'What in hell are you doing here?' she inquired courteously, in the tone of one who doubted that there could ever be a plausible explanation. I knew how to handle that. Quick as a flash I came back with, 'What are you doing here?'

It did the trick. A conversation was immediately engaged.

'We're going over to have tea with Lauren,' she said. 'Why don't you come along? Come on, hop in.'

The elevation from park bench to horse-drawn carriage was a pleasing prospect. I accepted the ride, but not the invitation. For one thing, Bogey might be there, and punch me on the nose, just to keep his hand in. Outside the spooky, and Gorey, Dakota building, where they shot, so to speak, *Rosemary's Baby*, Gloria, who was here on a brief trip with her daughter, repeated her invitation. Again I declined.

'Well, anyway, keep the cab,' she said, reaching into her handbag. Ever the gentleman, or anyway, concerned about my image, I seized her wrist, the one that held the five.

'Please,' I said, with quiet, manly authority, 'I'll take care of that.'

'OK,' she said, to my surprise, and ankled off, clutching the progeny by its small gloved mitt.

I drove airily off – these are open carriages – the horse heading, as horses like to do, for home base on Central Park South, where the piebald pigeons would come, uninvited, to share his nosebag. The fare was five dollars. I had exactly five dollars in the world. An expensive way of not meeting Lauren. I had salvaged some pride. Pride goes before Bacall.

Other afternoons, those on which I didn't meet expensive friends, I shopped for dinner: chicken legs and hamburger meat

277

on normal days, goodies from Bloomingdales and the French cheese shop on richer days. Then I walked with my arm-held paper bag, like Jack Lemmon in some dated comedy, down Fifth to meet the slim, eager figure of Patricia, her smile as unforced, as unfalse, as a child's.

Then home to the room which was mostly bed, and exercises from the new best-seller, the Royal Canadian Air Force 5BX paperback, and a shower. Then, to the music of WQXR, I worked my magic at the stove, sustained by a swig from time to time from the gallon jug of Gallo on poor days, or Almaden Mountain Red on better days. It seemed a full, rich life.

Lacking aim or purpose perhaps, I clung to routine, to the certainty of being loved, to the weekly hand-out, to the unthreatening, uncommitting notebook, concealing with outer form the lack of fire within. I was a dry sketch of a man, a man of negative, if any, capability, a Musil-man without qualities, a man for off-seasons.

Not all my friends were rich. Peter and Judy Hyun, the Paris runaways, now with a second child, were settled in an unlovely apartment on the West Side, in the kind of building where glassy-eyed junkies, mad for a fix, bumped you off the stairs (you didn't take the elevator if you were alone) as they rushed down carrying, with the strength of desperation, a stolen television.

On Sundays often, an old couple now, with habits, we walked across Central Park to a Korean lunch cooked by Peter who, being still employed in his fancy job of TWA ground steward, was better off than I. Once, while Peter fetched the jar of home-made and delectable pickled cabbage called *kimchee* from its isolation on the window-sill to fill the room with its unforgettable and pungent smell of swamp, decay and old tennis shoes, Judy murmured, with the match-making zeal of the happily matched, 'When are you going to marry that girl?' It wouldn't be in her lifetime, anyway.

Sometimes we went instead to a Chinese restaurant and let the authoritative Peter order for us, in Chinese which sounded fluent to me: but maybe he just knew the numbers. We took a cab one day, with the stunning Mia and her brother along for the ride. The boy was now more than a year old and Peter mentioned that he had not yet been christened, chiefly because they had not been able to agree on a name.

The cab driver, required by the New York cabbies' Code of Practice to join courteously in any conversation between passengers, half turned a shocked face.

'Did I hear right? Did you say the poor kid ain't got no name yet?' he inquired politely.

'Afraid not,' said Peter.

'That ain't right,' said the driver, shaking his head slowly in disbelief. 'Kid ought to have a name. Every kid's got a right to have a name. They're *entitle*, know what I mean?'

We rolled on towards our egg-roll, the driver in shallow shock.

'We thought perhaps Everest,' said Peter, with a polite smile. (What makes Orientals inscrutable is that since they are always smiling you can never tell when they're *smiling* smiling, if you see what I mean.)

'Ain't that a *mountain* some place?' asked the driver, unwilling to suspend his disbelief.

'Right. We thought a mountain or a lake would be nice. Himalaya, for example.'

The driver's back winced.

'Now you got to be kidding. That ain't no name for a kid. That ain't right. Poor little kid.'

It would be a story for his wife, perhaps, as he broke out a six-pack of Bud that evening in Bedford Stuyvesant. The handsome oriental father. The beautiful mother, white like you and me. The helpless, victimised offspring. Sure meet some funny people in this racket.

The boy was eventually christened Hogy, which is the Korean for tiger, which is the name Judy had given to the Siamese kitten I had mailed to her at the Château Garibondy in Cannes.

Judy worked part-time at the Metropolitan Museum now and asked me to drop by one day on my afternoon walkabout in the

Park. She said she would be greatly interested to have a look at my Great Thoughts, whose public until then had consisted of Dr McKinney. I took a heap of the stuff along, to humour her. When she returned it a few days later, she said, 'That's all very well, but why don't you *really* write something.' She gave me that long-drawn-out silent gaze that just managed not to be fey and added, 'You know, if you did I think you might surprise us all.' My public, however, has been disappointed. I mean, why try to write and find you can't, when you can keep the agreeable illusion of talent, and enjoy the guilt feelings hiding that one talent that is death to hide, as my fellow-scribe Milton cleverly put it?

Some weekends, if Junius Edwards sent five dollars for the fare, we took the train from Grand Central to see our black friend at White Plains. Junius, shortly after my departure, was fired from Ted Bates ('let go' is the official euphemism). As the second black in the Copy Department, his tenure had never been certain and without my protection he became vulnerable, and then one day redundant. With his deep-freeze packed, in the American way, with three-months'-worth of meat on credit from Macy's, and everything else on credit too, these were hard times for Junius. He had his revenge, though, in a most agreeable way.

In the summer there were trips to Amagansett, on Long Island, where Elliott Erwitt owned a house. Amagansett is gracious, neat, quietly prosperous America, all white clapboard houses in large, open-to-the-view gardens or incredible, one-off architectural feats overhanging the restless Atlantic. The popular summer sports are hard drinking, hard-court tennis and divorce-court adultery, and the sands are dense with advertising art directors, their tangled heaps fastidiously skirted by the staff men of the *New Yorker* and editors from the less commercial publishing houses.

It is a thing to which I have long been inured that when I am introduced to some total stranger that stranger says, 'I know your face from somewhere ...', or 'Haven't we met before ...', or some such deadly bromide. Blessed, if that is the word, with some kind of archetypal mug, I suffer with typical courtesy the peering,

280

stepping back and sideways, frowning and headscratching that usually accompanies this search for my true identity.

This little comedy, never a socko number with me, was given a new twist on the sands of Amagansett when Elliott introduced me to a handsome and kind-faced chap called William Cole, poet, anthologist and summer denizen of these parts. Bill said that although my face was totally unfamiliar, my name, for some reason, was not. We scouted around a bit for common acquaintances, turning up the hitherto unguessed-at fact that the Robin Jacques who had illustrated a book of sea-shanties for him was an old and valued friend of mine, but this did not seem to satisfy the questing Cole.

After an hour or so though Bill asked me if by any chance I knew a chap called Gavin Ewart, poet by trade. He had something there, I graciously conceded. 'That'll be it, then,' said Bill, turning his unconscious to other compelling matters. It appeared that the last-named poet had submitted a poem for the first-named compiler's anthology of erotic poetry, and this poem, it appears, was dedicated to a bloke of the same name as me. 'That's how I know your name,' said Bill, with quiet satisfaction. 'Nice poem, too. Pity I couldn't use it.'

This Bill, then, had been responsible for denying me that world fame which I have always secretly felt to be my due ('I would quite like to be quite famous,' I had written, young and foolish, in my Great Thoughts). All, however, is not lost. Rummaging the other day in a trunk I had left with my brother some twenty-five years ago when I quit the shores of England to seek that world fame to which I have alluded and which, as we have noticed, has eluded me, I unearthed, or untrunked, a piece of blue writing paper headed, 'KINGSWAY HALL, London, WC 2'. This, you may recall, was the address not only of S. H. Benson Ltd. the agency in which Gavin and I laboured, but also of the GHQ of the Methodist Church of England, headed then, as now, by the Reverend Donald Soper. I therefore publish, perhaps for the first time, the poem typed on this letter-heading with a warning to devout followers of the Rev. D. Soper to avert their eyes, for it is pretty hot stuff. Here goes:

TO AN EARL'S COURT BEAUTY
For Charles Hennessy

Sweater-girl, sweater-girl,
Couldn't-be-better girl,
Lovely French letter girl,
   Curvesome and clean,
Tempting young teen-ager,
Sweet in-between-ager,
Desireful and keen-ager,
   Sexy sixteen.

Pride of espresso bars,
Seduced in the backs of cars,
Peeling off pants and bras,
   Plump and serene,
Black frilly knicker girl,
Healthy high-kicker girl,
Come-hither, come-quicker girl,
   Delinquent Doreen!

When funds were too low for the fare to Amagansett, we went to Jones Beach, the endless stretch of sand and humanity you wing over as you come in to land at Kennedy, or to Fire Island, the world's largest inhabited sand dune. One hot Saturday morning, with just enough money in my pocket to take us there, I chanced to stroll up Madison as far as Marianne's new and vast boutique and salon complex. The elegant façade, with maroon shades on which was emblazoned, in a nice Bodoni face chosen by Borgie Baton, the name 'Spottiswoode', was only slightly diminished by the presence of the adjoining and less classically emblazoned 'Phoebe's Whamburger'.

Crossing the Avenue after my courtesy call, I plunged into the dark cold of a slightly louche bar called the Paris. As I was nibbling a wilting french-fry, and sinking a glass of draught Michelob, two figures appeared at my table. The Joneses were keeping up with me. Jim and Gloria were in town, they told me, for the publication of Jones's latest opus, a slim volume called *The Thin Red Line*. After a bit of fancy-seeing-you-here and well-what-a-coincidence, not to mention a small-world-isn't-it, Jones became restless, like a man who, strange as it may seem, had other things on his mind than the thrill of meeting old long-lost Chuck again.

'Know what I'd like?' he unburdened himself at last. 'I'd like to see my first book sold.' And he turned his warm but firm Marine sergeant's gaze on me.

Suddenly recalling how I had been taken for a ride, so to speak, on my last encounter with a Jones, I shifted uneasily, mentally totting up the bill for the comestibles recently lowered, adding it to the train and ferry fare to Fire Island and then seeing how that shaped up when you deducted the price of a hardback book. It didn't look too good.

'Hey, there's a book-store a block or two down,' his ever-helpful helpmate said.

Shanghaied, I left the joint with Jones, leaving Gloria behind (she had been joined by another woman, who may or may not have been Bob Mullen's wife from Paris: I was too gloomy to care). A couple of blocks down the Avenue, around 68th or 69th, there was indeed a bookstore. That was the bad news. The good news was that there was no sign of Jones's book in the window, nor inside either. But you don't put off a novelist who practically took Iwojima single-handed that easily.

'Do you have *The Thin Red Line* by James Jones?' asked James Jones. 'Ought to be out today.'

'Sure,' said the man behind the counter. 'Just have to unwrap the package.' He withdrew to a back room, and returned with a thin red book. That would be it all right. On the back of the wrapper was Jones's ugly handsome mug. The man looked at this and looked at Jones. That made his day. Just so long as someone was happy. I reached in my pocket and pulled out a five dollar bill, the only bill of any sort that happened to be in my pocket.

Thinking to rescue something from a disastrous morning, I

asked the famous author if he would mind inscribing a suitable legend in the expensive tome. Giving the matter that intensity of thought that makes noble minds so different from yours and mine, well, mine, the great man reached for a pen and, with hardly a pause between thought and act, wrote, with his fighter's sure fist, an inscription which has stayed with me to this day:

'To Charlie Hennessy,
who paid cash.
Jim Jones'

Chapter 37

The pleasing pattern of my days – the mornings writing, the afternoons walking, the evenings cooking and, *mirabile dictu*, if that's the dictum I want, the nights sleeping – I found entirely to my satisfaction. I was meant perhaps to be a dilettante. The warm, always magnanimous Patricia mildly observed that I was agreeable to live with when down and out but tended to get uppity when in the money.

The only snag about this near-idyllic state was that, since it never took me anywhere that such a desirable comestible might be found, I failed to bring home the bacon. Reluctantly, therefore, I drew up a list of agencies, and made out a résumé, and sent the latter to the former. Agencies, ever on the look-out for genius, receive practically anyone who requests an interview, and my curriculum vitae was studded with blue-chip names. But I would greatly have preferred polite refusals, and they didn't have to be that polite either. On nights before appointments I slept fitfully. I was beginning to perceive the advertising business, or any business, as a threat to my well-being and peace of mind. If that was the real world, they could keep it.

I was received one afternoon by a gentleman called Joe Sacco, Copy Chief at Norman, Craig and Kummel, an agency reputed to be of the rougher, tougher genre. He was a sallow man with lank dark hair and the looks of a tortured but decent George Raft. I spread my samples before him, mumbling justifications in an unconvinced and no doubt unconvincing way. My heart, you might say, wasn't in it. The proofs of the Cunard campaign, though, seemed to put a little colour in his wan cheeks, and as I rabbited inanely on, he began to gaze at me rather as that fat chap Cortez must have gazed at his platoon on that peak in Darien, with what the poet nicely called a wild surmise.

After a good bit of this wild surmising he leaned intently forward and said, 'Do you have a suit?'

I should perhaps explain that in unconscious, or even conscious, defiance of the code that governed such matters, I had presented myself in an odd jacket and trousers, this being the rig with which I kitted out my other, more agreeable persona, that of the contented bum. In reply to the question, I confessed to owning at least one suit, in tolerable condition.

'Go home,' said Sacco, 'put it on, and meet me in the lobby of the Pierre in an hour.' Then, using a line that George Raft would have felt quite at home with, he added, 'You just got yourself a job.'

Outside it was pouring and, as in all big cities when it rains, the cabs had been the first to scurry for shelter. I hopped, skipped and jumped through a symphony of doormen's despairing whistles that would have given Stockhausen an idea or two, and arrived home soaked. It was just as well I owned a suit.

In the hotel, Sacco grabbed my arm and said that he was going to fill me in, a choice of phrase that, pronounced as was his way out of the corner of his mouth by this stage Mafioso, increased my natural dread. NCK were, it seemed, having trouble with one of their most important clients, Hertz Rent-a-Car by name.

Everyone, it appeared, was talking about the new campaign now running for Hertz's great rival, Avis. This was a typical hand-wringing job from the hot shop, Doyle Dane Bernbach (I'm not short of commas but it is their affectation to write the name that way): the 'We're only No. 2' theme, with its scherzo, 'We try harder'. It seemed that it was the view of Hertz that this was rather more stirring stuff than the 'Let Hertz put you in the driver's seat' line their own agency was peddling, and they were making, almost as a reflex action, the kind of menacing noises that cause advertising executives to reach for the bismuth.

It just happened that on this rain-splashed night the agency was holding an all-pals-together reception for the Hertz head man, together with his son and heir-apparent and other representatives of the top brass. And lo, in the NCK of time a saviour had landed on the doorstep of the agency: me. I would now be presented as a red-hot creative man, cooking on all burners, who had been wrenched, after extensive search and heedless of expense, from the arms of such giants as David Ogilvy and Rosser Reeves, so that my powerful talent might be put to work on behalf of Hertz in its time of trouble. Could any agency do more?

'By the way,' said Sacco, squirming like a mambo dancer now as we advanced towards the important blue-suited backs that hid the bar, 'forgot to tell you – you're a Vice-President.' Here we go again, I thought. Bismuth as usual. Not, myself, wholly convinced of the wisdom of this ploy, I lowered a large whisky to brace myself for the highball-to-highball encounter with the *grand fromage*.

This last-mentioned, a big, powerful, hard-looking fellow with a 70-proof nose and a grip like a monkey-wrench, shook my hand severely, gave me one of those sincere, all-purpose, business-function looks and turned his back abruptly on me, the better to continue, in his six-cylinder voice, whatever fascinating monologue we had so importunately interrupted. Not exactly the dynamic breakthrough old Sacco had had in mind perhaps. Hardly the total impact we were hoping for. Well, it wasn't my script. I'd just been sent down by Central Casting, with a nice dry suit from Property.

Then Sacco introduced me, as a kind of courteous afterthought, to the Hertz-*führer*'s companion, a tall, lean man with the hungry, fanatical looks of Hugh Hefner, the founder of *Playboy*. This chap, it turned out, was Norman B. Norman, the founder of NCK, and hence my new boss. He took this dire news, and the improvised coup, in his large stride, with that kind of inspired superficiality that advertising men seem able to command at will.

'Heard a lot about you,' he lied sincerely. 'Welcome aboard.' And, gripping my hand, finished off the smaller bones the Hertz man had left, as a kind of 15 per cent agency commission.

It wasn't that it wasn't raining as hard when I got out into the street again, it's just that it didn't seem to be. All dressed up for the first time in months and, potentially – which would do for the Chase Manhattan – rich again, I took my sweet consort out to the Marmiton, figuring that the food there, being French, would be less likely to stick in my throat.

I told them what anybody else could have told them: that in the face of the Avis assault they should assume a posture of superiority – natural enough for a No. 1 – and ignore the attack completely. They should simply go on doing what they had done before. I added that there was a fair amount of evidence that advertising which drew attention to a rival brand, even by implication, tended to promote that brand: that the constant reference to No. 2 was bound to make people ask themselves who was No. 1, and, possibly, to ask themselves why.

Basic enough stuff, you'll agree. Run-of-the-mill, rent-a-Vice-President material. But it was enough to save the day and allow the ulcers to subside, and I was favourite for Creative Man of the Month again.

So I told them that, being as it were No. 1, I would need a No. 2, and I had just the chap for the job. Fellow name of Edwards, Junius Edwards. It wouldn't be easy, but I thought I could get him, if the money was right. It was thus that the unemployed and impecunious Junius joined me once again as *aide de camp*.

The thing didn't last though, for me, and, thus, eventually, for Junius. It had never had it in it to last. The whole bit just wasn't – how shall I say? – my style. For one thing, there were the *dramatis personae*. The account executive in charge of Hertz was a short, stocky, bull-necked man called Jerry Bissinger, who looked and behaved like that other Jerry, Eric von Stroheim. He had – like Stroheim, we are told – a kind heart, but he kept that tender organ carefully wrapped against any risk of shock.

He had nothing on Norman B. Norman though. This fellow had the disagreeable habit of calling unscheduled meetings in his corner office where, from a medieval pulpit that recalled James Jones's bar, he harangued even the most august of his employees in language that must have had the pulpit's original tenants spinning in their tombs.

I only ever had one conversation with Norman. (I use, of course, his surname: we were never close enough for me to call him by his first name.) I had found myself with him and Bissinger in an elevator. As is my wont when travelling in an elevator with my betters, I looked thoughtfully at my feet. So did Norman B. Norman. I mean, he looked at my feet, as if to discover what I found so fascinating in them. As we emerged from the grounded cage he turned and regarded me, for the first and only time in our not-brief-enough acquaintance, with a flicker of interest in his messianical eye.

'Where did you get those shoes?' he snarled courteously.

Ever one to help in the quest for sartorial perfection, I informed him that they were the handiwork of Peal's in London and could be obtained through the good offices of Brooks Brothers in this city. He grunted politely and veered off.

A couple of days later I strolled into Bissinger's office. He had his feet on his desk – my style rather, but hardly his. He gave me one of his Stroheim scowls, as if he had very few of them left and I was lucky to get one.

'Don't those goddam shoes kill you?' he asked.

I glanced at his feet, now greatly improved as feet by new Peal shoes from Brooks Brothers worn, for the occasion, in the unlaced, open-throated style favoured by infantrymen after a forty-mile forced march. All was clear. Bissinger, wishing to join the company of us patricians, had got off on the wrong foot and was paying dearly for his presumptions.

This same agreeable fellow called a meeting of the creative people on the Hertz account at noon one day. Everyone was there, except good old Jerry. After a bit of sitting around and chewing the fat, with a little shooting the breeze for variety, we started to get restless. One began to see the point of Duke Ellington's complaint about people stinking up the place with talk. Then the telephone rang. It was Bissinger's secretary to say that Jerry was detained at the client's and we were to wait there until he got back.

Now the more perceptive of my readers may have noticed in the course of this chronicle that I don't much like meetings. Well, I don't like non-meetings much better, and I found the detention of all that highly paid talent in that room somewhat debasing. Besides, it was the lunch hour, and hence sacred. At 1.30, with Bissinger still missing, and getting missinger, I made one of those decisions that can change the course of a man's life. As the ranking officer present, and feeling somewhat peckish, I dismissed the meeting.

Then I walked, as was my habit, a block or two down Madison to 55th and up to the St Regis and chose an armchair vantage point in the small bar to the right (it had the attraction, for me, of allowing women in at lunchtime, which the chauvinistic King Cole didn't) and ate a sophisticated hamburger and drank a glass of Californian *pinot noir* and watched the regal Dali (André Breton's Avida Dollars, over for the annual collection: that is, he did the collecting) hold court among the doting art groupies and then went downstairs to have my Peal's shined and strolled fatalistically back to the office and found a note asking me to report to Joe Sacco, who fired me, as he had hired me, on the spot.

He looked at me wonderingly, as he had that first time, squirming in his chair and pushing back the lank hair that fell over his sallow face.

'You just don't care, Charles, do you? You just don't care.'

And, you know, I didn't. But if you put some of the behaviour I've described here down to plain irresponsibility and lack of commitment, don't count on me to agree. Because you'd be talking about Society, and I'd be talking about Me, the one being the enemy of the other, and vice versa.

Things were not so hot. The world looked as if a grey wash had been brushed over it. Action was called for, even if it was only listening with one ear. My own kind of self-sufficiency taking the form of leaning on friends, I borrowed the price of a one-way ticket to Paris from Elliott Erwitt (remind me to pay it back) and Digby Neave, a widower still, came to Orly to take me to the house of the old penny-a-liner and gastronome, Dumas, while I looked around for a job.

Nothing turned up. I flew over to wet, cold, bleak London, a good city to feel sorry for yourself in, and dashed off a clutch of self-pitying letters to Patricia. At Mather and Crowther, Stanhope Shelton, Creative Director, looked at me curiously and said, 'What's holding you back?' Well, he was, for one, by not giving me a job, but maybe that isn't what he meant.

I flew back to Paris. At least it was Paris. On the round table in the hall there was a message: I was to call a Mr Weinbaum at Young and Rubicam. Y & R was the third largest agency in the world, and recently established in Paris. Mr Weinbaum offered me the job of Creative Director, at 25,000 dollars a year, which was worth twice what it would have been worth in New York. I was rich again, and I was in Paris. All I lacked for plenitude was Patricia and I cabled her to come.

Chapter 38

My new boss was a shortish, slight, moon-faced, balding man who walked with a slight cringe. He had narrowed, Donald Bradman eyes that darted warily, almost fearfully from side to side as he went. He gave the impression of one who had been kicked a lot at school, and had never fully trusted anyone since. He had good qualities as a father, family man and *bon viveur*, but found difficulty in manifesting these admirable traits in his professional life. You could say that he was his own worst enemy, but I ran him a close second for a while.

Young and Rubicam was known to be losing money in France. The office had been largely the creation of George Gribbin, the revered (though not by me: I don't revere easily) Chairman of Y & R, the World. The trouble with this sort of set-up, though, is that when there's an upheaval at HQ the tremors are felt in the field: when the head man goes, heads roll elsewhere. One of those heads was to be Sumner's; another, by a sort of reverse domino effect, was mine.

It should not be inferred that I have nothing but unhappy memories (luckily, I do not suffer from a good memory) of my stay with Y & R France. There were compensations. The Copy Department was headed by my good friend Bernard Galmiche, the priest *manqué* with whom I had worked at J. Walter Thompson. Helping Bernard was a young man of charm and wit, Philippe Woolf, a sort of black-haired talking Harpo Marx, who later left advertising to write successful novels. Another JWT alumna, Marie-France Bourdel, became my secretary. It was an agreeable ambiance and the situation, on the Avenue George V,

292

was devilishly convenient for Fouquet's, *chez* Mercier on the Rue Lincoln and *chez* Francis on the Place d'Alma.

It was also only a few hundred yards from the Hôtel Tremoille, the Plaza Athénée's bourgeois cousin, where, as the French say, we were descended. I had given instructions to an estate agent about the kind of place I was looking for: an apartment in the 4th *arrondissement*, for example, on the Ile St Louis, say, on the sunny side, perhaps, somewhere about the Quai d'Orléans, for instance. Forget it, they said, everybody wanted to live there, these days. Hopeless. They'd keep on looking, though, and let me know.

On the Saturday after my first week on the new job, Patricia and I walked down to this same Ile St Louis again, that we had last seen, leg-weary and dry-mouthed from too much champagne, at dawn on 15 July. We strolled again under the windows of my old apartment on the Quai d'Orléans. The windows were open on to the light river breeze and I thought that perhaps the *concierge*, who had also been my *femme de ménage*, might be cleaning the place and would let us in so that I could show Patricia where I had lived.

We went into the courtyard by the Rue le Regrattier and up the curved stone steps to the first door. I rang the bell. After a moment the door opened and the Modern Jazz Quartet emerged, going full blast on some hidden hi-fi: sacrilege in this shrine. They were followed by a bearded chap (you wore a beard to listen to the MJQ). I apologised for intruding, and explained the circumstances. He invited us courteously in, and, bellowing above the din, introduced us to his wife. Both were Americans, which, with Brubeck and the gang, made quite a lot of Americans in one small flat.

Patricia thoughtfully strolled the low-ceilinged, bent-with-age, grey-green-walled rooms that were laved in river-reflected, leaf-dappled light. It didn't seem right. Here was the apartment of any young couple's dreams, as they say in the ads, wrongfully occupied by these noisy usurpers, however nice and hospitable they might be. Made you sick. Manfully, and womanfully, disguising our chagrin, we took our leave, wishing the pair a happy *séjour*, as mine had been.

'Hell,' said the bearded fellow, 'we're just packing, moving back home. Leaving next week. Know anybody looking for an apartment, this one's free. Bye now. Take it easy.'

Back in the hotel that evening I called Madame Archibald, daughter of Madame Salle, owner of the apartment and well-known discarder of used husbands. She told me that her brother (or perhaps step-brother, the *ménage* being naturally a confusing one) now handled Madame Salle's affairs, so I called him and invited him to lunch at Fouquet's. Since I knew him to be an elegant *boulevardier*, in the English style so often affected by the *16-ème* dandy, and also a widower, I took Patricia along too.

A Remy Martin closed the stomach, and the deal. There was just one small problem, said my *invité*. The apartment was now handled by an estate agent, so that I would be obliged to pay not only two months' rent in advance, plus the customary one month's *caution*, but also alas one month to the agency. That was bad enough. What really stuck in the gullet was that this agency turned out to be the agency that I had charged with the job of finding me just such a desirable residence. *Merde alors*.

But I borrowed the money against my salary and moved into No. 1, Rue le Regrattier for the second time. Not much had changed since I had lived there. A carpet now covered the aged-in-the-wood parquet, to deaden the sound, the *concierge* explained, of the hi-fi after complaints from the highly-strung lady who occupied the lowly *sous-sol*. Remembering that the loudest noises during my previous tenancy had been the odd girlish giggle, the twang of a bed-spring or the suggestive chuckle of the bidet, I decided to uncover the lovely parquet.

'Roll up this carpet' I ordered, 'we shall not be needing it in our lifetime.' This, apart from being pompous, was a grave mistake.

Elliott Erwitt, whose turn it was to be President of Magnum Photos that year, came to stay, bringing with him his new blonde wife Diana and, as photographers will, a few tons of equipment packed in metal boxes against the termites. Now if you fill a lot of metal boxes with filters, lenses and things, and then shove them about on a bare parquet floor, you get a peculiarly abrasive, rather screechy noise. And if you happen to be one of those obsessive craftsmen whose favourite occupation it is, late at night, to check and polish these lenses, filters and things, necessitating the opening, closing and shoving about of metal containers, and if you carry on these activities a few inches above the head of a hysterical lady who has recently acquired a volatile Latin lover, you might anticipate trouble.

A preliminary skirmish should, in retrospect, have alerted us to the danger. One night the above-mentioned Latin lover, wearing for the occasion a long black leather coat, a pencil-moustache, a jaundiced cigarette and a scowl, had manifested himself at the door of the apartment. He informed me, without preamble, that in his opinion too much noise was being created above the head of the lady who lived below. I asked him with my customary courtesy what business that might be of his. The question reduced him to a black rage.

'*Moi, je n'aime pas les américains,*' he spat, his hand, it seemed to me, creeping towards the lapel of his gauleiter's coat.

'*Moi, je ne suis pas américain,*' I riposted, rather cleverly I thought.

Elliott, who had been standing behind me, reacted with patriotic fervour.

'*Moi, je suis américain,*' he said, '*et je ne vous aime pas du tout.*'

Feeling that the topic had now had a fair run I ended this international give-and-take with a cheery '*Eh voilà*', and closed the door.

We were dining at home the next night. In the small kitchen, on the courtyard side of the flat, the girls were preparing a simple repast (a few oysters, roast chicken, the world's finest ice-cream from down the street). I was setting the table when, glancing outside, I saw, standing under the street lamp on the cobbled ramp that led down to the inky Seine, a black-coated figure, the top bit of which was smoking a *caporal jaune*.

Suddenly, as the cliché goes, a cry broke the silence, leaving it in little jagged pieces.

'My God — somebody shot me!' sang out the unmistakable voice of E. Erwitt.

I brooded on this unexpected communication for a second, then rushed calmly into the living-room. Elliott was standing knee-deep among his camera junk, which now appeared to be liberally sprinkled with finely ground glass, holding one hand over his left eye and pointing dramatically towards the window with the other. There, near a standing lamp, in what had hitherto been a pristine pane of glass, appeared a small black hole. Quickly assuring myself that Elliott would live, I cunningly switched off the light and withdrew to the kitchen. There, addressing the busy backs of the two lovely girls, and having rapidly discarded various other formulations as being too flowery or melodramatic, I made a simple announcement.

'I say, Elliott's been shot,' I said, with that economy of words which has made my prose style the talking point of those salons where advertising men gather to discuss their craft.

The reactions of the two girls were interestingly varied. My own inamorata turned her lovely head just enough to give me one of those *'et ta soeur'* looks she had perfected since her sojourn in the City of Light, a look that conveyed not so much disbelief as affectionate long-sufferance. Diana, by contrast, impressed no doubt by my serious mien, said in her cool East Coast drawl, 'You know, I don't think he's kidding.' 'For once,' she added, a trifle unnecessarily I thought. Then they wiped their hands on their aprons, as women do before facing facts, though men don't, possibly because they rarely wear aprons, and followed me into the living-room where in the gloom the injured party was now dabbing his eye with a handkerchief.

He explained that he had received a quantity of powdered glass in this orb, the invasion being the result of a bullet, fired from outside, traversing the window — hence the hole. (The affected organ was, as I said, the left eye, which might seem to alleviate the gravity of the assault were it not that Elliott Erwitt is one of those rare photographers who focus with the left eye – rather an inconvenience when you consider that they don't make left-eyed cameras.)

While the girls fussed about the victim, I shuffled over to the telephone, one of the genuine antiques scattered liberally about the place, and called the police. Within minutes blue lights outside lit the apartment intermittently while sirens breathed their last beneath my eaves. On the other side of the flat the doorbell rang and I opened the door to allow seven neat, slim, blue-uniformed Parisian *flics* to file into the scene of the crime. Each saluted in turn, with a courteous *'Messieurs-dames'*, before removing his kepi and shaking hands all round, which, since we added up to a full football team, required some pretty intricate choreography.

The formalities over, I led them over to the window. Outside the *quai*, though full of police vans, was, understandably, empty of assassins. Inside they poked about a bit, looking, without much conviction (though as much conviction as we were going to get on the case) and totally without success, for the vital bullet. Tiring of this, they kindly offered to conduct Elliott to the chief Paris eye hospital, the Quinze-Vingt, which was handily across the river, near the Bastille. I said that I would accompany my old pal in his hour of need, which was pretty noble of me when you consider that dinner was cooking. Before they left, the cops went through their hand-shaking number again with the two ladies, rather as if they were leaving a presidential reception, which, in a sense, they were.

At the hospital the duty doc rinsed out the President's witty eye and said that he'd be snapping again in no time. The *flics*, who perhaps didn't like Americans either, never caught the culprit. The local paper carried the story. Madame Salle, apprised of the attempt, said, *'Mon dieu – on dirait Chicago!'* I put a simple plaque by the window, with the time and date, to inform posterity that the President had been shot here. It seemed the least I could do.

Chapter 39

If you are living on a *quai* of the Ile St Louis, with a doting companion and an income in the top 3 per cent in France, all you need to make the whole set-up unbearably cute is a dear little cottage tucked away somewhere in the lush countryside, bowered in apple-blossom and with only the odd bird-chirp or distant dog-bark to point up the surrounding silence.

Although never one to be small-minded in the constant quest for a better life-style, I had, for reasons connected with financial liquidity, not included the acquisition of a country seat, or *résidence secondaire*, as the French more prosaically put it, in my current fantasies. Somebody else, however, had been thinking for me along just these lines, and that person was Bill Murray, the American friend of Digby Neave, in whose cool mill-pond we had dunked our grateful bodies during that 14 July escapade. When the Americans established an air-base near his house, not far from Dreux, Bill had seen his chance. He acquired a few broken-down houses, fixed them up with all the basic necessities of American life except air-conditioning, and rented them to the airmen and their families. This happy arrangement, providing shelter for the servicemen and moolah for Bill Murray, was abruptly ended by none other than Charles de Gaulle. Without a word to Bill, the *Président de la Republique* withdrew the French forces from the NATO command and peremptorily ordered the American forces out of the country. With this cruel stroke Bill found himself without tenants for his properties and thinking about how to replace them he thought of me.

The cottage he had in mind was on the fringe (like me, half in, half out of society) of Bill's village of Blevy. Like the flat on the Ile St Louis, it was one of those places that charm immediately – charm being, I suppose, a quality that springs from something being absolutely and unselfconsciously itself, which is why all children, who have not yet learned to be someone else, possess it. It was a sway-backed seventeenth-century *fermette*, down a curving hedged lane, like Wordsworth's violet half-hidden from the eye. On the south side spread a vast unbroken vista of fields and rooky woods and at the back high hedges hid an orchard of apples and pears, holding promise of *calvados*, for this was Normandy. It looked like a child demanding to be adopted. You can't afford it but what can you do?

We went to this cottage almost every week-end, in all seasons, for many years, and spent summers there replete with tennis, sun, barbecues, friends and quietude. For the last few years, though, I have lived in it alone. You may be good enough to wonder why. Hang tough. We're getting to that.

While everything was coming up roses in Blevy, in Paris the ground was somewhat stonier. Work went on at Young and Rubicam. I supervised campaigns for Dash, a Procter and Gamble detergent, for the Playtex living bra, for Tricosteril, the French Bandaid, for the CCC, a now-defunct department store whose budget was so small that, to save on fees, they asked me to model the men's clothes. Don't tell Anderson and Sheppard. I also modelled for Modess.

Elliott was to shoot the picture, a night-on-the-town scene to illustrate the promise of freedom offered by the product. We were working under floodlights in the court-yard of Monsieur Prouvost's mansion on the Rond Point des Champs-Elysées. The girl, in evening gown, was to be handed down the steps of the house by her escort, twirling the while (freedom, right?), and into a great black Jaguar. The trouble was, the escort failed to show. Elliott, ever the quick thinker in an emergency, asked me to go home and get into a dinner-jacket. It was thus that the startled readers of *Elle* and *Marie Claire* saw me in my midnight blue, flashing a smile that nicely combined pride in my lovely companion with lecherous (and, under the presumed circumstances, surely misplaced) anticipation as I conducted her to my snaky car. It is a large claim, and one perhaps not acceptable to the *Guinness Book of Records*, but I may have become that night the first man to model for a sanitary towel. In the struggle for immortality, one does what one can with the talents at one's disposal.

Meanwhile, back in New York, George Gribbin, golden oldie, had become ex-Chairman of the Board of Young and Rubicam, though, by general consent, looking as Young and Rubicam as ever. It was announced, shortly afterwards, that the head of Y & R in Brussels, Bill Tragos, was to take over the Paris branch. In Paris, Sumner Weinbaum called me into his office one day and, addressing, as was his habit, the corner of the room which lay beyond and below my left shoulder, informed me that, brilliant as I undoubtedly was, enriching as had been the vast experience I had brought to the task, and invaluable as had been the very real contribution I had made, I was, unfortunately, too heavy a financial burden for the agency to continue to bear and he was therefore, with great reluctance and personal sadness, obliged to give me, as of then, three months' notice.

Now Sumner's training had been on the creative side of the business, and he had decided, no doubt in the interests of economy, to assume the responsibility of Creative Director. A rapid calculation told him that this would make a total of two Creative Directors in the agency, one of them, as they used to say in the army, being surplus to establishment. That one, in Sumner's mind, was me.

Worse was to follow. For when I arrived at my office the next morning, I found that it was no longer there. That is to say, the furniture, of the tasteful, metallic, grey-green kind I had learned, if not to love, at least to live with, had disappeared, to be replaced by an interesting collection of heavy Spanish gothic pieces, last seen on the chic executive floor above. The French, cleverly anticipating just this sort of situation, had invented a phrase for it:

what we had here was a *fait accompli*.

After about a second of profound thought, I took what seemed the only course open to me, or anyway the most agreeable one. I slithered down in the elevator, stepped out on to the sunny sidewalk, ankled across the Avenue George V and requested the barman at Fouquet's to pour me a *coupe* of the house champagne. I was free again.

(Shortly afterwards, Sumner Weinbaum was recalled to a post in the New York office, and then, I heard, he quit advertising for good — for his own good, Joes of advertising would say.)

Marc Riboud had taken Patricia on at Magnum (where Henri Cartier-Bresson, who trusted no one with his archives, trusted her) and with her salary we were able to stay alive by lodging with friends, and to keep on the Blevy cottage but not the apartment on the Ile St Louis. It was summertime, and the living was easy. If you booked your tennis court in Chateauneuf for 4 o'clock you were out of your bath and into your gin-and-tonic in nice time to plan your dinner. Vegetables came from the local market garden, fruit from the trees, and on Sundays the local artist who was our butcher trimmed a gigot before our eyes, carving on the fat a slender branch with leaves. You roasted it on the spit of your Le Creuset barbecue and while you sipped a Ricard you watched the branch and leaves brown and thicken like a living lino-cut. It beat television. There wasn't much more you'd need of a summer evening to make life dandy.

We were not alone in Blevy. All around the Maison du Verger were neighbours who, partly because the French had not yet become fanatics of *le* week-end and *la résidence secondaire*, and partly because most of them were tenants of the ubiquitous Bill Murray, constituted a sort of North American colony in the broad plains of Normandy. Tom Webb, the international lawyer who had been our neighbour on the Quai d'Orléans, had taken over the Moulin de Laleu from the bereaved Digby Neave. His wife Betty, although like him American, was chief designer at Rodier, the knitwear firm. Their son Matthew chose to live, as far as

301

anyone could ascertain, exclusively on mushrooms and chocolate cake.

A handsome young Canadian couple, Fred and Vicky Wanklyn, rented one of the lodge cottages in the park, when they weren't in Paris or in their villa on the Costa Smeralda. They had two daughters and a son, Freddy, whose godfather I became. Freddy kept me up to date with reports about the new stepfather of his school-chum, who kindly invited him to his château on the Loire. To Freddy his host was *l'oncle David*. To me he was David Ogilvy. It was OK down there, said Freddy: swimming pool, horses, good food, that sort of thing.

That summer was too good to last. A French agency called and made me an offer I couldn't refuse: a job. I would need a flat in Paris again. Fred had an aunt in Chantilly who had a friend, recently widowed, who was redecorating her flat in the Rue Jacob with a view to letting it furnished. I went to see this friend. One more beautiful landlady. One more beautiful flat.

Chapter 40

Those familiar with the life of the lesbian-de-luxe (a sort of godmother of the Sapphia) Romaine Brooks, and more especially with that of her *grand amour*, Natalie Clifford Barney, also known as *l'Amazone*, will need no introduction, as they say, to the precincts of No. 20 Rue Jacob. Books have been written by and about these famous ladies, but when I moved into the place – one of the great secret places of the world in one of its nobler streets – they were closed books to me. Burning Sappho had loved and sung here, and I'd heard nary a peep.

Delacroix had lived here and, until recently, a certain Dr Jeanneret, who had moved in after the death of the previous tenant, his brother Le Corbusier. The ground-floor apartment, stretching the length of the courtyard, boasted, or rather, modestly asserted, for this was well-mannered architecture, four tall windows. As its occupant I was thus well placed to observe the occasional and painful passage, across the ankle-twisting cobbles, of a very old woman, assisted by a henna-haired companion of, as they say, a certain age: this was Natalie Clifford Barney and her last, Romanian, lover.

Had I moved in a little earlier I could also have spotted, arriving for Miss Barney's famous Wednesday lunches, the like of Gide and Cocteau and Colette and Gertrude Stein with Alice B. and Hemingway and Virgil Thompson and a lot of lesser folk, such as ambassadors and politicians. But the person who had crossed this courtyard more often than anyone else, several times a day for forty-three years, was a small, round-faced, round-spectacled, alert-as-a-bird woman called Berthe Cleyrergue, who lived with her husband in a flat above the vaulted entrance. Bertha was maid, cook, woman-servant and *bibliothécaire* to Miss Barney, as she was always called, and, more latterly, a friend to me.

Miss Barney had arrived at 20 Rue Jacob in 1925 and was joined by Berthe, a fresh-faced country girl of sixteen from Burgundy, two years later. From that time, Berthe had known and cooked for, and been cherished by, all the famous visitors to this place. She told me that her favourite had been Colette, earthy fellow-Burgundian, whom she found honest and without pretence. When the writer came to lunch, while her fellow-guests were chatting with their hostess in a cultural way over canapés, she would grab Berthe's arm, take her aside, and ask her gravely, *'Berthe, qu'est-ce qu'il y a à bouffer?'*

Sensing that I was similarly appreciative of her art, Berthe brought to my door her left-overs, though that is too prosaic a word for her creations. There were pâtés rich and dark as truffles, tarts that tasted of summer, a pheasant or a partridge with its blood-thick sauce to warm up. She also brought me the latest news, most of which, those days, was bad.

Michel Debré, then a government Minister, had bought Miss Barney's *pavillon en viagé*, in a somewhat macabre arrangement whereby you contract with an aging proprietor, at a *convenable* price, to purchase the property on his death: thus, in effect, making a bet on that regrettable event. According to the *Canard Enchaîné* and other more sombre journals, Debré, anxious to move in, had started noisy and messy restoration measures. One result of these activities had been to drive the ninety-year-old Miss Barney and her companion out of the house and into the Hôtel Meurice. In his book about her, though, François Chalon contends that the final blow came not from the hammers and chisels but from the peritonitis that the hitherto-robust Berthe contracted during my last months in the Rue Jacob. For the first time in all those years she was taken to hospital. *'Plus de Berthe, plus de rue Jacob,'* said the wilful Miss Barney, and went to the Meurice, and died.

304

In my tall-walled apartment I had *tout confort*: a kitchen that might have been a squash court in a previous existence, an octagonal — which gave people something to talk about during dinner — dining room, with pale-blue walls and a Chippendale table in the usual brown, a bedroom in which you couldn't hear a hair-pin drop, lined with felt-backed aquamarine *toile de jouy* you could bounce off and sometimes did: it was rather like sleeping in an eighteenth-century vanity box. You woke to the optimistic chirping of the birds that took over the morning shift from the pessimistic *chouette* who, since he was leaving anyway, didn't give a hoot.

All I needed to complete the set was, say a silver Jaguar 3.8 litre, with, for example, walnut and red leather interior, to park on the cobbles by the kitchen door; and, never one to spoil the ship for a ha' porth of car, I obtained one such. In this bijou we vroomed to Blevy down roads that had no speed limits then — and on, and on; threading the whole coast of Brittany, through villages where small boys squealed, *'Oh regardie — la Jag!'*; down to Ramatuelle, to the sun-warm, peach-coloured terraces of Edward Behr's converted Belle Vue hotel; to Talloire, on the Lac d'Annecy, to savour the *omble chevalier* in the *jardin ombreux* of the Père Bise; to snowy Alsace to celebrate the Haeberlins' third star at Illhausern with *truffe sous la cendre* and our pick of seventeen white alcohols, including the one made from holly berries; to Tours, to meet the Ogilvy copywriters Cynthia Proulx and Ian Keown at the Tortinière, here to compile their *Lover's Guide To France* (the handsome young couple going into the gazebo in the book is us) and to dine *chez* Barrier, who makes his own walnut-studded bread to accompany the *plateau de fromages de chèvre*; to the airport, to fly to Senegal and the Ivory Coast, where the Hôtel Ivoire has the only ice-skating rink in Africa.

It wasn't bad, I tell you. Of course, you may be saying, yeah, pretty good, in fact, too good to last. And you'd be right.

'My life: a series of inspired mistakes': this gag, from a series of inspired one-liners by Mr Craig Raine, leader of the Metaphor

305

Mob, might serve as a motto for my own rake's progress. *Hubris*, if that's the word the Greeks had for it – that usually restrained arrogance that grows reckless when I am on the wordly heights – now brought me low again.

Here was I blessed with a companion who, had she happened to be a glove, couldn't have been better designed to fit me by the best talents at Lanvin or Charvet. For eight years now, as she sometimes gently observed, undemanding, uncomplaining, understanding, underrated, she had shared my life, in morning sickness (mine) and in health, for richer and for, more often, poorer. Fresh as the first day of spring, sweet-natured, punctual, adaptable, ready to pack and go or stay and enjoy, impeccably dressed and mannered, at ease with everyone and everywhere, liked by men and women and loved by children, she was – how shall I put it? – a credit to me.

Ha! There you have it. She was for me, as one of our friends was later to observe, the perfect accessory, helping to clothe, like the Savile Row suits, the Jag, the flats of the Ile St Louis and the Rue Jacob, the nakedness of my natural, my native insecurity. For under the bright chatter of the debonair wag who graced the salons of Mayfair, Manhattan and the Faubourg St Germain, might have been detected, if one listened carefully, a deeper, darker tone – the voice of Milton's Satan: 'Which way I fly is Hell; myself am Hell.'

Which way I flew just then, actually, was towards New York. My old stable-mate, Junius Edwards, routinely fired by NCK now that I, Whitey, was no longer there to protect him, had hit on the only way to make sure he was never fired from an agency again. He founded his own: Junius Edwards Inc., Junius Edwards President. Take that. His clients came from what is quaintly known in New York advertising circles as the black market, and all his employees were white. Pursuing this pleasant vein of, so to speak, black humour, he acquired two Mercedes convertibles, a jet one for himself, a white one for his Norwegian wife. He also acquired a chalet on Snow Mountain, handy for when they weren't skiing in Norway or Switzerland, and two adjoining penthouse apartments on the East Side. As a sort of crowning achievement, he became my employer.

Making one of those inspired mistakes referred to above (leaving aside the sheer cruelty of it: there are some things I'd rather not think too much about without a large whisky handy), I announced unannounced one evening to our Canadian friends the Wanklyns (invited to the cottage for a slice or two of *gigot rôti* accompanied by *haricots blancs à la bretonne*) that I was off to New York for a while. This, I now concede, oh boy, do I ever, must have been startling news to my fair companion but, being a girl of poise and dignity, not to mention pride, she said nothing, unless it was a quiet 'Oh really?' as she spooned a thoughtful bean or so on to her plate.

I explained to the assembled company that I had been persuaded by my old chum Junius to go and work on a campaign for him, all expenses paid. I might have mentioned that it is a quirk of mine that when in New York I am nostalgic for Paris, and vice versa. Yeah, you'll be saying to yourself, if that happens to be the way you talk, like to have your gigot and eat it too, right? Spot on. For while counting on the reassuring presence and support of the sweetheart at my side, I reserved the right to pursue a bachelor life when the mood took me. 'It's been eight years, do you realise, Charles?' she once had said, trembling at her daring, for it was not a promising opening for a conversation between us; and 'Other girls get married, you know,' she said, without pressing the matter further. She was twenty-nine then. I know, I know.

So it seemed expedient for me to forget that all my moments of, well, shall we say minimum misery? for almost a decade had been lived with her, from the home cooking in the one-room apartment in New York to waking, rich that week, in the Normandy in Deauville, sea-tang invading the room to mix with the sweetly acrid *café-crème* and the honey-smelling *brioche*; not to mention, or hardly, all those moments of extended bliss, heading towards some cathedral of gastronomy with, as Palinurus put it, her with the *Michelin* beside me, the wind in her

307

hair and the plane trees going sha-sha-sha through the open windows of the car.

(And that's another thing. She was unique in this: she was the only woman, hell, the only person, who, like me, found no comestible without merit* — always providing, of course, that it was good of its kind, and had been correctly cooked. And if you think such an achievement isn't rare, just test yourself or your companion. Liver? Kidneys? Tripe? Brains? Cabbage? Oysters? *Andouillette?* Ha! She never failed me. I must have been mad).

She came with me, as she always did when I made a trip, to the airport. You do a lot of thinking when someone has just left you at an airport, especially if you're a girl, and all the future seems to be happening for him, and you're not getting any younger. She might even have been thinking, though it wouldn't be like her, why do all the nice girls get drawn to the bounders?

In New York, at the suggestion of the Erwitts, who were summering at Amagansett, I picked up the key from Magnum and moved into their apartment, Central Park at my feet, New York like a giant picket fence enclosing it.

I went to see the Hyuns. Peter poured me a stiff whisky as, under the gravely interested gaze of Mia and Hogy, I waited for Judy to announce that she could be seen. She wanted to look nice for me, said Peter. Then she was ready and I walked into the bedroom, where she lay dying. She wouldn't have needed the make-up. Her beauty now was more ethereal, tinged with the unearthly, refined by pain. I kissed her for the last time. The children would be all right. Peter had long been reconciled with her parents. He was a vice-president at Doubleday now. If you could believe in a god, you'd have to admire his sense of irony.

Cynthia Proulx and Ian Keown gave a dinner for me. I looked down from the fifteenth floor on to the deep streets ribboned with red and white car-lights and out to the skyscrapers like black illuminated punch-cards and suddenly my nostalgic pleasure in all this became unpleasure and I knew that it was because she was not there to share it, not there for me to glance at with complicity,

* Yet she was skinny as a rake, and I speak as a rake.

not there for me not to need to glance at.

Later that night I called her in the Rue Jacob and asked her to join me straight away. She was untypically hesitant, and made excuses. Elliott had just flown in to shoot the perennial French tourist campaign and needed her to set up the shots and maybe to model. She said she'd have to see.

I spent the weekend on the beach at Amagansett with Diana Erwitt and the children and the art directors and the publishers. We drove over in the Volkswagen bus (you had to have a Volkswagen bus that summer) to a party in Easthampton. George Plimpton was there, with Freddy who, on seeing me arrive so unexpectedly, didn't bat an eyelid. James Jones was there, with Gloria, who was used to bumping into me by now, on the *quai*, in Central Park, anywhere. And I was there, with my thoughts.

> How did the party go in Portman Square?
> I cannot tell you, Juliet was not there....

Back at the Erwitt apartment someone had shoved a cable under the door. It read, 'IT IS TIME YOU STARTED YOUR ADULT LIFE. I WILL NOT BE AT THE AIRPORT TO MEET YOU. PATRICIA.' I took the first plane out I could get.

In the Rue Jacob next morning there was no sign that she had ever lived there. She had left as she arrived, quietly, neatly, with decorum. A note on the bed, in that standard American script, asked me in the classic way not to try to find her. It was better this way. Goodbye. That sort of note.

I lay back on the bed, my suitcase at my feet, staring at the ceiling, unblinking as Freddy Espy, as if there might be a message for me there. I lay motionless, unfeeling, like someone felled by something like grief. When I next moved, my limbs were stiff and cold and it was dark outside in the courtyard. The leaves of the plane tree had blended with the sky. The *chouette* gave a hoot. Well, at least somebody did. It had been a long day's journey into night, a long voyage home. Maybe tomorrow my adult life would begin. Again, maybe not.

Chapter 41

Those of you who have stuck with me this far, recalling perhaps my rather large claim that this narrative created an entirely new form of Eng. Lit. – i.e. and to wit, not to mention viz: fiction thinly disguised as autobiography – will possibly be muttering to yourselves about now, 'Right-ho. Got the idea. Chap's in charge of the overall picture. But shouldn't he then, at around this stage of the production, introduce some sort of crisis, climax, what-have-you, which, by bringing together the various strands of the plot, along with the assorted *dramatis personae*, resolves the conflicts and leads us on to reconciliation for the put-upon protagonist and a bit of – what's the word – catharsis for the loyal reader, i.e. me?' That's what you may be muttering to yourself. You might even point out that the Greeks, before they were into supertankers, were into the writing game in a pretty big way. And they were especially strong on this *deus ex machina* who gets into the action and sorts it all out, though why the Greeks chose to express themselves in Latin escapes me for the moment. Well, I say to you, don't go away mad. Hang tough. It isn't all that easy to arrange this sort of thing when you're dealing with a (let's face it) work of non-fiction, as opposed to fiction, but I think I've got something that will do the trick. In fact, talk about nature imitating art!

Revenons en nos moutons. The funny thing is that the disappearance of the fair, the chaste, the inexpressive she – i.e. Patricia – while having the immediate effect of making me feel pretty low, also produced one of those surges of the spirit that seem to accompany a sudden freedom, like a school half-holiday

310

you didn't expect, for example. Of course, I'm beginning to suspect that real freedom comes from commitment, that, for instance, a chap like me is never so free as when chained to his desk, with pencil and paper to hand – as long, of course, as he does the chaining. But I didn't think that then, and hence my resemblance, after a short slump, to a lark at break of day arising, all set to sing hymns at heaven's gate.

But first, to clear up the problem of the missing person. Naturally I telephoned around and about, broadcasting the while, of course, my disarray. All the world hates a loser. Finally Diana reported in to say that she was there, in the house at Amagansett. What a switch. She had found a job, with an advertising agency – now there's another switch – and had rented a room in Greenwich Village. Next Bill Murray, our Blevy landlord, called on her in the Village and pronounced her in good health. (Bill, having with difficulty collected the back rent, tended to take off in winter for America and Jamaica, where his neighbour, Noel Coward had impressed him on their first meeting by putting a manicured finger on his glass as he poured him a drink and saying, 'Just to the brim, dear boy, just to the brim.') Then Peter Hyun told me that Patricia had spent a lot of time at Judy's bedside and was with her almost to the moment of leukemia's bitter triumph.

There didn't seem much that I could do about any of this. Of course, there was, plenty, but, as so often when action is called for, I was paralysed by opposing feelings. I stayed put. Then, eager to try out my new, *soi-disant*, feelings, I headed, avid as a mainliner heading for a fix, towards the sun. I drove down to St Tropez. I took a room with terrace at the Baou, a new and expensive pile below the ramparts of Ramatuelle. Then I moved smoothly into gear for an act I knew well, the standard routine of the well-heeled bachelor in St Tropez (it is of course true that though I have been a bachelor for ever I have been well heeled only for weeks at a time).

Mouth-cleansing grapefruit, not too early, in bed or on the terrace. Smell of herbs, pines, woodsmoke all about. Jag down

311

the twirly road past the vineyards and the cork-stripped trees. Park with the other Parisian 75s under the raffia shades behind the hotel of the *plage de* Tahiti. Fifteen francs to the aging neuter beachboy for the orange mattress, headrest, parasol, title to the private plot of land – each man an island to himself – about the size of the one to which we all hold title. At noon, too early to be chic, a few oiled bodies lie, like stranded and bereft sardines. This is the first summer breasts are bared, and two or four of them are good to look at.

People begin to trail along the sandy gully from the car-park, kicking off sandals and espadrilles without looking down, dragging beach-bags along the freshly brushed and combed platinum-blond sand. Others power up in boats to the jetty from around the bay: Vadim and his disparate brood, Elsa Martinelli, famous for being famous, down with her Omo-dazzling teeth from her Omo-dazzling villa on Cap Camarat, Jacques Charrier, famous for having married Brigitte Bardot (but not Bardot, too famous to need to come here). The usual crowd. Nobody I knew, or would much want to know.

Time to shirt-up and lope the gauntlet – cold who-are-you stares from hot bodies – of the two rows of inland *chaises longues* as far as the round, thatched bar of the restaurant and order the house speciality, an exotic fruit cocktail called *un Paradis, avec ou sans rhum. Avec.* Under palm and parasol, bare feet in the table-shaded sand, do-it-yourself *crudités* served on curved bark platters, like Basque pelota throwers. A small, well-disciplined parade of *rougets grilles*, anchovy sauce, parsley, lemon, shaped boiled potatoes served from small hot copper bucket, half bottle of Ramatuelle *rosé* bobbing and using the ropes in large, cold silver bucket. The local dessert, the *tarte tropezienne*, two layers of sponge-cake, *crème anglaise* between, powdered sugar on top. Finger-licking good. Coffee small, rich and dark, like the Aga Khan. Over to the mattress to close the eyes and run the meal in play-back.

At four, change in the restaurant and drive up the sand-dusted roads to the port, buy the English papers and the *Trib*, unfold a

312

red canvas chair under the red awning of Senequier and order a Kronenbourg from the black-dressed, white-aproned, pale-faced waitress, who has seen it all before. Watch the talent pass between here and the backyards of the yachts, pursued or protected by preening males. Better than the movies. Should be, at the price of the beer.

Re-Jag. Up the hill. De-sand, shower, change. The pale blue pants, the dark blue shirt (shirt outside or inside pants? Decisions, decisions), navy moccasins. Skin glowing nicely, not red though, just the right brown, fifteen francs worth of sun, plus a bit of moonlighting. Senequier again, new boy in town, everybody else de-sanded, showered. Sun setting on schedule behind the Buffet angularity of masts, hanging there exotic yet familiar, like an orange to a child.

The yacht people, cocktailing it on their shaded poops, or whatever, like colonials on verandas in Hollywood movies. Down a Ricard or two, decide against Les Mouscardins (two stars then, how are the mighty fallen) as being too grand, and the Auberges des Maures (one star then and now) as being too poky, and settle for the less gastronomic Pirate next door but one as being chic, open-air, *mouvementé*.

Here's action man again. *Moules marinières? Bouillabaisse? Soupe de poissons? Loup de mer au fenouil? Dorade?* Decisions, decisions. Study the form. Post-prandial beer or calva or marc at Senequier, stroll through unisex Choses and Vachon to check on what you have to be wearing this year. Scouting over, up the cooling hill, out to the terrace, take in the view, the scent of rosemary and thyme, the faint revving of excited cars jockeying for parking space on the *place* in Ramatuelle, and sleep to the sibilance of cicadas.

The mind-emptying routine ('Enough, my brain, of these circles, circles, cease, caged enemy, cease!': old Tessimond, hitting the head on the nail again) goes on for a week or more, stretching time so that the charging minutes now crawl by like retreating infantrymen. Small events point up the longueurs: David Hamilton, the soft-focus whiz, who lives in Ramatuelle,

313

setting off in his Aston Martin with a gaggle of freshly pubescent Danes, all awkward grace and girlish gravitas; dinner at Edward Behr's, curry (he's an old Indian Army man), *Paris Match* journalists, a BBC producer, wives, mistresses; visit from my brother, his wife and son, over from Ste Maxime, the St Tropez for families; promise to see them back at Blevy, their usual stopover before London, not having any idea I won't make it.

On my last day − why? why not? − bill payed, cases in the boot, thoughts of the hot shimmering ribbon of the *autoroute* to Paris nudge me down for a last cooling swim. At Tahiti, salt water dripping from nose, chin and trunks, more self-indulgence: I study the menu nailed to a palm tree. Lunch here, or farther on, at Aix, say? Decision made for me. A pair of cool hands reaches round to cover my eyes and a female, East Coast voice says (guess what?), 'Guess who?'

It is Diana Erwitt. Not on the beach at Amagansett. On the beach here. Surprise, surprise, do admit. I look around fast − anything possible now − for you-know-who. She's not there. Thank God. Caught off balance. Not ready. Need time to think. Relief. Back into persona. Diana leads me over to a table. Elliott. Hi. Lady art director from Mather and Crowther, London, nice face. Hello. Eric Lessing, Magnum's specialist in artworks. *Guten Tag*. Financial columnist of *Figaro*, bare-breasted (bosom friend of Eric's?). *Bonjour*. They invite me to join them for lunch. How nice. Pleasant send-off. Elliott confers, apart, with lady director, then turns to me.

'How'd you like to do a bit of modelling for us?' he asks.

He is here to shoot pictures, one more time, for the French tourist campaign. The blonde Diana, chaste, or anyway, chased huntress, will be a model. An English girl model is expected momentarily, as we used to say on Mad Ave. What they needed was a male to escort, cavort with, dash along the sand with, sup with these two pretty girls. It sounded like a tough assignment, but we Hennessys have never ducked a challenge. The idea was to show the rest of the world what it was missing if it didn't vacation in the South of France. I said my impression was the rest of the world did vacation in the S. of F. They said, if they paid my hotel and expenses and laid some money on me for my time, could I stay on for a few days and help out? I turned this offer slowly over in my mind for a second. Beautiful girls. Free food and lodging. Agreeable company. Hell, I couldn't let down an old buddy like Elliott in his time of need. Putting as good a face on it as I could, I accepted.

So a star was born. For three days I played the fool, for money. Eating, running, jumping, standing still, swimming, dancing, canoodling. Diana murmured, during some clinch, 'Elliott says you look as if you're in training for something.' You had to be. It was demanding work, I can tell you.

I didn't mention absent friends. Play it cool in the St Tropez sun. See what she's missing. See if I care. That sort of rubbish. But Diana looked at me with one of those schmaltzy, girlish smiles and whispered, 'I hear wedding bells.' If she heard them around my belfry she must have been bats. But she wasn't talking about me.

All checked out, bag in the Jag again. I had a farewell drink with the group at their hotel in Port Grimaud. They asked me, for security's sake, to take the precious colour film to Paris for processing. So I threw a plastic bag containing hundreds of rolls of Ekta and Kodachrome into the back of the car and at about seven on a nice warm evening I was purring suavely northwards, with the pleasing prospect of a cool freshwater swim in the pool of Le Pigeonnet at Aix and a plate of ratatouille on the terrace afterwards and a peaceful dove-cooing night before joining the mad lemmings on the Paris road. That was my plan, and frankly I couldn't see much wrong with it. But, as they say in the kind of book where they say that kind of thing, it was not to be.

It was getting dark as I burbled through Fréjus but I wasn't missing much. It was never my favourite town. It certainly isn't now. Traffic lights in the centre of town turned red, halting the cars so the drivers could get good and hot. A girl (not bad) stepped off the pavement and skittered among the frustrated cars, putting leaflets that plugged some supermarket sale under the windscreen wipers. Angry at having the view obscured, I opened the door and stepped out to remove the paper, turning to shout at the disappearing girl. With my back to the traffic lights, I didn't see them change to green.

Fritz Lang was handling the next shot, young Orson Welles assisting. Ground-level camera, 28-mm wide-angle lens, pans slowly, sometimes in focus, sometimes out (puller must be drunk), around a circle of faces framed against darkening night sky and staring down from elongated bodies (that's the wide angle) with expressions of shock, sympathy, thrilled horror. Then I realised that the camera is my head and that something warm and sticky is leaking from it to form a pool on rough tarmac I couldn't have chosen for comfort. And I can't figure out why I can't lift my head, or move my body, or how to play the scene, or what the dialogue might be. They hadn't given me the script for this one.

Sirens sound, like keening women. Somebody dead, maybe. Written out of the film. Then two property men pick me up by shoulders and ankles. My head, cannon-ball heavy, lolls back vertiginously (Hitchcock here too?) and a sound like velcro ripped apart comes from my neck. Voices scream, *'Sa tête! Prenez sa tête, nom de dieu!'* Who wrote this stuff? Why are all the extras French?

Cut to interior of service elevator. Scratched paint on walls bares grey metal. Not cosy. Camera looks up hairy legs of man in shorts. Not a pretty sight. Seen better. Not my style. Swing out, up, sideways on to cold slab. Dr Kildare, impersonal, asks me to move legs. Sure. I give the necessary orders. Legs obey. So what. I can do it any time.

Arab music on sound track. Must be immigrant territory. Figuring it all out now. Aren't I the clever one. That's sticky blood and sweat matting my hair into strange-feeling shapes. My head begins to hurt, feels like a head again. The doctor wipes my forehead, dispassionately, sews up a piece of it, crudely, clumsily, if you're used to watching women sew.

He chats to a nurse the while, about her boy-friend.

316

Unbelievable. Chap suffering on slab and they're into her sex-life. I try to engage their attention, to point out that I am something other than a piece of *charcuterie*, to tell them I am custodian of valuable artworks and that they should alert Elliott Erwitt at Port Grimaud. I try to remember name of hotel. Not remembering so good. The Giglia. Ha! Try remembering that, and then pronouncing it, with your second cervical vertebra shot to hell.

They put a heroic, Crimea-veteran bandage round my head and levered me out of my *choses* from Choses and into a coarse white smock, like French hotel sheets. Then they dollied me past the wailing Arab wards and into a private room. You don't take chances with a Jaguar owner. They put a sloping wooden board behind my head and a von Stroheim brace about my neck. That and the board fixed my reluctant gaze on a crucifix by the red light bulb over the door. Ecumenical, this joint, I thought as I lay there, surrounded by Moslems, a surpliced altar boy again. They say they always get you in the end.

Left alone, my chief feeling was of rage. I'd never been a hospital patient before, never had an accident, never been ill – apart from feeling pretty sick most of the time, like everybody else. Pristine, I'd been, and now all spoiled. No fault of mine. Rotten show. But whose fault was it? Why does one chap step on the banana skin and not another? Who knows what path the urge for self-destruction might choose? There's more than one way to skin a head. Thinking these deep thoughts I fell into a fitful Mogadon sleep, waking in the night to try not to believe it, to pretend it all hadn't happened. God that my love were in my arms, and I in my bed again, as the chap said.

The next day, packed social schedule. Broken neck, pronounced the specialist, and his cohorts nodded sagely. The great man's done it again. All wheel out. Big deal. Then the chap who'd done the damage, bulleting off from traffic lights. Young Frenchman with Yugoslav girl-friend and glasses an inch thick. Hadn't seen me, he explained. Well, at least he was a hit-and-stay driver. Give him credit. Clumsy bastard. Canoodling probably. I would have been too, with that slant-eyed Slav beside me. Next.

Elliott and Diana came over. Fancy meeting you here. They picked up the film from the police, who had put the Jaguar behind bars. I asked Elliott to call Eileen Coffey, Patricia's colleague at Magnum, and have her inform all who needed to be of the tragedy. Digby, who insured the car but not me – shrewd cookies, these Lloyds fellas – sent his dapper and efficient man in Nice over, to get a statement. He had checked the scene of the crime (*lèse-majesté*, in my view) and said that when the lights changed our French friend, or fiend, had surged on to the centre line, currently occupied by me, as blood-marks confirmed. An unidentified girl, no doubt the supermarket hustler, had been spotted running from the scene in panic. Well she might. Leave everything to him, he said. Good show. In that case, I'd stay where I was.

Edward and Christiane Behr came over from Ramatuelle. They had a friend who was chief consultant at St Tropez municipal hospital, whose surgeons were a cut above, so to speak, the Fréjus chaps. Edward said he'd arrange for me to be transferred there as soon as I could be moved without my head falling off. He also promised to telephone New York and tell Patricia I'd broken my neck, or had it broken for me, which came to the same thing. (You may think I'd gone a bit far to get the girl back, but needs must when the devil, or whoever, drives.)

So there you have it. The twist in the plot we were talking about. Hard to see how you could take artistic integrity further, I reckon. I mean, there's our hero, riding high, top of the world, when pow! and pow! again – the classic double whammy. First, bereft of the loved one and then, when he's still reeling from the blow, cut down by a thunderbolt (in my case, a Renault 16, actually) and brought to the very threshold of death, or paralysis, or anyway left with a hell of a pain in the neck, and left, what's more, alone with his thoughts, which ought to prove pretty interesting.

Now, one's heard about this sort of thing. I mean, chap living frivolous, selfish, hedonistic life is suddenly brought low by blow of fate but saved to reflect in enforced leisure upon wasted years, false values, and thereby is changed, made over, born again to begin a new life of commitment, responsible adulthood and service to others. That's the plot, right? Well, maybe so, but it's not what happened to me.

Chapter 42

It may not be everybody's idea of an end-of-season junket in the South of France, but life in *l'Hôpital Municipal de St Tropez*, though not perhaps in your five-star or *palace* class, wasn't too bad at all.

I mean, when you've had a roughish night, lifting your own head with your two hands (have you ever tried lifting a head? Weighs a ton, though of course that may depend on the size of the brain) to shove it around on the pillow so that its more or less in line with the rest of you, it bucks you up no end to have a peasant's bowl of *café-crème* and a freshly buttered *baguette* to dunk in it brought to the bedside with a pert *'Bonjour'* by a suntanned nurse who, leaning solicitously over to pat a pillow, gives ample evidence that the topless fashion, though launched only that season, has, so to speak, taken firm hold.

A young American intern, boy-friend of the fetching, and carrying, *infirmière*, brought me the *Herald Tribune* from town each noon, and *Time* magazine on Wednesdays. For my birthday (and Scott Fitzgerald's), which I may have been lucky to see, they produced a bottle of champagne. Drinking champagne through a bent glass tube is better than not drinking champagne at all.

At last a cable came. She commiserated, wished me a speedy recovery, but said that, all things considered, she thought it best to stay in New York, and that a letter tackling the matter in rather more depth followed. The letter, a few years (it seemed to me) later, only confirmed this decision. Yet all that time, especially in the interminable, semi-drugged nights, I found it impossible to believe, almost as if it would be fatal to believe, that she would

320

not return, that someone who had shared my life for eight years could become, so soon, so detached.

Perhaps, I conjectured, she thought the whole thing was a ploy. Perhaps, there was, as popular fiction has it, someone else? The thought that lay below such brooding though was this: having been given the nudge by the old gardener in white, I was faced with the fact that there wasn't anybody else to whom that mattered vitally, that there wasn't anybody else who had to care. Home is the place where, if you have to go there, they have to take you in, said Frost's farmer. There wasn't any place like that for me on earth.

Christiane Behr, visiting me, was convinced, as any right-thinking Frenchwoman would be, that if Patricia realised that I had been, as she rather dramatically put it, *grièvement blessé*, she would be at the bedside *tout de suite*. So she roared in her resounding Triumph up the hill to get on the blower to New York, a neat trick from Ramatuelle in those days, for in France, the saying went, half the nation was waiting for the telephone, and the other half was waiting for the dialling tone.

One of those rare instruments rang the next afternoon. A nurse came to tell me that there was a call for me from New York and that I would have to take it in the matron's office, down the corridor. This amazed me. The last time I had been on my feet was at the traffic lights in Fréjus, and look what that had led to. But she got me up, head as big and heavy as a deep sea diver's helmet, and I tottered like an old man out into an unknown, never seen world, full of doors, down to a room with a desk on which a telephone receiver lay, black and silent and dangerous as a cobra's head.

I picked it up fearfully and croaked hello. Her voice was an instant comfort, like the touch of a familiar hand. She spoke gently, as if she felt, over all that distance, that I was fragile and might break. She said she had not realised that things had been so serious, but now that apparently I was out of danger she thought it would be better if she stayed where she was.

I was working painfully, being out of practice, on a reply to

321

this, when suddenly, from somewhere that seemed very near, a deep wail rose, broken by sobs, a noise as unbidden, as primal, as the long, terrible cry of the mother in *Pather Panchali* when she knows at last her child is dead. It grew to fill the room, the corridor, the hospital, the world. And then it changed, broke slowly down into something more earthly, more everyday, into the way words sound, ill-formed but intelligible, in the mouth of a child weeping uncontrollably. The words were coming from me.

Grief surging like a killer-wave in a calm sea had hit me once before, the day I heard my father had died, suddenly, unexpectedly. Years of unspoken, unadmitted love demanded outlet then, and would not be denied. The force of such buried, but never deeply enough buried, emotions shocked me now. As they calmed I heard the voice of Patricia, quiet, soothing, awed perhaps as I was by this visitation from the vasty deep, this archetypal howl. She didn't promise, but she would think it over, and I shouldn't worry, and I should go and rest now. I nodded abstractedly, as children do when you dry their eyes and tell them it's all better, and I hung up and shuffled feebly back to my bed, drained, purged, as I had been after LSD.

Next day, around noon, I was called to the telephone again. An old marathon hand now, I slippered more quickly down the hall. She sounded distant. I had forgotten about the French telephone system. If it sounds distant it must be France.

'Where are you?' I asked. Strange how the important phrases are the most banal.

'I'm here, at the airport, at Nice,' she said, changing the world situation with one sentence. 'Christiane was supposed to meet me, but she's not here. Don't worry. I'll take a taxi.'

The unthinkable no longer needed to be thought. I had got in under the wire.

I went over for the first time to the basin in my room and looked in the mirror. They should have told me. My hair was still matted with dried blood and I could neither comb it nor wash it. I couldn't brush my teeth, for my bones had not yet set, or *consolidés*, or whatever they said they had to do. All very well to be

322

up and about at last, but mustn't lose one's head. I wore pyjama trousers only (I think I've mentioned that this was the first topless year down there: go with the trend has always been my rule in sartorial matters). Funny to have ribs again, like a skinny kid. If I went down to the beach now they'd kick sand in my face, which might have improved the one, a stranger to me, that stared back at me from the mirror now. I removed it from public view and went and sat on the edge of my bed, front row of the stalls, looking out at the empty courtyard framed by the window, screen on which, for once, a fantasy might come true.

She came on screen left, suitcase in hand, Burberry trench coat swinging open, fresh, young, healthy, hair straight and neat. If you'd added a beret you'd have had Michele Morgan in *Quai des Brumes*. All she needed was a decent chap with the heart of Gabin. All she had was a skinny weakling. She came into the place through a door I'd never seen, quietly eager, unruffled by taxis, airports and night flights. She was her own country, my new found land, found again.

We talked shyly, as people do who have been close and then apart. She had lugged a life of Mozart and Keats's letters all the way from Doubledays. When Christiane Behr, who thanks to the French telephone system had not received her cable, came to take her up to Ramatuelle, I turned to the books, in every way content.

Next day they came to get me, eased me on to the stretched-out front seat of the sports car, and I followed the bends in the road by the tops of the trees that swayed and curved against the blue vault of the tropezian sky.

We had the guest room that we knew, French windows on the terrace, looking over faded apricot balustrade past gnarled vineyards and olive groves and bare red earth down to the blue hazy bay. All bones, I lowered myself gingerly into the bathtub where she tried, scared at every movement, to wash my hair, black hard specks of vintage blood mixing with the suds. We went for slow, invalid walks about the village, cooler now than when I'd left it, she supporting me as if I were some returned veteran of the wars, ghost of the singing boy who had gone for a

323

soldier.

The sun falls last in Ramatuelle on the high ground of the cemetery and we pursued it there, to end our evenings on a stone bench by the tomb of Gerard Philippe, local boy made god, who had gone to wherever young gods go. (Mozart and Keats would be waiting.) Life was smiling again, for me if not for him. All that was left for me to do now was kick it in the teeth.

Marriage, as I have noted, in my smartass way, in my as yet unpublished Great Thoughts, is two people being alone together. (That may give you a clue as to why they remain unpublished.) But what I say is, if it helps get them through the long day's journey into night, OK. Live and let live, though the proximity of marriage has always seemed about as cheery as the tepid breath on your neck of the old reaper himself, and that's a subject I now knew something about. Fear of commitment, fear of women, fear of life? Or fear perhaps of some important freedom lost? You tell me.

Still, if one had to get married – at shot-gun-point, for example – I would wish for the ceremony, or last rite, to take place quietly, privately, secularly and even secretly: among a few old friends, say, in the *mairie* of some small and remote French village. I would wish for my bride to be beautiful, kind, trusting, loyal, owing, like me, no allegiance to class, sect or nation, and sharing, or at least indulging, my perhaps dubious tastes. After the brief doings (another advantage of the French ceremony is that you get a free book, no doubt to give you something to do on your wedding night) I would wish good food for no more than six people in a civilized and, for memory's sake, picturesque setting.

Well, not only was this whole package available to me then, it was warmly urged upon me by those who might be thought to have my best interests at heart. Patricia announced, with that grave, controlled excitement that girls reserve for any topic bearing on the Big M, that the kindly *maire* of Ramatuelle, whom she had thoughtfully visited with Christiane while I unsuspectingly was resting the neck behind a chunk of Keats,

324

had, in honour no doubt of the long association of our hosts with his natal village, agreed to dispense, *exceptionnellement*, with the delays normally attendant upon the nuptials of *étrangers*. We could, it transpired, be married forthwith.

It is a matter of pride with me that when in deep shock I contrive, drawing on God knows what unsuspected sources of inner strength, to conceal this state from the outside world. So it was with a casual 'Oh he will, will he?' and a non-committal 'Oh we can, can we?' that I greeted these dire tidings. Men more heroic than I might say that at that moment a career notable for pusillanimity was crowned by a craven act of cowardice. Women, I suspect, would simply want to give me a good shake.

Passing my chair at dinner that night, Edward Behr, back from Paris for the weekend, and for all I know, the wedding, made two pistols with his fists and fired them silently at me, a gesture that puzzled me at the time. Christiane took me aside and said, *'Mais pourquoi tu ne veut pas épouser cette fille? Elle est toute jeune, elle est toute fraîche ...,'* which I contrived to find a trifle importunate, closing the mind against her temporary lapse from her own high standards of taste.

Wriggling desperately and unashamedly now, marooned in crunchville with no one to throw me a rope, I indicated to the doubtless disappointed, and possibly even humiliated, loved one that I did not want to go through such an important moment in our lives while I was still encased in my *minerve* (the rather pretty French name for the gruesome apparatus, after that goddess with the swan-like). Besides, think of what it would do to the wedding pictures! Playing for time now, my only hope, I proposed – *le mot juste* – that we put the whole thing off until Christmas, in Paris, when I would be fit again and all the arrangements could be properly made, without indecent haste. The subject was not mentioned again. I congratulated myself on having procrastinated with great cunning. I did not allow the thought that I might well be regarded with obloquy, if that's the word, by those around me to intrude upon my self-satisfaction and sense of relief.

The head man (in every sense) at the hospital said that I could now travel to Paris, as long as I went by ambulance to and from the airport. We were a smart crowd on the Air Caravelle. René Clair, small, lean, stooped, like a kindly miser, carried a small Louis Vuitton box that contained a packed lunch or the family jewels. Jacques Brel, windswept from his boat, was alive and well, with the quiet, firm presence of one who is his own man at all times and in all places. Françoise Giroud, still editor of *L'Express* then, intelligent, aware, good woman, all Parisian chic in her bi-sexual Chanel. I was the star, though. You get the attention when you walk around with a broken neck. I thought Madame Giroud stared more than most. Then I remembered that at nineteen she was script girl on Renoir's *Grande Illusion*. So I raised my glass of brandy to her, and tossed it back with a quick von Stroheim jerk. It must have brought back memories.

Back in the Rue Jacob I felt not unsatisfied with life. I had almost lost the inamorata, and then almost lost my life, and I'd got both of them back, more or less. And here I was, home with her in Paris, to prove it. I wanted to go down to Blevy, to show the world, to meet the friends I had not seen for so long. Patricia, most compliant of companions, refused absolutely to accompany me. That I didn't understand why gives you the measure of my insensitivity, of my near-to-monstrous egocentricity. (His brother Beppo said of Groucho's marriages, 'He just wanted someone to have dinner with'; maybe that was true of me, too.)

She said she had to get back to New York. I begged her to stay, claiming that I could not get around by myself. She was firm. She had found new strength – the kind that women have to gather before they can make a break that the mind but not the heart may want. In her letter to me in the hospital she had written, 'I have my own life to save too, you know.' As she got into the cab she turned to kiss goodbye and said, for my ears only, 'You know, I'm not coming back unless its to marry.' I mumbled reassurance. It couldn't have been too convincing. I never saw her again.

There were enthusiastic letters. Her father and step-mother, doubtful about me from the beginning, as any caring parents might be, were now happy for her. The office was giving a farewell party for her. She had been down to Princeton to stay with Joel and Marikay Raphaelson at their week-end place. Borgie Baton had been there.

I wrote to tell her that Sam White said the simplest thing was to get married at the British Embassy, cutting out a lot of the hooha attendant on such arrangements under the French system. (I'm not sure why Sam was putting in a plug, so to speak, for the Embassy. He had been *persona non grata* there ever since he revealed to a startled world that Lady Jebb, on moving in, had had all the bidets moved out.)

Then one day there was a letter that started with the same girlish eagerness as the others and then, halfway through, announced that this was all nonsense, wasn't it, that we really had nothing in common and that she had met this man who was kind and nice and whom she liked very much. For some reason – perhaps from a feeling that this must be some passing hysteria, perhaps from relief that a decision had been made for me – I did not reply immediately to this letter. She may have felt I would, though not avowing it, welcome an escape route, with map provided. 'Just think what you'll be escaping – ,' she wrote, 'marriage!'

A few weeks went agreeably by, as they do in Paris. Then the telephone rang in my office one day. It was Eileen Coffey, at Magnum. She said, 'I suppose you've heard about Patricia?'

'No,' I said, 'What about her?' Not perhaps on the highest intellectual plane, the conversation.

'I'm sorry,' she said, 'I was sure you must have known. She's married.'

He was a Frenchman, living in New York, younger than her, something to do with sound. By a nice irony, of you like irony, the wedding had taken place in Cynthia Proulx's apartment, looking out on the view I had wanted to share with her on my fatuous escapade. Our friends the Raphaelsons, Ian Keown, Inge and Junius Edwards, Borgie Baton were, as the expression goes, members of the wedding. The pictures were taken by Elliott Erwitt. Nothing but the best.

She had asked Junius to tell me that she was about to marry. He had tried, he said, to reach me, without success. When Eileen Coffey dined with the couple later in New York, Patricia said, 'He had seven weeks to come and get me.'

Chapter 43

Win a few, lose a few. Women are like buses, they said, there'll be another one along in a minute. That's all right, unless you happen to want, like Dorothy Parker, one perfect limousine.

There was Siw, the archetypal Swede: an English girl that's been dipped in bleach. I took her to St Tropez, scene of the crime. Swedish accessories were in that year. The Jaguar, its heart broken by the betrayal, died at Aix. She took me to Stockholm that winter. Streets all full of snow, stop, please advise. That cooled my ardour.

There was Anna, seventeen, like Siw. All old men are dirty old men. Child-woman, obsession of the writer, so they say. Anna was at a finishing school (yes Virginia, such things still exist) called Anita's, which sounded like a *bordel*, also known as the Convent of the Sacred Heart, which didn't. 'Oh really? When were you up at Oxford?' she asked. Forty-seven to forty-nine, I told her. 'Then you must know Daddy!' she squeaked. And, by God, I did. That kind of thing marks a man. Soon she had to go home in order to come out, if you follow me. Yes, that goes on too. It's all still going on, in England. Nostalgia is the English disease, or anyway, its symptom. I needed a break.

I had lost my freelance contacts during hospital and convalescence. I still had the use of an office, but there wasn't much going on. I'd have to move out of the Rue Jacob. God how I hate change. I went to dinner one night at the Neaves' and stayed over, for about a year. (Digby had remarried, a French girl, called Christiane.)

On a job-hunting trip to Paris I was sitting – I was doing a lot of it at the time – in the Drug Store at the Rond Point, getting my shoes shined, when I perceived, in the pharmacy section of the complex, a familiar and distinguished figure, wearing a long overcoat with a Diaghilev astrakhan collar. David Ogilvy. Turning to leave, having made his purchases, he saw me.

He advanced gravely towards me, reaching in his pocket the while. Then he proffered a package and said, 'Charles, I've been buying toothpaste. Have I bought the right brand?' Be memorable.

As we walked up the Champs-Elysées, I reassured him about his purchase. Macleans. Excellent brand. I had written copy for it myself, at Bensons ('Did you Maclean your teeth today?' was our immortal theme). I mentioned, à propos, that I had heard that when he had recently acquired Bensons, to add to his earlier acquisition, Mather and Crowther, Benson heads had clattered. He looked pained. That wasn't how it had been at all.

'You see, when the directors of Bensons moved in with Mathers, and saw what good management really was, they all threw themselves out of the windows!'

As we crossed the Avenue, he taking my arm, as he had on Fifth, he asked me whether I counted in old francs or in new. New, I said. Everybody did, except the French. So did he, he said, but it could lead to confusion.

'When I was leaving Touffou this morning I discovered I had no money on me, so when I saw my gardener in the grounds I asked him if he could possibly lend me twenty francs. *"Deux mille francs, Monsieur?"* the good fellow replied, *"Mais bien sûr."* Well, one can't take two thousand francs from one's gardener, can one?'

I was mulling over this tricky social problem when we arrived at the Travellers' Club. Ogilvy turned to me, said 'Goodbye!' and leapt up the steps of the club like a mountain goat who has spotted a particularly fetching she-goat. Memorable though.

Blevy was now my only home. One winter night there I went over to Tom Webb's *moulin*, the old Neave homestead, for one of our frequent *tête-à-tête* dinners. (Betty had died, following a stroke.) As I was about to go glowing into the night I remembered that I had nothing to read, a dire situation if your bed is empty, and even if it isn't, come to that. I looked around and my glance fell on a small, scruffily-printed newspaper entitled the *Sikkim Times*. (Tom, an international lawyer, represented Hope Cook, the winsome American girl who married the king of Sikkim, and presumably was keeping up with social events in Gangkok.) I borrowed the journal – whatever gets you through the night, is what I say.

Reading in bed, one cold arm at a time outside the sheets in my *chambre Stendhalienne* (two of the walls red, two black), I noted with interest, and then with mounting excitement, that a new dam had been opened, with a suitable speech, by the Indian Political Officer, a Mr K. S. Bajpai. Old Baj! For this could be none other than my Oxford buddy, Shankar Bajpai, whose name had appeared thus, in gothic white on black, at the foot of our staircase at Merton. I had not seen him for twenty-five years, though I had had news of him from Edward Behr, whom I had sent to see him when he was on diplomatic post in India and Pakistan.

Next day I wrote to Shankar, care of the *Sikkim Times*, Gangkok. My letter began, 'My dear Shankar, As I was browsing through my *Sikkim Times....*' His reply was rapid, warm and affectionate. He had tried to reach me over the years and the miles, in New York, Paris and London, but I'd always just moved on. He was coming to Paris, though, very soon. It would be nice if we could meet again. His letter ended, as I had half-expected, with a postscript: 'By the way, dear boy, I am wondering what on earth you are doing subscribing to the *Sikkim Times*!'

When I returned his paper I showed the letter to Tom Webb who said, 'Tell him, what do you mean, subscribe? Tell him you picked it up at the dentist's, like everyone else.'

Shankar came with his wife, Meera, a small, beautiful woman of gentle manners, fierce intelligence, wide culture and quick wit. His mother had chosen well. There were two lively sons, Mirko and Goupy. You would be lively with names like that. They were on their way to take up his first ambassadorship, at The Hague. That wouldn't be far, by the Autoroute du Nord, or the TEE.

The next day I took them out to Marly le Roi. Digby and Shankar, who had last met as undergraduates on the cobbled quadrangles of Merton, now embraced on the *pavés* of the Rue Champflour.

Soon we were all week-ending at The Hague. The Neaves drove up from Marly. Anthony Blond flew in from London. So did Michael Briggs, with his wife, Isabel Colegate, whose first novel had been published by Blond. Hilary Rubinstein, another Merton friend, who was now a literary agent (for Wodehouse – you wouldn't need any other authors), came and left a book he had written on insomnia. It worked for me. Tony Curtis, literary editor of the *Financial Times*, with whom I had shared my first English tutorial with Hugo Dyson, was asked and couldn't make it. Edward Montague was asked and could. It was one of the best times of my life.

I'd been suffering, it now became clear, from a kind of social and cultural malnutrition. Most of my fellow guests were people I regarded as my closest friends, with whom I had tastes, and feelings and humour in common – and yet I had not seen them, or tried to see them, or to live among them, for many years. Why? They seemed happy to see me. I was more than happy to see them. Had I been cut off? Or they?

At our last dinner there, a grand and dinner-jacketed affair for Shankar's birthday, there were speeches, which usually give me the heebie-jeebies. Edward Montague, used, no doubt, to piping up in the House of Lords, proposed a toast to Shankar from his Oxford friends. As half a dozen old buddies scraped back chairs and teetered to their feet I glanced at the dignitaries assembled at the vast table and wondered what deductions they might be making, from our flushed faces, about the imprint made upon us, if any, by our alma mater. What on earth did we have in common?

There was someone there I had something in common with,

though, and that was the second Lady Montague, a South African of quiet charm whom I met for the first time. Discovering that I was in advertising, she wondered if I might know her ex-fiancé, or at least his father, who was pretty big in the business. Fairfield Ogilvy was the name of the former, the name of the latter being David of that ilk, as I believe they say up there. Heard of the former, I said, knew the latter. Fairfield, a highly successful lawyer, was still unmarried. They were still good friends, she said, and recently when she and Edward had stayed at Touffou Fairfield brought with him a new and, according to Fiona Montague, whose judgement I respect, admirable girl-friend.

At the end of their stay, David Ogilvy had driven the Montagues in his Volkswagen bus to the airport at Bordeaux. During the drive he asked Fiona what she thought of his son's new girl. Fiona, a frank and honest lady, or Lady, replied that she found her a splendid girl and a fine companion for Fairfield.

There was a silence that lasted for several kilometres. Finally Ogilvy spoke. 'I wonder what brand of chewing gum she uses,' he said.

After dinner we strolled in the gardens of the residency. It wasn't Versailles, but then Shankar was only an ambassador. A narrow canal crossed our path. Michael Briggs wondered what its function might be. I didn't hesitate. You have to catch these things on the wing, and they fly by only once.

'That must be one of those diplomatic channels one's heard so much about,' I said.

I hadn't lost my touch. Maybe they'd let me back into society. Maybe they'd throw me in a canal.

The Bajpais came down for Christmas with the Neaves and in the summer Shankar took a house in Oxford. I drove over with Digby, Christiane and their son Lionel. Alan Cooke, now a BBC television producer, came up from Richmond with his American wife and two sons. My brother Tom, another Merton man, came with his wife and son.

We went over to Bicester for drinks with Airey and Diana Neave, had beer and sandwiches at the Trout and dinner at the

333

Bear at Woodstock, where we had taken our golden girls before the Commem Balls. Digby, Shankar and I trod the lawns of Merton again, more soberly, perhaps, more solidly this time. We peered through the windows of our old rooms, as if we would find our lost youth there, or anywhere.

Emboldened by my excursion with Digby and Shankar, I ventured out and into England more, renewing contact with old friends. The news was not all good, but there were survivors.

I stayed for a while in his Chelsea house with Robin Jacques, my Ebury Street room-mate of twenty years ago. He was still doing his little dots for books and the *Radio Times*.

I spent a weekend with Bernard Gutteridge, walking and talking, in his Sussex cottage. Freed now from J. Walter Thompson, he wrote for the *London Magazine* and had recently published a new book of poetry, *Old Damson Face*.

I had dinner with Gavin Ewart and my beautiful god-daughter Jane, whose pure and Christian upbringing I had assured for nineteen years by self-sacrificingly keeping my distance from her. Gavin's poetic star continues to rise, and he has a nice side-line in dirty limericks.

I had lunch with Colin Hunter, Mary's brother, in his house in Cheyne Row. He was bowing out as Chairman of the London Press Exchange, which had been taken over by Leo Burnett, the Chicago agency. He showed me a picture of Mary as I had known her, and as she was now, in Milan. It is rare for beautiful girls to become beautiful women. She has.

I drank a reminiscent Ricard with John Mellors, who had sagely leapt from the bridge of S. H. Benson before she was steered on to the rocks from which she was salvaged by David Ogilvy. He had recently published his memoirs of his life in advertising. Before I left he said, 'Why don't you write yours? Should be interesting – Paris, New York and all that.'

I stayed heavily with my brother in Barnes. He had dined with Patricia and her husband in New York; my sister-in-law had dined with them in their new home, in Hollywood.

I was still alone, or as alone as you can be with devils still to be

334

cast out. For, in Tessimond's words,

> He who has eaten the golden grapes of the sun will call
> no sour fruit sweet.
> He will turn from the moon's green apples and run,
> though they fall in his hands, though they lie at his feet.

I didn't see John Tessimond. They found him dead, in his basement flat. The neighbours had noticed the milk bottles.

I thought about Mellors' suggestion. He hadn't been the first. It had been a leitmotif of my life. 'My goodness, why aren't you writing?' Marianne's soothsayer in London had said. 'You ought to be hitting that typewriter,' said his colleague in New York as I dined with Reva. 'I think you might surprise us all,' said Judy Douglas. 'I'd say that way lies your salvation,' said Dr McKinney.

In my brother's house I read an essay by Stephen Spender. I don't know if Rousseau, Restif de la Bretonne, Henry Miller and the rest of the boys would go along with it, but it made sense to me:

> All confessions are from subject to object, from the individual to the community or creed. Even the most shamelessly revealed inner life yet pleads its cause before the moral system of an outer, objective life. One of the things that the most abysmal confessions prove is the incapacity of even the most outcast of creatures to be alone. Indeed the essence of the confession is that the one who feels outcast pleads with humanity to relate his isolation to its wholeness. He pleads to be forgiven, condoned, condemned even, so long as he is brought back into the wholeness of people and of things.

It made you think. Chap was right. I needed to shout: stop the world, I want to get on. Because baby it's cold outside, even if I've got my self-love to keep me warm. The unexamined life was not worth living, one of those Greeks had said. Proust, they tell me, was on to the same idea. Well, why not Charlus H.?

So, back in Blevy, I went down the hill to the village store and bought three pencils, 2B pencils, and an exercise book. In the cottage I sat at my desk with the same easy nonchalance as a man might sit in an electric chair, back to the view, face to the blank wall, cold sweat, for some reason, on my face. Should I open the exercise book, the exorcise book? Dare I pick up the pencil? 2B or not 2B?

Then I started to write. Nothing much happened. Suddenly nobody burst out singing. Nobody laughed. I didn't die. Emboldened, I went on squiggling, sending out my timid messages to mankind. Perhaps someone would notice them and I might at last be saved. For I was not as far out as they thought, and not drowning but waving.